PCs made easy

STAGE 3

A PRACTICAL COURSE

Microsoft® Windows®
xp
edition

PCs made easy

STAGE 3

A PRACTICAL COURSE

Microsoft® Windows®
xp
edition

PUBLISHED BY THE READER'S DIGEST ASSOCIATION LIMITED
LONDON NEW YORK SYDNEY MONTREAL

PCS MADE EASY
MICROSOFT® WINDOWS® XP EDITION
A PRACTICAL COURSE – STAGE 3

Published by the Reader's Digest Association Limited, 2003

The Reader's Digest Association Limited
11 Westferry Circus, Canary Wharf, London E14 4HE
www.readersdigest.co.uk

We are committed to both the quality of our products and the service we provide to
our customers, so please feel free to contact us on 08705 113366, or via our Web site
at www.readersdigest.co.uk
If you have any comments about the content of our books, you can
contact us at gbeditorial@readersdigest.co.uk

®Reader's Digest, The Reader's Digest and the Pegasus logo are registered trademarks
of The Reader's Digest Association Inc, of Pleasantville, New York, USA

For Reader's Digest
Project Editor: Caroline Boucher
Art Editor: Julie Bennett

Reader's Digest General Books
Editorial Director: Cortina Butler
Art Director: Nick Clark
Series Editor: Christine Noble

PCs made easy – Microsoft® Windows® XP Edition was fully updated for
Reader's Digest by De Agostini UK Ltd from *PCs made easy*, a book series created
and produced for Reader's Digest by De Agostini from material originally published
as the Partwork *Computer Success Plus*
The new edition was adapted by Craft Plus Publishing Ltd

© 2003 De Agostini UK Ltd

Printing and binding: Printer Industria Gráfica S.A., Barcelona

ISBN 0 276 42754 8

CONTENTS

Windows®

Keep a healthy hard disk

With Windows' disk tools, you can ensure your computer is always achieving its optimum performance by preventing problems and putting them right if they occur.

A computer is a complicated, fragile piece of equipment, and every now and then things can, and do, go wrong. It can get accidentally knocked, for example, just like other electrical equipment in your home. When a PC is switched on, even what might seem like a small knock could affect the computer's hard disk, where all your programs and documents are stored. Such knocks can interfere with the data that is stored on the disk and this could make a single file – or even whole areas of the hard disk – impossible to use. As a result, any data stored there could be lost.

● Don't just switch off

Similar problems often arise when the PC is switched off before open documents are closed. Make sure that everyone using your computer – especially any children who share it – knows that the only safe way to switch a computer off is to select the Turn Off Computer option from the Start menu. If you do this, Windows will check to ensure that any open documents have been properly saved before shutting down.

Less frequently, hard disk problems can also occur as a result of faulty software, quite outside your control.

Even when it is working properly, your computer's hard disk can become clogged up. As a result of this, you might find that it seems to slow down, and operating open and save commands takes longer than it did when the PC was new.

All these problems are easily cured with Windows' suite of programs called System Tools. There's a tool to deal with each problem.

● Instant cures

When a document file stored on disk has been damaged, it is said to be corrupted. Sometimes the file won't be accessible at all: you might,

for example, see an error message appear when you try to open a corrupted letter in Word. Even if the document isn't that important, you should always repair the damage to the disk so that it cannot affect other documents in the future. The error-checking tool can check your hard disk for errors and will automatically repair any damaged areas it finds.

If your computer seems to be running slower than it used to, you can tune it up and get it back up to speed by using the Disk Defragmenter. This reorganizes the data on your hard disk so that programs can start, and your documents can be opened or saved, as quickly as possible. It doesn't change the way you have arranged the documents and folders on your disk, so you'll still find everything where you left it.

We'll also look at Disk Cleanup, another of Windows' System Tools. This program can automatically delete unused and unwanted files that are taking up disk space.

PC TIPS

Backing up

It's an unfortunate fact of life that computers can go wrong and your data – Word letters, Excel workbooks or graphic layouts, for example – might be lost. Because of this, you should always keep copies of your important documents on floppy or, if more storage memory is needed, Zip disks.

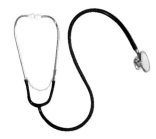

Checking your hard disk for errors

If you suspect that files on your hard disk have become damaged or corrupted, Windows' built-in error-checking tool might solve the problem.

ANY OF the files and data stored on your hard drive can become corrupted. In most cases you can repair this damage, although it is likely that the files can only be recycled as free space rather than reclaimed. ScanDisk is the tool to use for such tasks.

1 To start Windows' error-checking tool, first open the My Computer window by clicking on the Start button and then selecting the My Computer entry on the right of the Start menu.

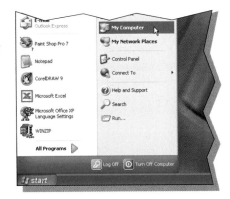

2 When the My Computer window appears, select your hard disk – on most PCs this is the C: drive, and it appears in the centre of the My Computer window. Then click on the File menu and select Properties from the menu.

3 When the Properties dialog box for the hard disk pops up, click on the Tools tab at the top. Then click on the Check Now button in the Error-checking section at the top of the dialog box.

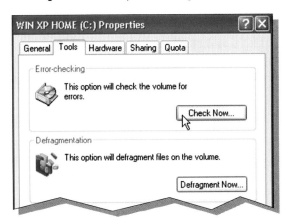

4 You must now tell Windows what errors you want it to fix. It's best to tick both Check disk options before clicking on the Start button.

5 Because the error-checking tool requires full and sole access to your hard disk, an information dialog box pops up (see Exclusive access box, below). Click on the Yes button (if you click on the No button, the error-checking process is cancelled).

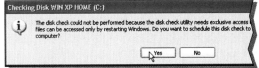

6 Now select Turn Off Computer from the Start menu and click on the Restart button to check the hard disk for errors. A program called CHKDSK runs automatically before the Windows Desktop appears. It carries out five types of check, including the way data is indexed on the disk, the integrity of all the data and program files, and the amount of free space on the disk. You can follow the results of the tests on screen. The process takes a while – 15 minutes or so on some hard disks. At the end, a summary screen appears, telling you the results and your PC restarts, loading Windows as normal.

Defragmenting your hard disk

Your hard disk can slow down as more programs and files are stored on it, but a simple operation will soon have it running at maximum speed.

THE MORE files you create and new programs you install on your computer, the slower it will work. This problem, caused by fragmentation, is not too serious but can be avoided if you use Windows' Disk Defragmenter tool to reorganize your hard

disk. It does this by moving files around on the hard disk. Don't worry about not being able to find them: the files appear in exactly the same place, but your hard disk can now find them more quickly.

1 To start Disk Defragmenter, press the Start button and select Accessories from the All Programs menu. Select System Tools from the Accessories menu and click on the fifth option of the drop-down menu: Disk Defragmenter.

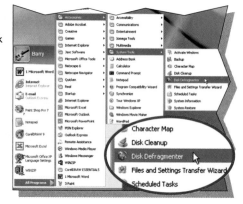

2 The first thing to do is select your hard disk in the panel near the top of the Disk Defragmenter window. To see if defragmenting this disk is necessary, first click on the Analyze button.

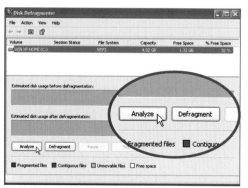

3 After a few moments, the Disk Defragmenter displays a summary of your hard disk in the form of a colour-coded bar. The red parts indicate data that could be more efficiently arranged on the hard disk – the more stripes you can see in the bar, the more fragmented the disk's contents.

4 If your hard disk could benefit significantly from defragmenting, a message box appears suggesting that you defragment it now. Click on the Defragment button to start.

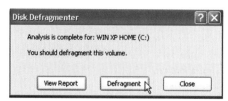

5 The defragmentation process will start and you can see it happening by watching the illustration bar in the lower half of the dialog box. You can run other programs at the same time, but you'll find your system will operate rather more slowly while defragmentation is going on.

6 When the reorganization of the hard disk data is complete, a dialog box pops up. In this case, there are a few files that could not be defragmented. Click on the View Report button to see more information and check on the files concerned.

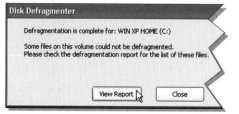

Cleaning up your hard disk

As you use your computer, many files are created that you will never need again. Here we see how to get rid of them to free up valuable disk space.

WINDOWS COMES with Disk Cleanup, a special program that automatically roots out useless old files in just a few minutes, saving you many megabytes of hard disk space in the process. When you run Disk Cleanup, it lets you choose which types of file to look for and delete. You can, for example, select temporary files created when you access the Internet.

1 To run Disk Cleanup, click on the Start button and select Accessories from the All Programs menu. Select System Tools from the Accessories menu and click on Disk Cleanup.

2 Immediately, the Disk Cleanup program starts to analyze your hard disk to see how much space it could save. Wait for a few moments.

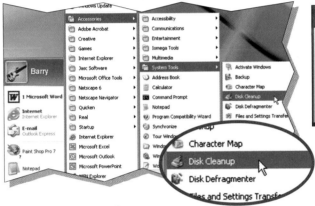

3 Disk Cleanup shows you the types of files it can clean up. Initially, only three options are ticked. Temporary Files include hidden files created by your programs that are no longer needed, but that have not yet been deleted.

4 You can click on the boxes to the left of each entry in the Files to delete list to add or remove the tick. As you do, the figure under the list changes to reflect the amount of space you'll save.

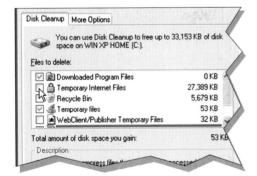

5 Not all of the options listed are deletions; scroll down the list and you'll see a Compress old files entry. This lets you tell Windows to squeeze rarely used files so they occupy a smaller amount of space on the hard disk. In this case, it will only save 1KB, so it's not worthwhile, but check the figure for your own PC.

6 Press the OK button and confirm your choice when Windows asks you to. It then deletes and compresses the various files you have identified as being redundant. It takes only a few minutes to recover the disk space.

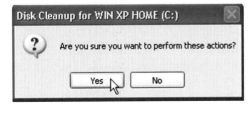

Change your view of Windows

Windows gives you the tools to control how the Desktop is displayed on your monitor. Here's a guide to show you how simple it is to make adjustments to your Desktop display settings.

Show off your Desktop to its full potential simply by adjusting the colour and resolution settings.

You have already seen some of the techniques to customize the way your Windows Desktop looks (Stage 2, pages 12–13). There is also another level of control over the way your Desktop is displayed on your monitor, which involves changing the display settings. There are two main display settings you can control: display resolution and the number of colours that can be shown on screen at any one time.

The resolution is the most important display setting that you can change. This tells Windows how many pixels (or dots) to use to form the image on the computer monitor. By using more pixels to make up the picture, you will see more detail. The limitation here is the computer monitor – some cannot display high resolutions. For example, you might find that Windows lets you try, say, 1280x1024 pixels, but the screen image then appears garbled and you can't see anything at all. If this happens, don't worry: Windows will switch back to your old setting automatically after a few seconds, so you can experiment freely.

● Number of colours

The other important display setting is the number of colours used to display the image. More colours mean that more memory is used on your computer's graphics adaptor; on some older PCs you might have to choose between a high resolution or lots of colours.

The easy way to change display settings

There are subtle ways of adjusting the Windows Desktop to suit your own tastes. Here we show how you can make Windows look smarter and work better on your computer at the same time.

1 The place to go to control how Windows looks on screen is the Display Properties window. This is available by clicking on the Start menu, then Control Panel and Display. However, the quickest way is to right-click on any free part of your Desktop and choose Properties from the menu that appears (right).

2 The settings for your display are controlled from the Settings tab of the Display Properties window. Click on the Settings tab and you'll find the things over which you have control: you can alter the number of colours used by adjusting the Color quality, the size of the Desktop area by changing the screen resolution and – via the Appearance tab – the size of text used throughout Windows.

3 The Color quality setting controls how many colours Windows can display on the screen at once. Click on the down arrow at the right end of the Color quality text box and select Highest (32 bit). On PCs with old graphics adaptors, Windows has only a limited amount of memory available to store the on-screen display, so you might have to compromise (see Old graphics adaptors box, below right).

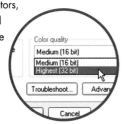

4 Now you can alter the Screen resolution setting by moving the slider. As you move this slider, the monitor preview picture at the top of the dialog box reflects your choice. A good setting for 17-inch monitors is 1024x768 while 1280x1024 is better for 19-inch monitors.

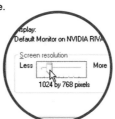

5 To alter the size of Windows text, first click on the Appearance tab near the top of the Display Properties box (inset). At the bottom of this tab is the Font size setting; click on it and select one of the other options. The monitor preview picture demonstrates the effect of your selection.

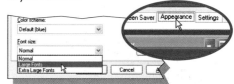

6 When you've finished making changes to your display settings, you can click the Apply button to see what your new Desktop looks like. The new-look Desktop appears within a few moments, and Windows asks if you want to keep the new settings. Click on the No button if you want to try other settings, otherwise click on the Yes button.

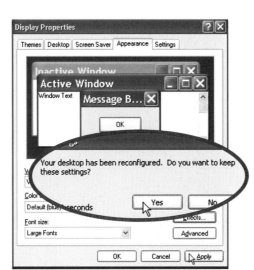

7 The larger font sizes can be especially useful when you have a large monitor. They allow you to opt for a high screen resolution, without on-screen text becoming so small that it's difficult to read. Experiment until you get the best combination. With some settings, the screen may appear to flicker, but this is also easy to fix (see PC Tips, left).

Installing new software

Whenever you buy a new piece of software, you have to load it from the CD-ROM or DVD-ROM onto your PC's hard disk. Here we show you how easy it is to install new programs.

Loading or 'installing' new software is much the same as putting any new data onto your PC from a CD-ROM or DVD-ROM. But instead of copying the files yourself, your PC will run a set-up program to install the new program on your PC's hard disk for you.

When you insert the new program disk and go through the installation process, all you are doing is transferring these instructions, bit by bit, from the software disk onto your PC's hard disk. Once they are on the PC, they provide it with a new range of instructions that you can use directly, just as you use any of the programs already installed on your PC when you bought it.

● Hard disk space
With a small piece of software, you might be transferring only a few files. With a major software package, you might be transferring most of a CD-ROM's contents. It depends on how the program will be used. Reference programs that provide you with data, images and sounds, such as Microsoft's Encarta series, require only a little hard disk space because the program reads the data directly from the CD-ROM disk (the CD-ROM actually needs to be in the CD-ROM drive for the program to access the information on it). But major programs, such as Word or CorelDRAW Essentials, can take up several hundreds of megabytes of space on your hard disk when they are fully installed on your PC.

● Installation time
The time it takes to load software varies from program to program. Clearly the larger the program, the longer it takes to load. But some

You'll be able to install most software successfully simply by inserting the CD-ROM supplied and following the instructions given by Windows.

major programs take much longer to install than others as they ask a lot of questions before they even begin to install the files. This is because these types of programs are also used in offices where it is important to know who is using the software and whether it has been properly licensed. Even with the largest programs, though, the installation process rarely takes more than half an hour – and is usually much quicker.

● Installation options
Most programs let you choose how much of the software you wish to install, but home users usually install the entire program. With the CorelDRAW Essentials program, for example, the default option for installation is called Typical and, as the name suggests, it will install all the files that most people typically use. Other options are Compact, which

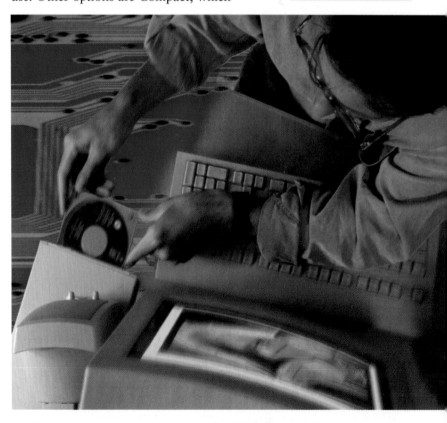

Installing a new program can often seem daunting, but usually it involves nothing more than answering a few on-screen questions put to you by Windows. Any changes to your PC set-up are made automatically.

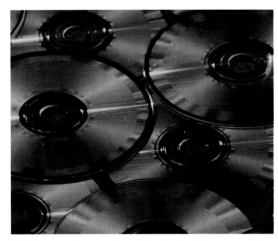

Installing new software will seem less of a daunting prospect when you understand what happens during the installation process.

installs only the essential files to save disk space, and Custom, which allows you to choose exactly which files to install. The Custom option is really intended for advanced users. Unless you have very little space on your hard disk, it's best to use the Typical option. This also applies when installing other Windows programs.

● Installing other software

Many large programs have a number of extra applications as well as the main program functions. These include items such as fonts and clip-art. While you should install all the main program functions, check how much space these extra files take up before you install them. If they take up a lot of disk space, and you don't think you are going to need to use them, you can leave all these items on the CD-ROM. If you are in any doubt, *always* leave them on the CD-ROM – you can install them if and when you need them at a later date.

All you have to do to install most of the software you are likely to buy is to insert the CD-ROM. This starts the program responsible for managing the installation process. Almost all Windows

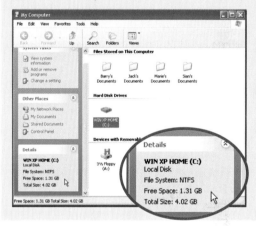

The icon for the CD-ROM drive features an image of a CD-ROM, with the letter that signifies the drive underneath it.

XP-compatible software comes on CD-ROM and installs itself, but a few older programs – and all programs on floppy disk – lack the autostart procedure. With these you must start the installation process yourself.

Don't worry, however – it's easy to do and doesn't take long to learn (see page 17).

How to install CorelDRAW Essentials

In Stage 2, pages 68–89, we introduced you to the graphics program CorelDRAW Essentials. Here we show you how to install the program from CD-ROM, a process that involves steps common to other installation programs.

1 To start the installation, you need to insert the CorelDRAW CD-ROM labelled 1 into your CD-ROM drive. The CD-ROM will autostart and a window will appear, giving you several options. Click on the Install option.

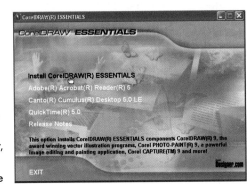

2 The Install program will analyze your system to see how much memory you have, how fast your processor is and so on. When it's finished, another window will appear, asking if you are sure you want to continue. To do so, click on the Next button.

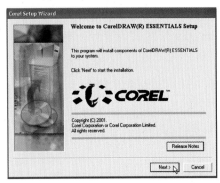

3 The next window displays the License Agreement, which asks you to agree not to copy or lend the software illegally. The following window asks you to type in your name and the name of your company (if relevant). This information is not really essential and merely helps to register the product. Click on the Next button and a window will give you a chance to check your entry; click on Next if everything is correct.

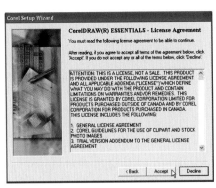

4 The next screen asks you to enter the product serial code for your copy of CorelDRAW; this code is different for each copy of the software and it is important that you don't lose it (the code is printed on a registration card that you'll find in the CorelDRAW box). It is a good idea to copy it down somewhere else in case you lose the original. When you've typed in the code, click on the Next button to go on.

5 You will now be presented with the installation options. There are three options from which to choose. The Typical installation will be selected for you by CorelDRAW by default, so click on Next to proceed.

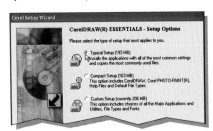

6 The next two screens let you choose which spelling dictionary to install and which fonts and symbols. Use the two panels to check and/or alter the suggested settings and click on the Next button.

7 The program tells you where on your hard disk the CorelDRAW Essentials software will be installed and then where on the Start menu the program shortcuts will appear. It's best to accept these settings.

8 As the software files are copied to your hard disk, a progress bar appears. When the copying process is complete, the set-up program takes you online to register your copy of the software. You can skip this step by clicking on the Different Registration Method button and cancelling the registration process.

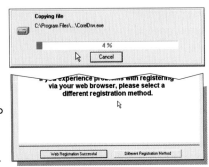

9 At the end of the process, the set-up program's window disappears. Click on the Start button and Windows XP gives you a useful reminder that you have installed a new program. It also highlights the new sub-menu in orange on the All Programs menu to make it easy to find.

Installing software manually

Sometimes your PC won't automatically know you are trying to install a new program. All this means is that you have to make a few extra choices and inputs yourself.

SOME SOFTWARE doesn't start automatically which means that you will have to install the program manually using the set-up or install file on the CD-ROM (the software manual will tell you the exact name of the file to look for). In the exercise below we show you how easy it is to load programs manually.

1 For software that doesn't autostart, you need to locate the set-up or install file on the CD-ROM. To do this, click on the Start button and select My Computer from the menu.

2 When the My Computer window opens, you will be able to see the CD-ROM drive. It has a small picture of a CD-ROM and the letter that the drive has been designated is underneath (in this case, D:). Double-click on the icon to open the CD-ROM drive window.

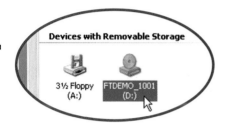

3 The contents of the CD-ROM will then be displayed. Often, the file you need to double-click on to start the set-up process will be called Setup and you'll spot it straight away. Sometimes, this file is called Install and you might have to look through many files and folders to find it.

4 When you double-click on the Setup (or Install) file, the installation process will begin. As the installation proceeds, you might have to answer some simple questions about your computer's set-up, or confirm that the software is making acceptable choices about where and how it will work on your computer.

PC TIPS

Readme files

If you have a CD-ROM software disk that doesn't start automatically, and you're unsure how to install it, look for a Readme file. Although the exact name varies from program to program – it may be readme.txt, readme.htm or readme.1st – the content and purpose is the same: to give you installation instructions.

Double-click on this file and you'll see a description of how to install the software, including which file to use to start the installation process manually.

A second manual installation method

1 If a program you have just bought doesn't install automatically there is an alternative method to the one shown above for installing a program manually. Click on the Start button and choose Run from the menu that appears.

2 Now Windows needs to know the location of the file, so click on the Browse button.

3 Next you will see a dialog box that allows you to look at the contents of your hard disk and the other disk drives on your computer. Choose your CD-ROM drive from the drop-down menu at the top of the screen.

4 It is now just a matter of locating the file that starts the set-up process. Because this process usually involves running a computer program that monitors the installation for you, the file will be called either Install or Setup. Double-click on it to begin the installation process.

Uninstalling software

If you try a program and decide you don't need it, it's best to remove it from your PC's hard disk. However, you must use the Uninstall or Remove command instead of deleting the program manually.

When you install any new piece of software (see pages 14–17), the set-up or installation program copies the software's many files to your hard disk. It also makes changes to vital system files buried deep within Windows.

It does all of this automatically so that, when the process is complete, the software and Windows work perfectly together. If the files were simply copied to a folder on your hard disk, the program wouldn't work properly. For example, you would find that the new program's icons and program entries simply wouldn't appear on the Start menu. More importantly, however, Windows XP wouldn't be able to keep track of your software, and make sure that it has the resources it needs to run.

● Don't delete programs

If you decide to uninstall software, it is vital that you follow the correct procedure rather than simply dragging a program to the Recycle Bin to delete it. In fact, this point is so crucial that Windows XP reminds you not to do it if you ever try (see Useful pointers to prevent problems, opposite).

This is because the changes made to your Windows system files when the software was installed must also be undone to restore the the files to their original state before you installed the software. There are so many changes – typically several dozen – and they affect so many different files that you can't possibly hope to do this manually. Instead you must use the proper Uninstall or Remove command (see pages 20–21) which will run a Windows program that automatically undoes all the changes for you.

● Why uninstall at all?

Only a few years ago, the limited size of PC hard disks – typically 2–4GB – meant that most people had to uninstall programs in order to make space for other software. With today's PCs weighing in with hard disks of 20GB or more, few people are likely to run out of space. However, there are other reasons why many PC users need to remove software.

For example, you may have installed a trial version of a program and then decided that it isn't suitable for you. Similarly, you may have bought and installed the full version of a program and subsequently sold the package

WHAT IT MEANS

SYSTEM FILES
These are the many files stored within the Windows folder on your hard disk. They include thousands of Windows XP program files, and many others added by software you have installed. Often these are more recent versions of files that were originally included with Windows XP; the new versions add extra features required by the software you are installing.

and CD-ROM. In both cases, you are obliged to uninstall the program – such clauses are often included in the small print of the licence agreement that appears when you install the software (see page 14).

It's also possible that you may buy a program that simply doesn't work with Windows XP. Some programs seem to install themselves perfectly but may crash or refuse to work at all when you try to run them from the Start menu. Check with the software manufacturer or the dealer where you bought the software for advice on Windows XP compatibility; you may find the only option is uninstalling the program and getting a refund.

Look closely at the hard disk locations that appear in a panel while your software is being installed and you can see that files are being added to the Windows folder.

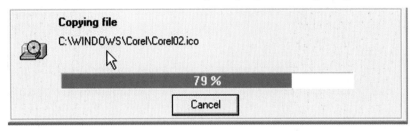

● Uninstalling for efficiency

Generally, it's advisable to uninstall software you no longer use in order to help your PC to run more efficiently. The reason is that every piece of software that you have installed adds a small burden to Windows. The more software you have installed on your PC, the more significant the cumulative burden, and the poorer your PC's performance.

With half a dozen programs, the burden isn't worth worrying about but, with the very large hard disks available on modern PCs, there's a natural tendency to install more programs. Each program increases the size of some very important system files that are opened and closed every time you use your PC. The larger these files are, the more time it takes to access them, and therefore the slower your PC runs.

Uninstalling unwanted software helps keep these file sizes down. Windows XP makes it easy to see which files you rarely use, so it's a simple issue to keep on top of (see page 21).

Useful pointers to prevent problems

Deleting documents you no longer require is simple, but removing unwanted programs involves changing system files and is best left to the appropriate uninstall command.

When you install programs on your PC they appear as extra entries on the Start menu, and, in some cases, extra icons on the Windows Desktop. Clicking on either of these items starts the software.

However, these icons and entries do not represent the software itself. They are merely shortcuts to the program's files – a pointer to tell Windows where the real program is located. Try deleting a program's Desktop shortcut icon and Windows reminds you that it can delete this icon but the software remains on your PC (left).

When you delete a shortcut, Windows reminds you that the program itself remains intact and unchanged, and provides a link to the correct program files so that you can remove the program from your hard disk if that is what you intend to do.

It also provides a link to take you to the relevant program (see page 21). The software installed on your PC is actually stored in the Program Files folder on your hard disk. First double-click on the C: drive in

the My Computer window and then double-click on the Program Files folder. Windows initially hides the contents of the folder and tells you not to make changes (below). The Windows programmers have also added a link in the System Tasks box on the left of the window which enables you to remove programs using the correct method.

Windows XP hides the contents of the Program Files folder from view, and warns you not to try to change its contents manually.

Uninstalling software from the Start menu

Many programs add their own uninstall option in the form of a command on the Start menu. Here we've used CorelDRAW Essentials as an example, but the process is similar for many other programs.

1 Click on the Start menu, then All Programs and then CorelDRAW Essentials. In this case, the main program entries – CorelDRAW and Corel PHOTO-PAINT are visible, but there's also a sub-menu called Setup and Notes. Click on this and then select the Corel Uninstaller entry.

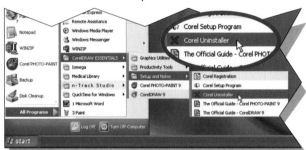

2 The first screen of this uninstall program suggests closing all other programs. This is good advice – it ensures that any files that the uninstaller wants to delete are not in use by other software. Close any open programs and click on the Next button.

3 Some uninstaller programs let you choose which elements of the software you want to remove. In this case, you can click on the small crossed (+) box on the left to see the choices available.

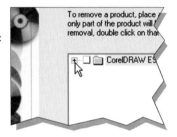

4 The choices you see vary from program to program. Here, we've chosen to remove just the Corel PHOTO-PAINT program, leaving the other parts of the CorelDRAW Essentials software intact. Click on the Next button when you have made your selection.

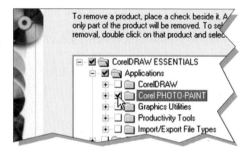

5 The program confirms that it will remove the file and directories (or folders) that Corel PHOTO-PAINT uses as well as the shortcuts it made when it installed the program. Click on the Next button.

6 The next screen shows the uninstall progress in much the same way as the install program. The progress bar moves from left to right and details of which files are being changed appear. Click on the Finish button when the process has completed.

7 Because the Corel Uninstaller program had to make changes to some of the most fundamental Windows system files, it informs you that your PC must be restarted to completely uninstall some of these files. Click on the Yes button.

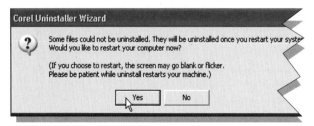

8 Check the Start menu after your PC has restarted. The program options you chose have disappeared from the Start menu.

PC TIPS

Although most software includes an uninstall program like the Corel Uninstaller, you may occasionally come across a program that doesn't have an entry on the Start menu (see Step 1). In this case, you must uninstall it by using the Add or Remove Programs window (see page 21).

Using the Add or Remove Programs window

This useful Windows program lets you uninstall programs, and has the added advantage of helping you locate infrequently used programs and see how much space you'd save by uninstalling them.

1 Open any window on your PC and locate the System Tasks panel on the Task Pane on the left. Click once on the Add or remove programs link in this panel.

2 This opens the Add or Remove Programs window. The main panel lists the software currently installed on your PC in alphabetical order. This includes programs you have installed yourself and any software pre-installed by your PC's manufacturer.

3 Click on one of the programs listed. It is highlighted against a blue background and some extra information appears to its right. In this example, Windows tells us that this program consumes just over 12MB of disk space, that we use it regularly, and the date that we last used it.

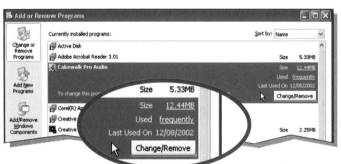

4 This information is useful if you want to locate software you no longer use. To sort the programs accordingly, click on the Sort by box and select Date Last Used from the drop-down list.

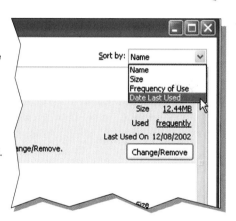

5 The list is reordered, with software you don't use at the top. Here we want to uninstall the long-neglected Netscape 6 program. Select the program you want to uninstall and click on the Change/Remove button.

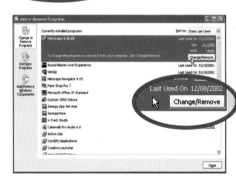

6 Windows locates the uninstaller program and starts it – the window that appears on screen varies from program to program. Select the uninstall option and follow the prompts that appear on the screen.

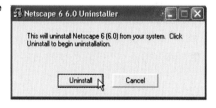

7 In this case, unlike the Corel Uninstaller program (see Step 7, opposite), the program doesn't require us to restart the PC. Within a few seconds, the program is deleted and we are returned to the Add or Remove Programs window.

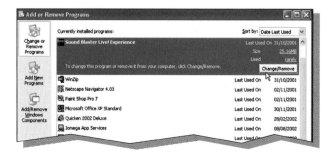

INSIDE WINDOWS

To gain an insight into why uninstalling software is best left to programs that know precisely which Windows system files to change and delete, take a look at the sheer scale of the task. Open the My Computer window and double-click on the C: drive. Then right-click on the Windows folder and select Properties from the pop-up menu. The dialog box that appears shows just how many system files there are – typically 10,000 or more. Clearly, far too many for manual changes.

Windows timekeeping

Your computer's clock keeps going even when you switch off your PC. It knows when you load programs and when you save files. Here's your guide to how Windows keeps track of time and, therefore, your work.

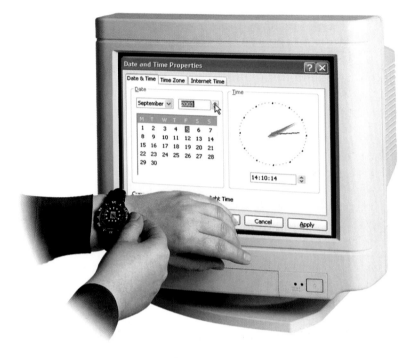

Keeping track of the time and date, even when the computer is switched off, is an important function that your computer performs almost invisibly. The small clock in the bottom right corner of the Windows screen might be the only thing you have noticed that indicates your computer's timekeeping.

The ability to tell the time comes from your computer's internal clock. This clock has its own battery that keeps the clock ticking, even if you don't use your PC for several months. The time stored in this clock is displayed in the Notification area of the Taskbar in Windows to give you a convenient on-screen clock to refer to while you're working.

● Clocking on

Windows also uses the clock for its own purposes to timestamp and datestamp files and folders every time you create, modify or save them. You can see how this works at its simplest by selecting My Computer from the Start menu to open the My Computer window. From this window, open your computer's hard disk (C: drive) window by double-clicking on it. Inside, you'll see a number of folders. Move your mouse pointer to

If you go to the View menu on a folder window and select Details, you'll see the last date and time you modified the files in that window.

You don't have to alter the year on your PC – it happens automatically. Your computer has calendars programmed with all the dates up to 2099.

the View menu and select Details. You can then see the time and date of when the folders and files were last modified. As Windows uses the time and date on your PC's clock to update this information, it's important to ensure that both are set accurately, otherwise the modified date will be useless to you. Windows gives you the power to do this using the Date and Time dialog box (see How to change the time and date, opposite).

● Putting the clock back

The Windows Date and Time dialog box also includes the option to adjust automatically for Daylight Saving Time. This is what the Americans call the system of putting the clocks forward in spring and back in autumn. If you leave this option switched on, Windows will automatically put your PC's clock backwards or forwards an hour on the right date.

The first time you switch on your computer after there has been a time change, Windows will warn you about the adjustment it's about to make and give you the chance to check that it's correct. It is important, therefore, to ensure that not only the time and date are correct but that your PC is set to the right time zone.

Once the correct time has been entered into your computer, all the changes you make to your documents will be timestamped by the PC's internal clock.

WHAT IT MEANS

TIMESTAMP AND DATESTAMP
Every file and folder stored on your PC includes information about the time and date when it was last modified. Whenever you modify a file or folder, Windows updates this time and date information. Updating the time is called timestamping, while updating the date is called datestamping.

How to change the time and date

Here we show you how easy it is to set the date and time on your PC. You'll also find out how to set up or alter different time zones.

1 Like many other Windows settings, time and date can be managed from the Control Panel. Click on the Start button, and then Control Panel. Double-click on the Date and Time icon to open the Date and Time Properties dialog box.

2 We want to change the month to September, so move the mouse pointer to the arrow on the right of the panel with the month displayed (in this case, August). Click on the arrow, scroll down the menu and click on September.

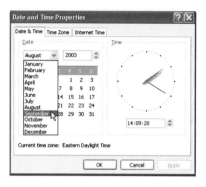

3 To change the year, click on the up arrow by the year window to add one year at a time, or the down arrow to subtract a year. To change the day, click on the number of the day you wish to use in the main window.

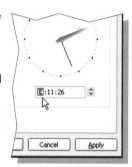

4 Changing the time can be done by double-clicking on the hour (in this case 14) and entering the required hour. Move along to the minutes, double-click and change as required, then do the same for the seconds, if necessary.

5 One thing to pay close attention to is the Current time zone, which is at the bottom of the window. In our example, it says Eastern Daylight Time, which is fine if you live in New York, but most people don't. Click on the Time Zone tab to change this.

6 This is the Time Zone screen. Click on the arrow to the right of the current time zone and a long list of all the world's possible zones will appear (far right). Choose the one that suits your location by scrolling down the list (we've selected Greenwich Mean Time).

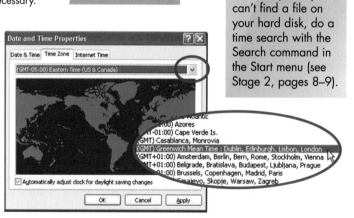

7 When you have altered the date and time, click the Apply button and the clock in the Notification area of the Taskbar changes to reflect your choices. Click the OK button to close the Date and Time Properties dialog box.

FINDING DATED FILES

When you look at the contents of a folder using the Details option from the View menu, you'll see the time and date each file or folder was altered under the Date Modified

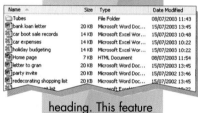

heading. This feature has hidden powers. For example, if you can't find a file on your hard disk, do a time search with the Search command in the Start menu (see Stage 2, pages 8–9).

PC TIPS

Internet time

The third tab in the Date and Time Properties dialog box is Internet Time. This feature automatically synchronizes your PC's clock and calendar with a server on the Internet when you go online. Be aware that if you alter the time or date and go online, Windows will occasionally correct the time and date to match your Time Zone setting. This is a handy feature, but you can turn it off if you prefer.

Software

CorelDRAW®

Printing on envelopes

Now that you are using your word processor to create perfectly presented letters, why not complete the picture and give a great first impression by printing professional-looking envelopes as well?

Y ou don't need any extra software, a special printer or computer-compatible stationery to have your envelopes printed by your PC. In fact, Word helps you produce them quickly and easily. You can even select the address from your finished letter and have Word place it in position on the envelope. Word will also print your own address (the return address) in the top left corner of the envelope, which looks neat and professional. Let's have a look at how easy it is to get Word to help you print your own great-looking envelopes.

LET THE WIZARD HELP YOU

You may prefer to use Word's Envelope Wizard, which you'll find by going to the File menu, clicking on General Templates in the New Document task pane, selecting the Letters & Faxes tab, then clicking on the Envelope Wizard icon (left).

Envelope Wizard

The Wizard is useful if you need to print an envelope for something you didn't use Word to produce. You simply enter the recipient's address in one window, the return address in the window below and then click on Print. You have the same options that we feature opposite, as well as the paper clip icon (right) which you can click on for help.

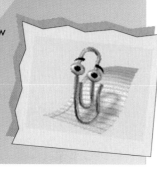

● Creating an envelope

There are two methods of using Word to print envelopes. You can either use the Envelope Wizard (see the Let the wizard help you box, left) or, if you have already created a letter which includes the recipients's details, you may prefer to employ Word to do some of the work for you (see opposite). With this method, Word copies the recipient's address straight from your letter and positions and prints it on the envelope.

● Laying out your letter

We have already seen how to lay out a formal letter using Word (see Stage 1, pages 34–35).

You place your address in the top right corner of the letter and the name and address of the person to whom you are sending it on the left, above the 'Dear ...' line. To use these details on your envelope, all you have to do is highlight this name and address, then go to the Tools menu, click on Letters and Mailing and then select Envelopes and Labels. The recipient's details will be ready and waiting for you in the window that appears.

There are lots of different shapes and sizes of envelopes, but Word can handle anything you can fit into your printer, and has ready-made templates for most common sizes.

You can produce such clear and well laid-out letters that it would be a shame to send them in poorly presented envelopes.

Producing professional envelopes

Sending mail in clearly printed envelopes is a good idea for everyone, not just business people. Here's our guide to making that great first impression every time.

1 Here is our sample letter and, as you can see, the name and address of the person to whom the letter is being sent appears on the left of the page below the date.

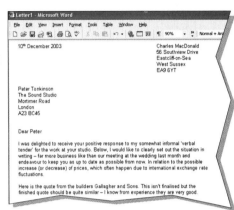

2 To let Word know the recipient's address, you highlight both the name and address. Do this by holding down the left mouse button at the start of the name and dragging the cursor to the end of the address. Then release the mouse button.

3 Now, move the mouse pointer to the Tools menu, select Letters and Mailings, then the Envelopes and Labels option.

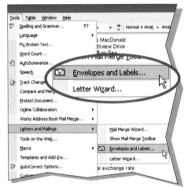

4 You will see a dialog box displayed in the centre of your screen. The address you highlighted has been transferred to the Delivery address panel. The first time you do this, the bottom panel (the Return address box) may be empty. When you enter a Return address, Word remembers it and uses it in future letters.

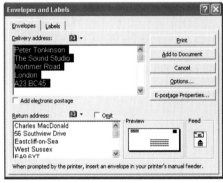

5 You need to check the size of your envelope. The standard size is 110 x 220mm (also known as DL). Click on Options in the Envelopes and Labels window and on the Envelope Options tab. Click on the down arrow for the pull-down menu under Envelope size. You may then select the envelope size you want.

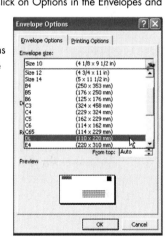

PC TIPS

Add to Document

If you want to save a customized envelope with the document you designed it for, click on Add to Document in the Envelopes and Labels window. Word will then insert a new page at the start of your document in which it saves all the details.

6 Now let's reduce the size of the font for the return address to avoid confusion with the main address. In the Envelope Options window, click on Font under Return address (see inset) and use the Size scroll bar to select a smaller font size. You can also change the font style by clicking any of the 11 Effects boxes. However, some of these effects could make life harder for the postman – so use them sparingly.

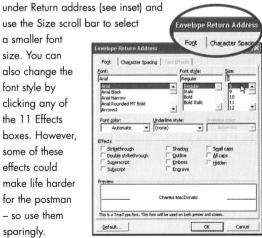

7 Some printers only accept envelopes fed into them in a certain way, but with most inkjet printers it is possible to have some say in the matter. Click the Printing Options tab in the Envelope Options window (right) to check the orientation of the envelope and which way up it goes into the printer (inset, above). If the setup is correct, click on OK, which returns you to the Envelope Options window, and then click on Print (left). You must ensure that your envelope is placed in the printer in the correct way (see Stage 2, page 97 for guidance).

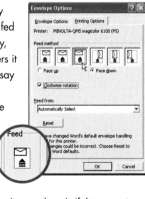

Putting text in columns

Big blocks of text running from one edge of a page to the other are hard to read and look far from enticing to the casual browser. So liven up documents and make them user-friendly by putting text into columns.

Whenever large amounts of information have to be presented in an easy-to-read format, or several different items need to appear near one another, you'll find text divided into columns.

Newspapers and magazines, for example, rely heavily on this format. Both need to display lengthy articles alongside shorter stories in a way that lets the readers find their way around the page with the minimum of fuss and confusion.

Since these columns are narrower than a single page (usually 70–100mm wide), you can scan the page and take in the information far more quickly than if the line extended to the full width of an A4 page.

When the text is spread over longer lines, readers risk losing their way; at least with columns, they know where they are.

● When to use columns

In Word you can easily format your documents into columns, although this will probably not be appropriate for all the documents you write. A single-page letter, for example, would look silly and confusing spread over two or more columns.

However, there are many occasions when placing text into columns can give a document a rather more professional appearance. For example, business reports and club or society newsletters would all benefit from being put into a more accessible column format. We'll take an in-depth look at such documents on pages 30–33. For the time being, however, we'll concentrate on how to format a section of a longish document into columns.

Structured columns of words are far more pleasing to the eye, and therefore easier to read, than large chunks of text that run from pillar to post.

EASY READING

It is quicker and easier to absorb large amounts of information when it is presented in short lines. When text is printed across a wide measure, the eye finds it hard to follow the story from one line to the next, and it becomes all too easy to lose your place on the page. For example, see how much easier it is to read the main text on this page, compared to the words in this box. Another big advantage of using columns of text is that they can be arranged around a picture if required and the reader will still have no difficulty in following the order. Pictures of any shape and size can be used without disrupting the flow of text.

Formatting into columns

You can use any document with a reasonable amount of text for this exercise. Ideally, you need three or four pages to see the true benefits. If you don't have a longish document, simply copy and paste chunks of text to make up the length.

1 Highlight all the text that you wish to format into columns.

2 Go to the Format menu and select the Columns command.

3 The Columns dialog box now appears, as shown below.

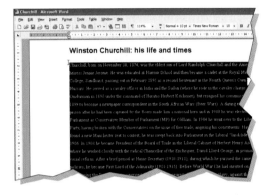

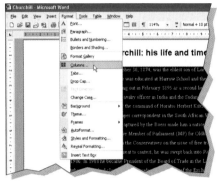

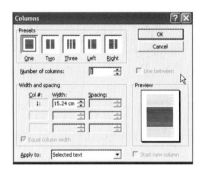

4 At the top of the box are thumbnail images of a number of preset column styles. Click on the Three column option and you can see what it will look like in the Preview panel. The two right-hand images, labelled Left and Right, give you the option of imposing unequal column widths, although these are very rarely used.

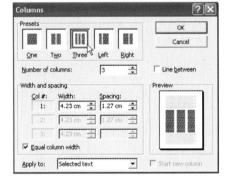

5 You can easily alter the column width and the space between the columns by clicking on the arrows next to the relevant figures to increase or decrease the measurements of column width or spacing. Word will automatically adjust the other measurement so that all the text fits inside the page. Click on the up arrow to make a slight increase of 2mm in the space between the columns.

6 Above the Preview panel is a checkbox labelled Line between. If you click here to select it, Word will automatically draw a thin vertical line between the columns to emphasize the division between them.

7 Now click on the OK button to see the columns in your document. The heading for our document is not affected by the Column command because we did not highlight it in Step 1.

8 If you need to get an overall view of how these pages will look now that they are formatted in columns, change the Zoom figure to show more of the page. To do this, click on the Zoom box in the centre of Word's toolbar and select a lower percentage. On most PC monitors, a setting of 50% shows the whole page.

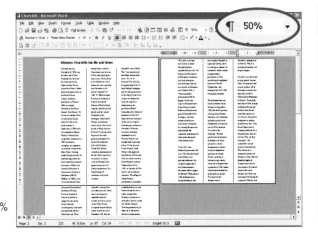

DISAPPEARING COLUMNS

You will notice that columns disappear from view when you select Normal from the View menu. This is because in Normal View, Word tries to display the document as quickly as possible. By using a single column on the left, it can show line breaks without taking time to draw all the columns.

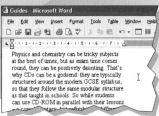

Creating a newsletter

Newsletters for the local youth club or school PTA don't have to be dull, typed pages. Here we show you how to make your club look like it means business.

We've seen in Stages 1 and 2 how to change fonts and add pictures and, in the previous pages, how to use multiple columns to make large chunks of text more interesting. Now we are going to use all these tricks – and a few more – to create a newsletter.

Of course, not everyone needs to produce a newsletter. Yet it's amazing how the same principles – captioned pictures, headlines and box rules, for instance – can make a world of difference to many everyday Word documents. Homework essays and student dissertations, CVs and even basic memos or lists to be pinned up on a noticeboard can all be enhanced with these simple tricks.

● Make your own
It used to be the case that if you wanted to create anything livelier than the most basic document, you would use your word processor only to input and check the text, then you would have to transfer the words to an expensive and complex desktop publishing package to create the finished article. But today you can achieve equally impressive results using Word, so saving yourself a good deal of time and money in the process.

You could even create something similar to *PCs made easy* in Word. All you have to do is get to grips with the necessary tools and you're in the publishing business!

The newsletter we're going to create is based on a Word Wizard-created document – but don't be afraid to experiment as it would be a very dull world if every publication had the same design.

Finally, an important design tip: don't be afraid to borrow ideas from the pros. Flick through magazines and choose the design features you like. Mix these ideas to create your own newsletters. It may sound like cutting corners, but it will save you several years at design school.

Hold the front page! Create your own news with Word's Newsletter Wizard.

Adding floating text boxes

Once you start using text boxes in more adventurous layouts, you'll discover just how versatile they can be.

THE KEY to any newsletter layout is using boxes for the different elements, particularly text. It gives you the flexibility to create columns of text that flow between different parts of the page.

By linking two text boxes together, when one box is full the excess text flows over to continue into the next box. You can change the size of the boxes at any time, and you can easily move them around until you get a balance that you like. When you alter the size or shape of the boxes the text automatically reflows. As text boxes are the most important elements of any newsletter-type layout, here we will show you how to use them in your Word documents.

Microsoft® Word

FLOATING BOXES

All boxes, including those we are adding in the exercise on this page, 'float' on top of the normal Word page. The space where you would normally type text sits underneath these boxes.

If you type without selecting one of the text boxes, the new text will appear at the current cursor position in the underlying Word text. If your document is blank (as it is here, underneath the text boxes), this text will appear at the top left of the page.

1 The text box tool is part of Word's drawing tools, so click on the Drawing button on the toolbar. When you do so, Word changes from Normal View to Print Layout View.

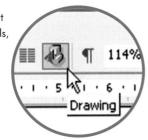

2 The view can change so that the whole page is visible on the screen. This is usually a 50 per cent view. To see more detail, ensure that the view is set to 100 per cent.

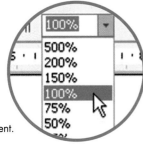

3 Click on the Text Box icon on the Drawing toolbar. It's in the centre of the toolbar below. You can create the text box wherever you like.

4 To do this, click and drag the mouse to create a rectangular text box anywhere on the Word page.

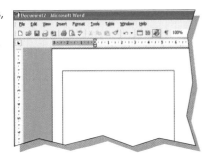

5 Click on the new text box, and type in a paragraph or two of text. To produce enough for this exercise, cut and paste it several times within the box until the text overflows the end of the box.

6 Now create a second text box, to the right of the first, by using the text box tool as you did in steps 3 and 4.

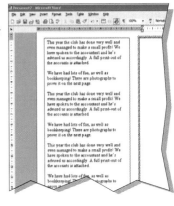

7 Click on the first text box to select it, then click on the chain icon on the Text Box toolbar. You will see the cursor change into a jug icon.

8 Move your cursor over the second (empty) text box – it will change into a pouring jug – and click. The text will then overflow from the first box to the second.

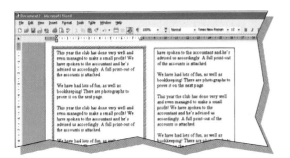

Using the Newsletter Wizard

Let's look at how we would go about creating a newsletter for a local football team. Word helps us make a start by providing the Newsletter Wizard.

1 Start Word and click on Templates on Microsoft.com in the New Document task pane on the right of your screen. Follow the dialog boxes that appear.

2 The Microsoft Template Gallery page appears in your Web browser. Click on the Newsletters link in the Marketing section. The next page lists the newsletter files available. Click on the Newsletter wizard link (see inset).

3 Read the licence agreement on the next page and click on the Accept button. You will then see a preview of the newsletter. Click on the Edit in Microsoft Word link to start downloading the Wizard.

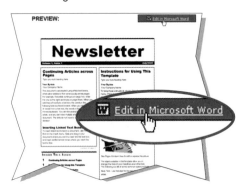

4 When the download has finished, the Newsletter wizard appears. Disconnect from the Internet and click on the Next button.

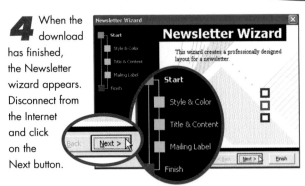

5 The flow chart on the left of the window will show that you have moved to the next stage, where you are presented with a choice of three styles of newsletter: Professional, Contemporary and Elegant. We're using Professional because it is the most straightforward in design and the easiest to use. Leave the other settings exactly as they are and click on Next.

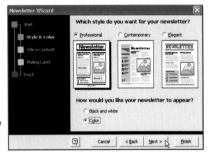

6 The next screen lets us type in the name of our newsletter, 'Up the Park', and add a date and issue number. You can either accept Word's suggestions or type in your own. If you don't want any details at all, click on the tick boxes to remove the ticks. Then click on Next.

7 The following screen allows you to print mailing labels. Click on No, as our newsletters are going to be handed out at the ground. Then click on Next.

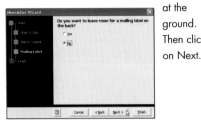

8 The final screen will tell you that the Newsletter Wizard has everything it needs. Click on the Finish button.

9 Word will create a newsletter with your title at the top, plus lots of dummy elements for holding text and pictures. At present, the boxes hold instructive dummy text. On the next page, we'll swap these dummy elements for our club newsletter information. But first check the paper size and change it if necessary (see PC Tips, right).

PC TIPS

The Newsletter Wizard creates documents based on US letter-sized paper. If you are using another size, such as European A4, you might have problems printing it. To change the page size, click on the File menu and select Page Setup. Click on the Paper tab and change from US Letter to A4. Click on Apply to: whole document and then click on OK.

Customizing your newsletter

The Newsletter Wizard does a lot of the work for you as it has the pages already laid out – all you have to do is insert text over what's currently there.

ONCE WORD has created your basic newsletter with dummy text and pictures, it's a good idea to print it out. This will give you a ready reference for the layout – just in case you accidentally delete something you may want later. What's more, the text on the page is a handy reference guide to creating the different items used and a breakdown of all the preset customized text styles, such as headlines, body text and quotes. There are two ways of adding and formatting your own text in the newsletter. You can either select and delete the document text, paste in your own and then format it afterwards, or you can change it bit by bit so that it keeps the styles already applied. The second method gives you more control and is suitable for creating text from scratch.

1 Replace the dummy text in the newsletter by simply highlighting it and typing over it. You can select complete paragraphs by triple-clicking (three rapid clicks of the left mouse button).

2 You could just replace all the text in the newsletter, but we want to jazz up a few of the headings as well. Highlight the heading in the first column and type in a new one. Then, from the Format menu, select Font. Choose a suitable font, size and colour and check how it will appear in the Preview panel. Be careful not to make the font too big, however, as it will unbalance the page.

3 Once you are happy with the format for this heading keep the text highlighted and switch on the Styles and Formatting task pane. First select Task Pane from the View menu and then select Styles and Formatting from the list at the top of the Task Pane. Scroll down the long list of styles that this newsletter contains, until you see Heading 1 – Professional. Move the mouse over this style and a small blue button appears to its right. Click this button and select Update to Match Selection. Now, all the headings that use this style match the choices you made in step 2.

4 Now we're going to insert a picture. As there is already a picture on the page, click on that, and then select Picture from the Insert menu. Choose which type of picture you want – we're going to use a clip-art image, so we click on Clip Art.

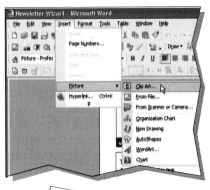

5 A Search For dialog box appears in the Task Pane. Type in a key word or description of the picture you are looking for in the Search text: box (here we have typed in '1st place'). Click on Search. All the appropriate results are displayed as images. Select one and click on it to replace the template picture.

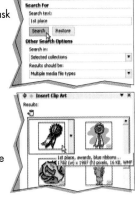

6 The size of the picture is not quite right for our newsletter, but we can resize and trim it to fit. Click on the Crop button on the Picture toolbar and then click on one of the picture handles and drag it in. Repeat this action until you are satisfied. If you want to move the picture to a different point in the text, use Cut and Paste to rearrange items until you're happy with your first publication.

Talking tabs

The [Tab] key is useful for moving text across the page, but it can be customized to do so much more. Set up as many invisible stops as you wish, wherever you want, to create professional lists and documents.

I n an earlier example (see Stage 1, pages 34–35) we used the [Tab] key in Word to make some simple indents in a letter. By pressing the [Tab] key several times at the beginning of each line of our address, we moved it to the right of our page to create a very simple letterhead layout.

It is easy to use tabs for this simple purpose, or even for indenting the first line of each paragraph to make a letter look more presentable. However, tabs are far more versatile than that. They have many other easy-to-use applications which can be utilized on a wide variety of documents.

● Tab behaviour

If you press the [Tab] key when the text insertion point is at the beginning of a line of text, Word shifts the text to the right. Try it again on another line of text and you will see that Word shifts the text by exactly the same amount. Press it again and your second line of text will be indented to twice the distance of the first.

Now try typing the following on a blank line: 1 [Tab] 2 [Tab] 3 [Tab] Four [Tab] 5. You will notice that Word doesn't space the entries evenly – the distance between the 'r' of the word 'Four' and the number '5' is shorter than between the '1' and the '2'. This example demonstrates an important facet of tabs: a tab doesn't actually add space; instead, Word shifts the text to the next of a series of invisible tab stops (which are placed at half-inch intervals – roughly 1.3cm).

The [Tab] key will enable you to place words exactly where you want them on the page, making lists and documents neater and easier to read.

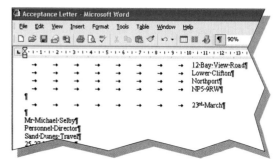

Here you can see the dozens of tabs we've had to use to move our address to the right of our letterhead. Once you've mastered tabs, you can do this with a single tab for each line.

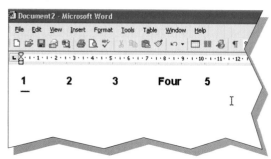

Despite initial appearances, tabs don't actually add any space. Instead they just shift text to the next invisible tab stop on the page; that's why the 'Four' appears to be closer to the '5' than the '3'.

● Changing settings

While these default tab stops are usually fine, there might be times when you require different settings. For example, Word can normally fit only 11 tab stops on an A4 page. Therefore, if you ever wanted to line up 12 or more columns of text, you would run out of space. To overcome this kind of problem, Word lets you specify both the position and the number of tab stops.

● Alignment options

There's another way in which Word's normal behaviour might not be quite right for creating neatly aligned tables of information in your documents. If you press the [Tab] key to move to the next tab stop in a document, Word will align the text so that it starts at the tab. This is called left alignment. Type more text and you'll find it starts at the tab stop. As usual, this is the default – because it is the most popular choice. However, you may want to align your text differently so Word places other useful options at your disposal, such as creating special tab stops that help align each piece of text in subtly different ways.

For example, if you were creating a price list, you might use a tab to separate the item name and its price. Normally the table would look like this:

New engine	£695.00
Air filter	£5.99
Oil filter	£17.95

However, it's not clear at first glance that there's a big difference between the prices of these three components. It's a lot easier to see the difference when they are aligned on the decimal point:

New engine	£695.00
Air filter	£5.99
Oil filter	£17.95

Now it's easy to see the prices in relation to each other. By using a special decimal tab stop, you can get Word to line up information just like this. There are also right and centre tab stop options that can help to clarify the entries in other tables.

● Professional results

Other options can help make your tables of information look really smart. Most contents pages of books and magazines lay out the list of chapters or articles with their title, a tab and a page number. However, to make it

easier to read across a wide column, the designer will often fill the space between the titles and page numbers with a continuous line of full stops.

Word lets you achieve the same results through its tab options. If you're creating a newsletter (see pages 30–33), adding a contents list as described above can help give it a polished and professional look.

● Following the rules

Adjusting the tab stops and choosing different alignment options is a very simple matter. By using the ruler (located just under Word's toolbars) you can add and remove any kind of tab stop with a few clicks.

You can also use the Tab's dialog box to add lines of full stops, or any other characters, to your contents lists. On the following pages we'll show you how to do all of this.

MEASUREMENTS

When setting tab stops or working with Word's ruler, you might have a preference for either centimetres or inches. Fortunately, Word lets you switch between these units as often as you like.

Click on the Tools menu and select Options. You will see a dialog box. Click on the General tab and at the bottom of the dialog box a drop-down list box will appear.

Select whichever measurement unit you want to use and then click on the OK button. You will usually need to use only Centimeters and Inches. The Picas and Points options are measurements that are generally used in the publishing and printing industries.

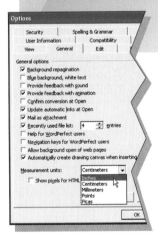

PC TIPS

You don't have to use tabs to indent the first line of paragraphs in your documents. If you want every paragraph to have an indented first line, you can save yourself time and trouble by applying this command as a default setting. Start with a new Word document and, before typing any text, click on the Format menu. Choose the Paragraph command and select the Indents and Spacing tab from the dialog box that appears.

Find the Special box on the right-hand side and choose First line from the options. Use the By number box to choose the amount of indent that you need, and then click on OK.

As you type, you'll find that the first line of each paragraph is indented. However, if you want to apply indents to paragraphs that have already been created, you just need to click the text insertion point in the relevant paragraph before choosing the Paragraph command from the Format menu, as above.

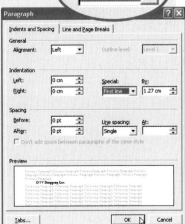

Setting tabs using the ruler

The simplest way to add, change and remove tabs is to use Word's ruler. With a few clicks you can align your text and see the effects immediately.

1 We've started with a simple DIY shopping list as an example of something that would look better with the item name and price in two columns. If we used Word's normal tab stops, we'd have to use a different number of tabs for each line, depending on the text length of each item. For example, we'd need just one for the long 'Nails, screws, tacks' item, but several for the short 'Paint' item.

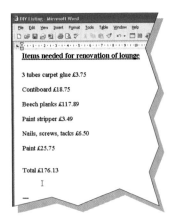

2 However, it's possible to do all this with one tab. Start by using the Select All command on the Edit menu.

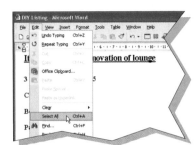

3 Now that all the text is selected, we can apply our tab settings to it. Move the mouse pointer over the ruler. When you're roughly in the position you'd like your tab to be, click and hold down the mouse button.

4 A dotted line will show you the position of your new tab stop. Move it left or right and, when it is in the desired position, release the mouse button. Word will indicate your tab stop with a small L-shape on the ruler.

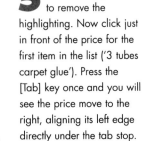

5 Click once again to remove the highlighting. Now click just in front of the price for the first item in the list ('3 tubes carpet glue'). Press the [Tab] key once and you will see the price move to the right, aligning its left edge directly under the tab stop.

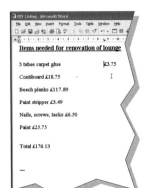

6 Now do the same with the other prices. Only one tab will be needed each time.

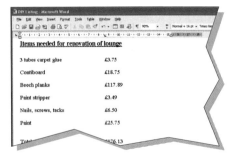

7 The table looks OK, but it would be even better if the prices lined up on their decimal points. Start by selecting all the text again. Now remove the tab stop we put in by clicking on its L-shape on the ruler and dragging it onto the document; as you do, it will change from black to grey. Release it and it will disappear. The prices in the table will move and appear even more ragged than they did before, but don't panic – we'll soon fix that.

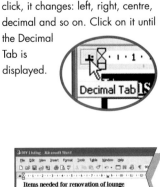

8 Change your style of tab stop by clicking on the square on the ruler's left side. Each time you click, it changes: left, right, centre, decimal and so on. Click on it until the Decimal Tab is displayed.

MIXING YOUR TABS WITH WORD'S TABS

If you had already used Word's normal half-inch tab stops to format your list or table you will probably find that there are now too many tabs in your table and these extra tab characters will make your table look ragged. You can delete unwanted tab characters one by one until the table lines up under your own tab stop. To see the tab characters, click on the Show/Hide button on the Toolbar (right).

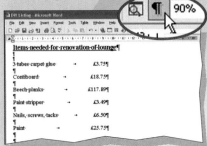

9 Now, making sure that all the text in the document is still selected, move the mouse pointer to the position on the ruler where you placed the first tab. Click the mouse to position the decimal tab in the same place.

10 When you release the mouse button, the prices in the table will immediately realign from their ragged state. Word looks at the items and positions them so that their decimal points lie directly below the decimal tab stop.

Fine-tuning your tab settings

Now we have worked with tab settings, let's make some changes to improve the look of the document we created in the previous exercise.

Microsoft® Word

PC TIPS

You don't have to set tabs for the whole document all at once. In fact, if you have several different types of table in one document, you'll often have to fine-tune tab stops for each table.

You can set tabs for a single paragraph or line of text simply by selecting it before you use the ruler or Tabs dialog box, and then adding, moving or deleting the tabs. The settings will then only apply to the text you highlighted.

1 You can create and alter tabs via the Tabs command in the Format menu. This has all the options of the ruler – and more besides. Start with a new Word document. Click on the Format menu and choose the Tabs command.

2 A dialog box will appear. At the top you will see a box which you can use to change the Default tab stops. As you can see here, Word is set to 1.27cm (half-inch) tab stops.

3 You set tabs by typing a figure into the Tab stop position box. Type 5cm into the space provided and click on the Set button below.

4 You'll see this tab stop position appear in the box just underneath. You can add more tab stops by repeating Step 3. As you press the Set button, each tab position appears in the list.

5 Deleting a tab stop is simple. Just highlight it in the list, then press the Clear button. Clear all the extra tabs until you have only the 5cm tab remaining.

6 You can also select the type of alignment for each tab stop in the Alignment section. Highlight the 5cm tab stop and you'll see that the Left alignment option is selected. Select another option and click on the Set button. Here, we've chosen Decimal.

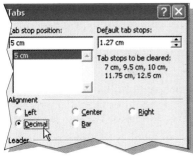

7 The other section of the dialog box is called Leader, and it's here that you can tell Word to fill in the space between tabs with characters. There are four options, the second one of which uses full stops and is often seen in contents and price listings. When you add a tab stop, Word doesn't normally use leader characters: the '1 None' option is selected by default. Select our 5cm tab stop and then click on the full stop option. Click on the Set button.

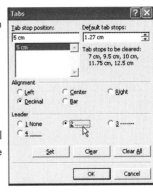

8 We can apply this new tab trick to the DIY listing that we made on the previous page. When you have finished that exercise, select all the text by clicking on Select All in the Edit menu. Go to the Tabs box and clear the tab you set previously, as we did in Step 5. Change the tab stop settings by adding a Decimal aligned tab at 5cm and selecting the second option from the Leader options. Press the Set button and then press the OK button. You'll now see a neat and easy-to-read list.

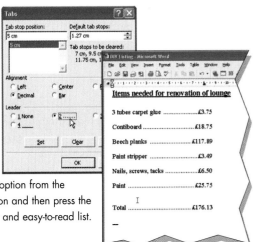

Inserting special characters in text

Word doesn't limit you to using ordinary letters and numbers in your text documents. You can also add foreign characters and a whole range of useful symbols and icons to create the right effect for your intended message.

One of the advantages of a personal computer over a typewriter is that it allows you to use all sorts of extra characters as well as the ordinary alphabet letters and numbers. This makes it as easy to produce an informal letter, adorned with little doodles and pictures, as it does to write a letter in a foreign language with accents, or a business letter with symbols.

Most of these special characters don't appear on your computer keyboard, apart from the punctuation and currency symbols. But, by using special commands, Word puts as many as 200 different characters at your disposal – and even more can be added with extra fonts.

● Improving letters and documents
This versatility gives you the ability to produce documents with a professional finish or with an element of fun and frivolity.

Special characters can be divided into three main categories: foreign characters (such as ç or é); business symbols (such as © or ™); and fun symbols (such as ♥ or ✗). There are two ways to insert these characters. The first is to pick them out from a grid, via the Symbol command on the Insert menu. Some characters can also be entered by pressing a combination

Your keyboard can contain up to 200 hidden characters and symbols – all you have to do is find them!

of keys on the keyboard. Although this method is quicker if you use foreign characters a lot, it is more complicated as you will need to remember the key combinations.

It's easy to see how different types of work – whether correspondence or other documents – can benefit from these additions. A letter in a foreign language, for example, could not be written correctly without these characters. Equally, business letters will look more professional if you use ready-made symbols, such as those for copyright or trademark. Fun symbols may not be as important, but they can pep-up a letter or a party invitation.

AUTOMATIC SYMBOLS

Word automatically helps out with some symbols and foreign characters. For instance, if you type 'cafe', as soon as you type a space, Word adds the accent to the 'e' automatically. Similarly, Word automatically replaces (c) with the copyright symbol. Both are instances of Word's AutoCorrect feature (see Stage 2, page 32), but the exercises on these pages show how to get any character you want, whenever you want.

Adding symbols

Use foreign characters and fun symbols to enhance your letter-writing.

TO ILLUSTRATE how special characters can be both useful and fun, we'll write a love letter to an absent girlfriend. Here is an example using both accented characters and symbols:

My Dear Gisèle,

Was it only yesterday we said goodbye? Je pense à toi. Les feuilles mortes sont tombées des arbres, mais mon amour reste toujours vivant. Ça me soulage que tu reçoive ma lettre. Je serai encore une fois avec toi, ô mon trésor éternel.

♥ Je t'embrasse ♥

Christian ✗✗✗✗✗ ☺

1 Type in the text until you reach a special character. Then select the Insert menu and choose Symbol.

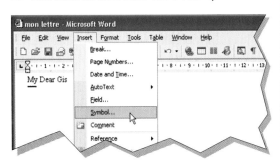

2 When the Symbol window opens, select the Symbols tab and choose (normal text) from the Font drop-down menu.

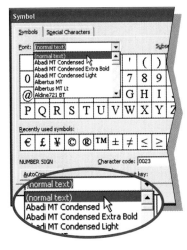

3 Now look at the grid and select the character you are looking for, in this case è, by clicking on it with the left mouse button. When you click on the Insert button, the character will appear in the text document (inset).

4 Close the Symbol window and carry on through the letter, entering all the letters with accents in the same way. The next special character is the heart symbol. This is entered in a similar way, but is lower down in the table of special characters. Select ZapfDingbats from the Font drop-down menu.

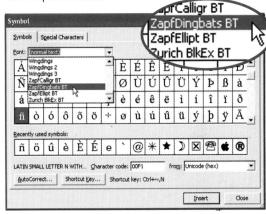

5 Click on the heart in the Symbol characters grid, then click on the Insert button. When you come to insert the second heart, save time by copying and pasting the first one. Have a look at all the symbols in this grid to see the variety available for use in different types of document.

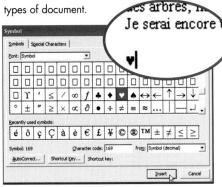

6 If you want to add other embellishments, try an '✗' for kisses after the signature. This is part of the Wingdings font, so select this font and choose from the grid as before. Again, you don't need to insert each '✗' separately, just copy and paste the first one.

7 Another symbol is the 'smiley' face. This is contained in both Wingdings and normal text fonts, so you can use either. Insert this at the end of the document. All the special characters appear in the font size you are using to write your letter, but let's make the 'smiley' face bigger. You do this in exactly the same way as with an ordinary character. Select the 'smiley' and increase the font size to 48.

Finding and replacing text

Are you looking for a quick way to get to the right part of your document, to add some formatting to frequently occurring words or to correct a name misspelt throughout it? If so, Word's powerful find and replace tool is what you need. It will even search for 'sound-alike' words.

It can sometimes be difficult to locate the part of a Word document that you need to work on, especially if it is a long document. The most obvious way is to scroll right through the document until you find what you're looking for, but this can be very time-consuming. Thankfully, Word has a much more flexible way of dealing with this.

Word includes a Find tool that allows you to search for words or phrases within your document. This means that you only have to remember a relevant word from the part of the document you want to work on, then you can use the Find tool to skip through the occurrences of that word until you reach the one you want. This tool can also be handy when you want to find certain key words or phrases in documents that you need to change.

● **Changing words and phrases**

Word's Find tool is not just a search tool for locating words and phrases – you can also use it to replace them with different words or phrases. For instance, you could replace all the occurrences in a document of British Broadcasting Corporation with BBC in one swift operation. Or you could correct all the occurrences of somebody's name if you discover that you've spelt it incorrectly.

In fact, it's not just words and phrases you can replace – you can actually replace any sequence of characters. For instance, many typists were originally taught to add two spaces after the full stop. If this is a habit you just can't break, you can search for two consecutive spaces and replace them with one.

There are also other special characters that you can replace, such as paragraph marks, tab characters and page breaks. The Word Find and Replace tool also includes some other advanced features. For example, if you're not sure of the spelling of a word you need to look for, you can ask Word to search for a word that sounds like the one you type in. You can also get the Find and Replace tool to look for words that appear in a particular format (for example, typeface, size, bold, italics and so on). You can instruct Word to replace these words with different words in the same format or the same words in another format.

Word also lets you match case. This means that if you want to replace the name of a company called 'FAST', but leave the ordinary word 'fast' as it is, Word can oblige. You'll soon wonder how you managed without it.

WHAT IT MEANS

CASE
This is the technical term for the style of letters used in text. Upper case text refers to CAPITAL letters and lower case text refers to normal, or small, letters.

Using Word's Find and Replace tool

The Find and Replace tool helps you locate and replace any sequence of text, including numbers and special characters. It makes it easy to move around long documents and change misspelt words in a single action.

1 Here's a letter that we've been working on. There's a mistake in one of the names – the first George Smith should be Andrew Smith. Let's use Word's Find and Replace tool to put things right.

2 Position the text cursor at the start of the letter so that Word will search through the whole document from the beginning. Now select Replace from the Edit menu.

3 The Find and Replace dialog box appears: type the word George in the Find what: text box at the top of the dialog box. Then type in the word Andrew in the Replace with: text box. If we wanted to change all the occurrences of the name George to Andrew, we would just press the Replace All button. However, we won't do this here because we want to show more advanced replace options.

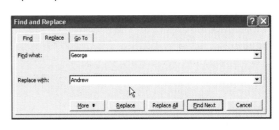

4 Let's exploit the different formats used in the letter – one 'George' is in italics, the other is not. Click on the More button and the Find and Replace dialog box will extend to reveal more options. Click once in the Find what: text box, then click over the Format button and choose the Font option.

5 Use this dialog box to specify the format of the word to replace. We chose 12pt Arial with an italic style (to find George in italics). Select suitable settings for your document and click on the OK button.

6 Position the cursor in the Replace with: text box, click on the Format button and select Font again. Repeat the choices we made in Step 5 and click OK. Notice how both text boxes have identical Format lines below them.

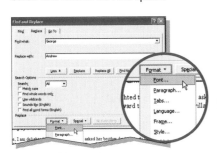

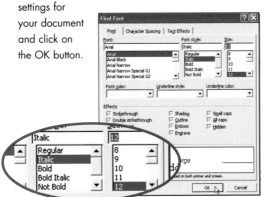

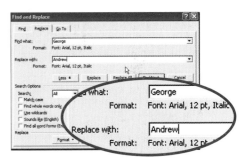

7 If you click on the Replace button Word will locate all words in the style specified in Step 5 and ask you to confirm each replacement as you go. For this exercise, click on the Replace All button. Word makes all the replacements (one in this case) and reports back to you. Click on the OK button in the dialog box that reports the number of changes (below).

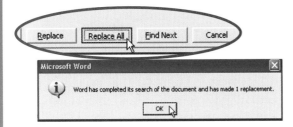

8 Click on the Close button in the Find and Replace dialog box and you'll see your modified document with only the one George changed to Andrew, as intended.

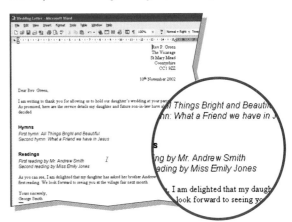

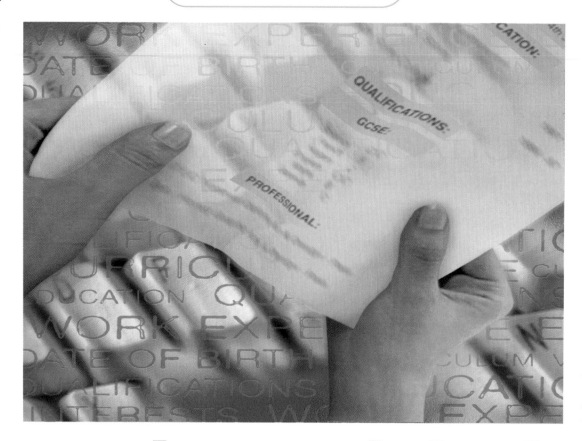

If you're applying for a job, why not take advantage of your PC's capabilities to make your CV look as good as possible?

Borders and shading

Adding borders and highlights to give your curriculum vitae a really professional look couldn't be easier when you're using Word.

If there is one document you just have to have professionally presented, it is your CV – your curriculum vitae or life history. The CV is the document that clinches an interview for a job or college place – or ruins your chances – and it is absolutely vital that it creates the right impression.

● The computer advantage
All too many CVs are simply typed out in a haphazard way or, worse still, handwritten. With a PC and a printer, however, you have the power to produce a clean, neat document that will make the most of your chances. Even better, by spending a little time making your CV as clear, concise and attractive as you can, you will increase the chances that yours will stand out from the rest, and help get you that all-important interview.

With a PC, it is easy to make last-minute corrections to your CV to ensure every detail is right. You can also update it to incorporate your most recent work experience or each new qualification – putting an end to handwritten corrections that make your CV look scruffy. You can modify it, too, to suit the different types of job that you may want to apply for. And, perhaps most importantly of all, you have complete control over the way it looks.

Over the next few pages, we give you a few tips on preparing a CV. In particular, we'll show you how to use Microsoft Word's tools to create a really professional look – adding borders and shading to emphasize specific features and to encourage the reader to look at the more important sections.

When creating a CV, it is vital to present everything in clear, easy-to-understand

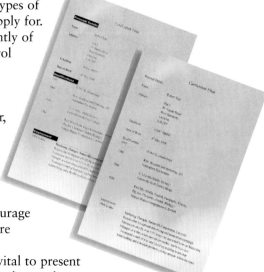

CHECKPOINT

MAKING THE MOST OF YOUR CV

As well as the formatting ideas covered in the step-by-step examples (see pages 44–45), there are a few general principles to consider when creating a CV. Follow the tips here and your CV is less likely to end up in the reject pile as a result of poor presentation.

☑ Try to avoid using capital letters and italics for large chunks of text. Both make your information harder to read than normal text.

☑ Avoid the temptation to use decorative typefaces. They might be fun for the odd letter or jokey poster, but most potential employers are looking for efficient, business-like employees.

☑ Be wary of using humour in your text – it's not what the CV is for.

☑ Always get your referees' permission to put their details on the CV. Neither they nor a potential employer will be impressed if you haven't.

☑ Keep your CV to a maximum of two A4 pages, unless you are specifically asked to do otherwise.

sections so that it is easy for the reader to immediately see your academic qualifications, recent employment history, and so on.

Borders are an excellent way of sectioning off different parts of your CV. They also make it look bolder and more interesting, and this can help make a rather lightweight CV look a little more substantial, without distorting the facts.

● Dividing your life up

You should always start your CV with your name, address and contact numbers (phone, fax, email and so on). Follow this with your date of birth, nationality (if relevant) and other background details.

Some people prefer to put all this information in the centre of the page, using the centre alignment button. Others prefer it on the left of the page, which is known as ranged left text.

The rest of the CV then divides into three main areas: education and qualifications,

employment history and related experience. The idea is to give the reader a clear outline of your life, so each entry in these three sections begins with the relevant dates. With the employment history, keep entries brief and to the point, but make sure it is clear what you were doing in each job, listing in order: dates, your job title, your employer's name and address and what your job entailed.

● The right order for you

Recruitment experts advise putting your employment history in reverse order. That means that you begin with the most recent jobs. Remember, when potential employers are reading through lots of CVs, they probably want to see what you're currently doing, without having to wade through your entire career of holiday and temporary jobs.

Others think that your employment history should be in chronological order down the page for absolute clarity. It is really up to you to decide which works best with your life history and also shows potential employers the important facts most clearly.

The final sections should cover your personal interests, which can be surprisingly helpful at getting you that interview, and the names and contact details of two referees who will give you good references. These are usually work-related, but some employers also like a personal referee.

WHEN TO USE UNDERLINE AND WHEN TO USE BORDERS

Most of the time you will use the Borders tool to add horizontal lines under some text in your documents. But you might also have been using Word's Underline tool (below) to achieve the same effect. Which one is better?

Underlining

In Word, you can emphasize any amount of text, from a single word to the whole document, by using the underline command, which places a single line under the text selected. Some people also use the underline character '_' (the character you get if you press [shift] + [-]

Once you're used to adding borders, you'll probably only use Word's Underline button for adding a single underline to individual words and short phrases.

together). By filling the page width with this character, a border is created. While this might look fine, it's a time-consuming approach. There are other potential problems, too: for example, if you increase the size of the text used in the document, you will find that this line of underline characters overlaps onto another line.

Borders

When you use borders for such lines, however, you'll find you have much more flexibility available at the press of a few buttons. For example, you have a wide choice of different line widths and you can choose from a variety of styles, including solid, dotted and even wavy lines. When you work

with borders, you'll discover that you can use them on any side of your text. You can put lines on one, two or three sides of the text, or even completely enclose it.

As you experiment with the borders options, you'll find that in most cases they're more suitable than either the Underline tool or the underline character. On the whole, while underlining is the best option for emphasizing a word or phrase in formal letters and documents, the borders options are much more suitable for making paragraphs or longer sections stand out.

Special effects, such as wavy lines and 3D edges, won't suit all of your documents, but they show the extra flexibility of Word's border options.

Adding borders to separate sections of your CV

To show you the basic steps of producing a CV, we've created an imaginary example for someone applying for the job of supermarket manager. You can either copy the format of this CV or create your own.

1 Type in the text of your CV, following the guidelines given (see Checkpoint box on the previous page). For the moment, don't add any formatting other than tabs to create columns. All the formatting commands will be added later on.

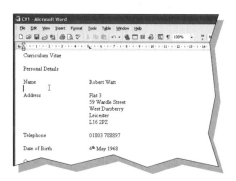

2 To divide the CV into clear sections, you can create lines across the page under each separate heading with the Borders and Shading option. Start by clicking on the line beneath Personal Details (or whatever your first heading is).

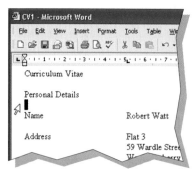

3 Now go to the Format menu at the top of the screen and pull down the menu. Select the Borders and Shading option to bring up the Borders and Shading dialog box on the screen.

4 The Borders and Shading dialog box shows a Preview, plus a choice of styles, including hatched, dotted and solid border options. We shall choose the default option, which is a simple solid line.

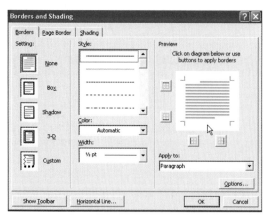

5 Click on the button which shows a top border and a line will appear across the top of the text in the preview panel. Click on OK to put this in your CV.

6 The Personal Details section should begin with a neat line (inset). Now go through the rest of the document adding a border at the beginning of each section in turn – Qualifications, Employment History, and so on.

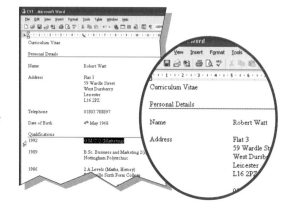

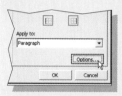

PC TIPS

Spacing borders

When you add a border to a section of your text, you will see that Word leaves a standard distance between the text and the border. Usually this distance will look fine, but you might find that you need the border a little closer or further away from the text. In fact, Word lets you change the distance in any of four directions. First, open up the Borders and Shading dialog box as before and click on the Options button in the bottom right-hand corner (top). Another dialog box pops up with a number of options (right). In the From text section, you can set the distance you want the border to appear from your text, at the top, bottom and on both sides. The easiest way to adjust these settings is to click on the up and down arrows next to each figure (left).

Adding emphasis

Shading is a great way to make words stand out.

TO MAKE each of the section headings stand out clearly, you can use Word's shading option. One way to use this is to reverse the normal colours so that the headings are white text on a black background. For our fictitious CV, we want to make all the section headings, such as Personal Details, Qualifications and Employment, stand out to make the CV easier to read.

1 Click just to the left of the heading you want to highlight, in this case, Personal Details. Choose Borders and Shading from the Format menu as you did for Borders (see page 44).

2 When the Borders and Shading dialog box comes up on the screen, look for the Shading tab at the top and click on it. This brings up a box with coloured squares in the Fill section.

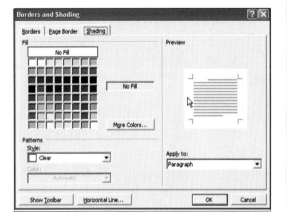

PC TIPS

Most of the Border commands can be accessed from the toolbar. Press the Outside Border button (top, right) and the current paragraph will be bordered or you can highlight the text you want to border and then press the button. Choose the border type you want by clicking the bar to the right of the Outside Border button and selecting your choice from the pop-up box (bottom, right).

3 The Fill section allows you to select the colour of the shading. This is white by default. To make it black, click on the black square. The Preview on the right will now change to black to show you the effect. If you like it, click on OK.

4 The whole line now goes black. To shade only the words, click on the Right Indent marker on the ruler and drag it to the left.

5 As you drag the Right Indent marker to the left, the dotted line shows the width. Release it when it corresponds with the inner margin.

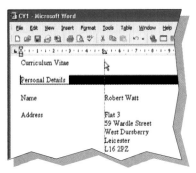

6 To see the effect, click anywhere in the document. Notice that the line beneath the shading is visible again and the text is white on black.

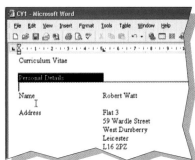

7 Repeat the procedure outlined in Steps 1–6 for all the other section headings in your CV. To finish the document off, you could embellish the text by selecting an attractive but business-like typeface, such as Arial.

Using Word's drawing tools

If a picture paints a thousand words, then why not make the most of the possibilities offered by Word's drawing tools? Use them to liven up documents such as letters, CVs and newsletters.

We have already demonstrated how you can add photographs and illustrations to text (see Stage 1, pages 46–49). However, both of these exercises assume that you have access to the type of graphics you want to use. The examples we used were perfectly acceptable, but when you want to do something specific, such as create a professional-looking logo, they may not necessarily be a great deal of help. Not only will they probably not look quite right, but other Word users will recognize them for what they are straight away.

● **Better graphics**
Fortunately, Word has a number of advanced tools with which you can create all manner of individual graphics. In fact, it not only has some of the core tools of a drawing package such as CorelDRAW, but also contains some rather clever and fun-to-use three-dimensional features.

Combining these tools with the basic options, such as coloured fills, coloured lines, patterned rules and customizable preset shapes (to name just a few), will give you more than enough scope to create some highly impressive graphics. It will be quicker and easier than working with a separate graphics program to achieve the look you want. Word's design tools are very straightforward to use and you'll soon master all the basics. Once you have the know-how, you can easily create personalised party invitations and change of address notices in a few moments.

● **Personalized portfolio**
Another extremely useful facet is that all the graphics you create can be edited. This means that you can gather together your own portfolio of graphics, each one of which is slightly different, to theme an extensive document or to make variations on your logo for use on letterheads or compliment slips.

This editing facility allows you to come back to the designs whenever you like so you can make further variations as your needs change. It also means that you can adapt one design for another purpose, potentially saving lots of time in the future.

Stand out from the crowd. Use Word's drawing tools to give documents a professional look.

The drawing tools

Word has an impressive selection of tools hidden in its Drawing toolbar. When you know where to find them, your Word documents could take on a whole new shape.

THE DRAWING tools can be broken down into a few broad categories. There are buttons you can see on the Drawing toolbar, and there are tools and commands which are available through drop-down lists.

Look along the toolbar (shown below) and you'll see buttons that look, and work, like those in other packages: lines, arrows, rectangles and circles, plus line style and colour and border options. Using these could not be more straightforward. You just need to click on the appropriate button, then move the mouse to the page and click and drag the mouse to draw the object on the page. Other buttons allow you to change the colour of the objects and their outlines, or even their shapes.

● **For Word's next trick...**
Word also has some tricks of its own, one of which is AutoShapes – shapes and lines that you draw in much the same way as the simple drawing tools but which have a built-in intelligence, making them very easy to customize to your exact requirements. Finally, there are shadow and 3D commands that you can apply to boxes on the page with very little effort.

Microsoft® Word

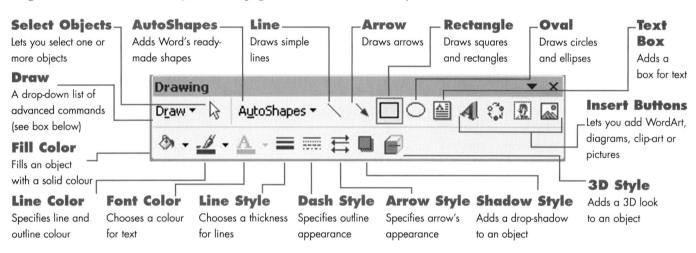

Select Objects Lets you select one or more objects

AutoShapes Adds Word's ready-made shapes

Line Draws simple lines

Arrow Draws arrows

Rectangle Draws squares and rectangles

Oval Draws circles and ellipses

Text Box Adds a box for text

Draw A drop-down list of advanced commands (see box below)

Insert Buttons Lets you add WordArt, diagrams, clip-art or pictures

Fill Color Fills an object with a solid colour

Line Color Specifies line and outline colour

Font Color Chooses a colour for text

Line Style Chooses a thickness for lines

Dash Style Specifies outline appearance

Arrow Style Specifies arrow's appearance

Shadow Style Adds a drop-shadow to an object

3D Style Adds a 3D look to an object

ADVANCED DRAWING TOOLS AND OPTIONS IN THE TOOLBAR

The drop-down list of options in the toolbar's Draw menu is concerned with how the objects 'sit' on the page and how they relate to each other. The grouping options let you combine or separate objects, although these objects must be selected for the commands to be highlighted. Group combines them; Ungroup breaks them up again.

The options under Order let you move objects in front of, or behind, each other. Bring Forward and Send Back shift the object, one level at a time; Bring to Front or Send to Back move the element straight to the front or to the back, jumping through any other layers or objects with just one click. Objects you draw usually

float on top of the Word document you are working on. However, the Send Behind Text command puts an object under the Word text. This is useful for adding a tinted panel behind the text.

Word usually helps you line up objects on the page when you draw or move them by snapping them to an invisible grid. Grid lets you turn this facility off if you want to line objects up by hand. Nudge commands shift objects by tiny amounts. With the Align or Distribute commands you can get Word to position objects. You can

choose whether to line them up or have them evenly separated. The Rotate or Flip commands allow you to rotate an item by exact amounts or flip it to make a mirror image (you can do this horizontally or vertically). Use the Edit Points command when you want to subtly alter the shape of any freely drawn object such as smooth lines or irregular boxes. The object must be selected for Edit Points to be highlighted in the options list.

Change AutoShape lets you change one AutoShape into another – a circle into a multi-pointed star, for example.

Set AutoShape Defaults allows you to customize a shape so it is exactly how you want it each time you draw it. For example, draw a square and change the thickness of its outline to 6pt. By clicking on Set AutoShape Defaults, any shape you subsequently draw will also have a 6pt border, saving you time.

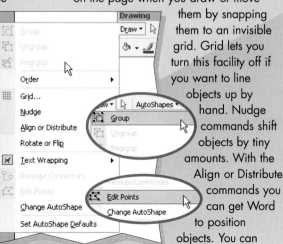

Drawing simple pictures in a letter

Word's drawing tools should not be underestimated. Not only are they powerful enough to enable you to be creative, but they are also available at the click of a mouse button.

1 Let's set up an imaginary example, adding some simple pictures to a letter explaining some work to be done on the garden. Once you've entered your letter text, click on the Drawing button on the toolbar.

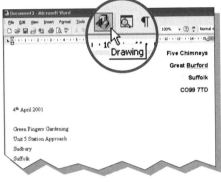

2 Now select the Rectangle tool from the pop-up Drawing toolbar and draw a rectangle within the drawing area Word places on the page. We'll use this as our garden outline. Unfortunately, the text of the letter runs under the rectangle.

3 Click on the outline of the drawing area with the right mouse button and select the Format Drawing Canvas option from the menu that pops up.

4 Click on the Layout tab in the Format Drawing Canvas dialog box that appears. Select the Square option under Wrapping Style and then click the OK button. You will now see that the text wraps to create a new line, instead of disappearing under the rectangle.

5 Now we'll change the colour of the garden. Make sure the rectangle is selected, click on the Fill Color button on the toolbar and then select a suitable square from the drop-down palette. The rectangle will fill with your chosen colour. Now we want the green to look patchier, so that it reflects its poor state.

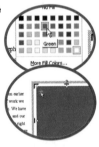

6 Click the Fill Color button and select Fill Effects. This dialog box lets you add many different types of effect. Click on the Pattern tab.

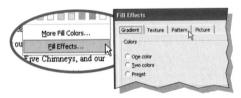

7 You'll see a variety of patterns. Choose one that looks a little patchy. Click on the OK button and your rectangle will then change.

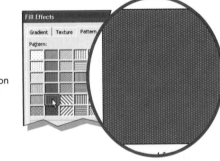

Sticky buttons

You'll notice that when you use the tools on the Drawing toolbar, the buttons 'unclick' themselves after you have drawn each object. This can be very inconvenient when it's necessary for you to draw several lines or shapes one after the other.

To get around this problem, double-click on the button. This will make it stick down; you can now draw several shapes in a row.

When you want to use another tool, just click on the button again to unstick it.

8 Now we want to add a shed using the same steps. Choose a roof colour and pattern.

9 We used the horizontal lines for our pattern, but now we want brown planks with white lines – not the other way round. To do this, bring up the Pattern tab of the Fill Effects dialog box (Steps 6 and 7) and switch the Foreground and Background colours. Click on the OK button to see the effect on your shed.

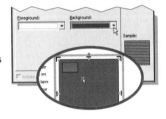

10 We're going to finish our first plan by adding the paved walkway from the back of the house to the garden shed. Now we're ready to use Word's more advanced drawing tools to draw a diagram that will show how we want the garden to look (opposite).

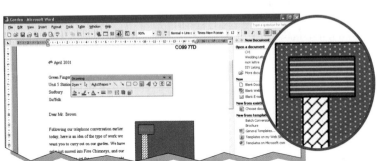

Using advanced drawing tools

We can use some more of Word's drawing capabilities to finish the garden plan started on page 48. Here we'll show you how to add some fine details.

1 Start with the letter we created opposite. Use this to make a similar garden layout to which you need to add several small dark green circles (using the circle tool) to indicate small shrubs.

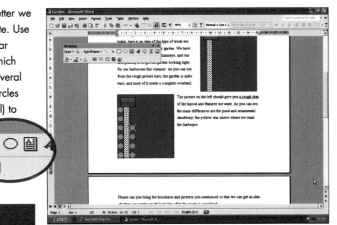

2 We want to add a special object that will draw the attention of our gardener to an area for a barbecue. Click on the AutoShapes button then select the Stars and Banners option and click on the first shape: Explosion 1. Then use the mouse to drag the shape to the top of the garden (inset right).

AUTO SHAPES

Word's basic shapes are easy to add to your documents, but there are times when you will need more complex shapes, which Word also supplies. You can select one of these and then tweak it to form the exact outline you need.

Click on the AutoShapes button and you'll see that Word has six categories. For example, there are ready-made star shapes, arrow-heads and speech bubbles.

AutoShapes' Lines options are also very useful when you need more than straight lines. The Scribble tool lets you draw lines by hand and will follow the exact path your mouse takes on the mouse pad. Use the Curve tool to smooth the line or try the Freeform tool to combine Curve and Scribble.

3 Use the Fill Color palette to colour in the explosion shape. Make sure it's a shade that will be easily noticed to avoid it being confused with the other existing garden objects.

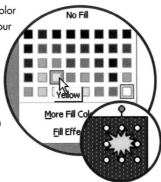

4 Now we'll use another of Word's AutoShapes to create an ornamental pond. Select the Moon shape from the Basic Shapes collection and drag the crescent into the blank area of the garden.

5 The Moon is a special kind of shape: there's an extra handle (the small yellow diamond) in addition to the usual handles along the edge. AutoShapes with these special handles can be tweaked. Click and drag this handle to the right.

6 This handle controls the curvature of the concave side of the Moon, making it more or less bowed (experiment with other AutoShapes to see other ways these diamond handles work).

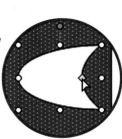

7 Use the Pattern tab of the Fill Effects dialog box to fill the pond. Choose suitable blue colours and the wavy lines option to represent the water surface.

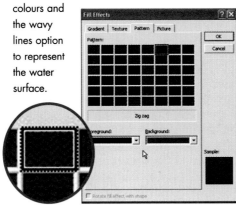

8 Here we've added the final touches (right) – some more shrubs by the pond and a patio area. Use the Rectangle and Oval tools to add these. Such simple diagrams give you an idea of what you can achieve in a few minutes, without even firing up another graphics program.

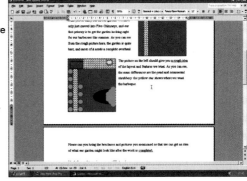

Using mail merge

Sending the same circular letter to a group of people can be extremely time-consuming as you have to personalize each one. Fortunately, Word can lend a helping hand, with a special feature called mail merge.

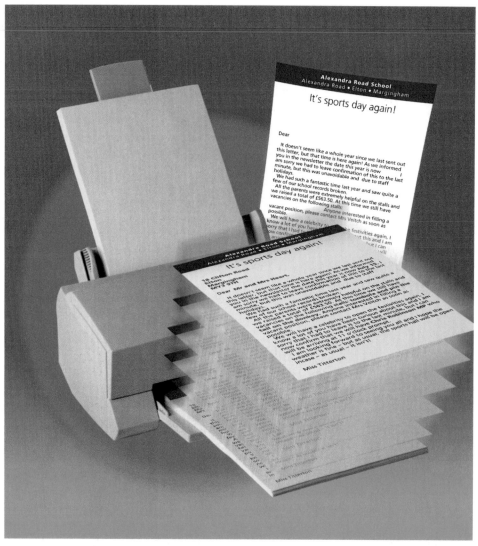

Professional, personalized and relatively painless...mail merge can save you time and effort.

There are various occasions when you need to send similar letters to several people. Sometimes, a basic form letter will do. Often, however, although most of the text can remain the same, it is much better if each letter is personalized. For example, party invitations or speculative letters to potential employers look much better when they are individually addressed.

● Changing information
You can amend each letter by hand but Word's mail merge facility makes the job much easier. With mail merge you need only write the document once and then tell Word what you want changed, so you can print hundreds of personalized letters with a single operation.

The principle behind mail merging is that you store the parts of a letter that change (such as the name, address, and so forth) in a separate database. This information can then be incorporated into a letter (or other document) in positions that you specify. All you need to do is create the basic letter, inserting special codewords in the places where

you want the variable information to be inserted from the database, and then bring the two together.

You've probably seen examples of 'junk mail' created this way. Such letters usually set the data up in another program, which is one reason you sometimes see letters addressed to 'Dear Mr 10 Park Rd'. Thankfully, Word makes everything far simpler.

Although Word still creates two documents – a form letter and a data source – everything is done in one program. Word also has an easy-to-follow dialog box – called the Mail Merge Task Pane – to take you through the whole process in detail.

● A simple example
For our first step-by-step exercise, we are going to take the example of a school circular informing parents of the forthcoming sports day. This is a very simple mail merge and only requires basic data to be entered, but even this example illustrates another advantage of mail merging. If you want to send another letter to the same people – providing the sports day

results, perhaps – you can re-use the names and addresses from the database without having to retype them.

● Setting up mailing data

Although this example uses simple data to create a brief letter, the same principles apply to longer or more complicated data and documents that you want to generate. All you have to do is insert in the document the meaningful markers that Word understands, or fields, which correspond to the entries in your database.

You can have as many fields as you like. You can even sort or filter the mailing according to the data that appears in them. In our first example, we want everyone on the list to get the same letter. But in the second example (see page 53), we will see how to use more

advanced options to ensure that only members of the PTA council get a letter.

Mail merges can be as complex as you want, depending on the details in the database. For instance, when mailing a club membership, you could include information on whether or not a subscription has been renewed and so write only to those who haven't paid up!

The mail merge facility is so efficient that it can incorporate many different types of variable information in the same document. For example, a self-employed home PC user could use a database of customers and create different sets of letters for good customers and late payers on a monthly basis.

When you start mail merging you go straight into setting up your database, but don't feel nervous – Word gives you a lot of hand-holding to ensure quick results.

(see page 53)

WHAT IT MEANS

FIELDS

In a mail merge document, a field is a block of data that is held in a database. When you are preparing a mail merge, Word automatically sets up your data in separate fields that might include entries for, say: title (Mr, Miss, Dr, etc); first name; surname; first line of address (house number and street name); second line of address (district); city; postcode; and country.

Word also uses fields as special place markers in a document. These fields indicate places that are reserved for information, which Word automatically adds, e.g. a field can automatically insert the current date or time.

In the case of a mail merge, when you prepare the letter for merging you can include fields that correspond to the blocks of data in your database. The fields in the letter can then draw upon the data and place the correct details in the document when you complete your merge.

Creating data for your mail merge

The mail merge process is divided into two main parts: creating fields to use in your mail merge and adding the fields to the letter or document you want to merge.

1 Start with a new blank Word document, then select the Mail Merge Task Pane from the drop-down list on the right of the Word window.

2 The Task Pane displays the first panel in a six-step guide. To start, select Letters as the document type and then click on the Next: Starting document link at the bottom of the Task Pane.

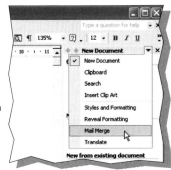

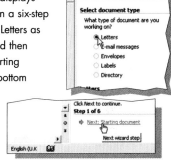

3 Because we haven't yet created the letter for our mail merge, select the Use the current document option at the top of the Task Pane. Then click the Next: Select recipients link at the bottom of the Task Pane.

4 Because this is our first mail merge, we need to create a new list of recipients for our letter. Select the Type a new list option and then click the Create link.

5 The New Address List window lets you type in the recipient details, but first click the Customize button. In the Customize Address List dialog box, you can select Word's suggested fields and click on the Delete button to remove the unwanted fields, such as Company Name.

6 Shorten the list of fields to those shown here. Don't worry about ZIP Code – we'll use it for the postcode and change the field name later (see PC Tips, opposite). Click on the OK button.

7 Now use these fields to enter the recipients' names and addresses. When you finish each one, click the New Entry button to type the next person. When you've finished typing in recipients, click the Close button.

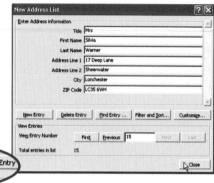

8 Word asks you to save your address list as a Data Source. Type in a file name and click on the Save button. Word shows your list in table form; click on the OK button to return to your Word document.

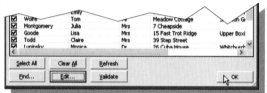

Creating a merge letter

1 Once you've typed and saved your address list, click on the Next: Write your letter link at the bottom of Word's Task Pane. The first job is to insert the fields for the recipient's name. Word lets you do this in one step – click on the Address block link in the Task Pane.

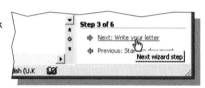

2 Word asks you to confirm the format of the address block. If the preview is correct, click on the OK button. Word inserts the AddressBlock field right at the top of your document. Press [Enter] twice to create two lines and then type in 'Dear' followed by a space. Then click the Insert Merge Fields button on the new toolbar that has appeared.

3 Select Title in the Insert Merge Fields dialog box and click the Insert button. Word adds this field to your document. Type another space and then repeat this step to add the Last Name field.

PRINTING MAIL MERGES

As soon as you select the Print link in Step 5, Word lets you choose exactly which letters to print. It offers the choice of all pages, just the current page, or any range of pages from the database you created. Make your choice and then click on the OK button.

4 Type in the rest of your letter. When you have finished, click on the Next: Preview your letters link in the Task Pane. Word now shows your letter with the first recipient's name and address details in place of the fields you inserted.

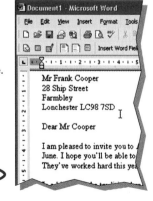

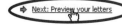

5 Click the Next: Complete the merge link in the Task Pane. You can now print these letters by clicking the Print link in the Merge section. Word will produce one letter for each of the people whose details you typed in (see Printing mail merges box, right).

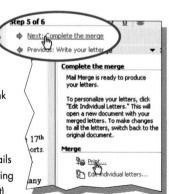

Advanced mail merge techniques

THE FIRST step-by-step exercise demonstrates how a mail merge consists of two documents, the form letter and the data source. These combine together to create the finished document, which can then be printed out (or faxed or emailed). We've explained the essence of the form letter so now we're going to look in more detail at the data source to show how you can sort your records and customize your mailshot. For this example, we're going to create a new field, specifying whether or not parents are members of the school PTA council, and then create a mailing that goes only to those who are council members.

1 With your mail merge letter open, click on the Mail Merge Recipients button on Word's Mail Merge toolbar. The table of names and addresses you entered appears: click on the Edit button.

2 Click on the Customize button when the data screen appears. In the Customize Address List dialog box, click on the Add button.

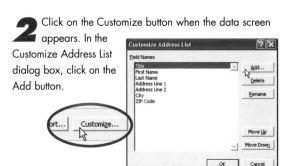

3 Type the new field name – in this case it's 'PTA council' – and then click on the OK button. To change the position of this or any field, select it and use the Move Up and Move Down buttons to move it to its most logical position. In this case, we've moved the PTA council field to the bottom. Click on the OK button.

4 Now you're back to the data entry screen. Use the Previous and Next buttons to move from one recipient's details to the next. Type 'Yes' into the PTA council field for some of them, leaving the others blank. Click on the Close button.

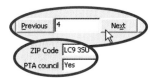

5 You can use the Mail Merge Recipients window to filter the people in your database according to this new information. Scroll along to the right until the PTA council column is visible. Click on the downwards-pointing arrow just to the left of PTA council and select Yes from the drop-down list.

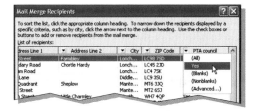

6 Immediately Word filters the recipients according to the value in this column. All other people are hidden from view, leaving only PTA council members visible (two in our example). Click on the OK button to return to your mail merge letter.

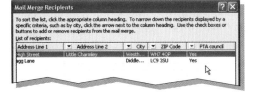

7 Use the links at the bottom of the Task Pane to go to the fifth step in the mail merge procedure. This lets you preview the results of your mail merge: click on the Previous and Next buttons near the top of the Task Pane and you see that only those people who are PTA council members appear.

PC TIPS

You can rename the fields in your database by first selecting the field in the Customize Address List dialog box (see Steps 2 and 3) and then clicking the Rename button.

8 It's also important to remember to remove the filters you apply when you don't need them or you could accidentally mail merge a sub-set of your database. To turn off the filter you applied in Step 5, go back and select All from the drop-down menu for PTA council.

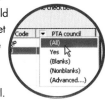

CENTRALIZING YOUR DATA

As you start to use your computer for making small databases, such as the names and addresses in this example, you may find that the information overlaps with other databases – perhaps a basic address book that you use. The best idea is to put all the information into a central pool. The information can then be used for letters, invitations and newsletters – in fact, any mail merge document that you wish. This means that you don't have to type in the same details several times.

Working with percentages

Percentages are used in all sorts of calculations, from personal finance to a detailed business plan. So whether you are trying to sort out your tax or tackle some maths homework, here's how Excel can help you to get the right answers.

Working out percentages is one of the most common mathematical operations after basic addition, multiplication, subtraction and division. That's why many calculators have a special percentage key. In a similar way, Excel makes it very easy to calculate a percentage.

On the next page, we'll work through some straightforward problems to see how to do this. In practice, it's probably quicker to use a calculator for such simple examples. But, as with other tasks, the beauty of learning how to use Excel is that you can set up a detailed worksheet containing large numbers of figures that will be recalculated automatically every time the data changes. This is the basis of the complex tables that are used for calculating the profit on a small business venture, for example, or even the odds on a series of bets.

Many common sums are expressed as percentages. Obvious examples are the VAT rate (currently 17.5%), interest rates (10% a year, perhaps), or a business profit margin (30%, say). All these factors can be included in a spreadsheet calculation and are easy to enter into Excel.

All you need to do is use the % symbol together with the percentage factor and type this into the cell where it applies. Suppose you want to find out how much VAT should be added on to a base price of £63. This can be written out in the form of a simple calculation: £63 x 17.5%. To input this into Excel, you would type it in as =63*17.5%. If you enter this into an empty cell in Excel, it will work out the result for you and display the answer: 11.025. Opposite, we show how to set up some helpful percentage calculations in your worksheet.

Excel automates the calculation of percentages with a special percent button, so you will be able to plough through your work in no time at all.

CALCULATING PERCENTAGES

The word percentage comes from Latin and means 'out of a hundred'. It's used as a simple way of showing how any two numbers are related by referring them to the single standard number 100.

The advantage of this is that it makes it very easy to compare wildly different sums. For example, it can be hard to say whether 9/13 is bigger than 747/1189 without working them out, until you are told that one figure is roughly 69 percent and the other 62 percent. These figures are worked out by calculating the fraction (e.g. 9/13 is 1 ÷ 13 x 9 which equals 0.6923) and multiplying by 100 (to get 69.23%).

Any fraction can be expressed in this way. If it is less than 1, it will be expressed as a percentage less than 100 (so a half is 50%, three-quarters is 75%). If it is more than 1, it will be a percentage more than 100 (so 2 is 200% and 4½ is 450%).

Calculating percentage increases

One of the commonest uses for a percentage calculation is to add a factor to an existing sum and display the result. Here we show you how.

1 It's your lucky day! You have been given a pay rise of 8.5%, and you want to find out what difference this will make to your yearly salary. Start your worksheet by typing in some simple text labels in three consecutive cells (A1, B1 and C1) for Salary, Increase and New Salary. The cells underneath these headings will be used for our figures and calculations.

	A	B	C	D
1	Salary	Increase	New Salary	
2				
3				

2 Type your salary, say £18,000, into cell A2 and then move to the next cell across to type in the percentage increase of 8.5%.

	A	B	C
1	Salary	Increase	New Salary
2	18000	8.5% I	

3 Move to the New Salary column and enter the formula that will calculate your new salary. Multiply the old salary by the percentage increase and add the answer to the old salary. Type the formula =A2*B2+A2. This works without brackets because Excel does the multiplication before the addition.

	A	B	C	D
1	Salary	Increase	New Salary	
2	18000	8.50%	=A2*B2+A2	

4 When you press the [Enter] key, Excel will calculate the correct answer. Now, if you change the number in cell B2 – perhaps you negotiated a better pay rise – the result will change automatically.

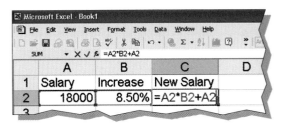

	B	C
	Increase	New Salary
000	8.50%	19530

Calculating a percentage discount

1 You are considering setting up 10 special telephone numbers to save 5% off your bill. However, as the scheme costs £5.00 per quarter, you need to know whether this would be of benefit to you. Type in four column headers, and enter your quarterly bill and discount.

	A	B	C	D	E
1	Quarterly bill	Discount	Saving	Profit or loss?	
2	180	5%			
3					

2 Move to the Saving column and enter the formula to calculate the expected savings: =A2*B2. Press the [Enter] key to see the result.

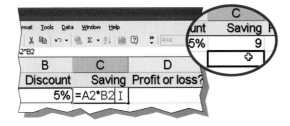

	C
unt	Saving
5%	9

B	C	D
Discount	Saving	Profit or loss?
5%	=A2*B2 I	

3 Now move to the Profit or loss? column and enter a formula to see if you will save or lose money. Type in =C2-5, which is the saving less the £5 running costs. You will save £4. Now try changing the quarterly bill. If the answer is positive, this is how much you save each quarter. If it is negative, the scheme will cost you money.

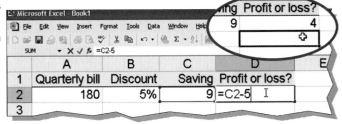

	A	B	C	D	E
1	Quarterly bill	Discount	Saving	Profit or loss?	
2	180	5%	9	=C2-5 I	
3					

HOW TO SUBTRACT A DISCOUNT

A common problem is to find out how much is left after applying a discount. One easy way to do this is to take the percentage discount away from 100, which shows the percentage remaining. For example, a 5% discount would leave 95%. Type =180*95% into a cell and check that the new bill is £171.

Excel at mini-databases

So far, we have used Excel for accounts and financial purposes, but Excel can handle text as well as numbers and will help you organize anything from a Christmas card address list to a gem collection.

Excel's worksheet is made up of rows and columns of cells. So far, we have mostly put numbers into these cells, but Excel is designed to organize text information as well as numbers. In fact, Excel can be used to create what is called a database, which is basically a list of items organized into different categories. There are other full-scale database programs, but Excel is capable of doing the work just as well for small-scale jobs.

For example, a database makes the perfect electronic address book. Opposite, we show you how to set up a database address book in Excel. You can use it for tasks such as making Christmas card or wedding invitation lists, or any other occasion where you might need separate lists for certain events.

● On top form

Excel's database has many other useful functions. If you are involved with a club, for example, you'll find it a great way to store a membership list. Or, if you collect things such as stamps or minerals, you can use the Excel database to catalogue and label them.

What makes an Excel database so useful is that it makes lists easy to sift through, even when they have become long and involved. One way it does this is with a facility called Form view, which lets you see one record or entry at a time. To look at data in Form view,

first click on any record within your list. Next, select the Form option from the Data menu. You will see a new window pop up in the middle of your Excel screen. It shows one record at a time, starting with the first one. Each field is shown in its own box. A set of buttons on the right-hand side allows you to flick backwards or forwards through your list, one record at a time. Other options let you add new records and delete old ones. This way of viewing information is extremely efficient and easier to work with as you only have to concentrate on one record at a time.

Using an Excel database for an address book helps you to get rid of all those scraps of paper on which you have jotted down new addresses, cab companies and so on.

PC TIPS

Finding information in a worksheet

It could be difficult to find the information you want when a worksheet is full of data, so Excel includes a search tool. Select Find from the Edit menu. In the dialog box that appears, type the text you want to locate in the Find what: text box and press the Find Next button.

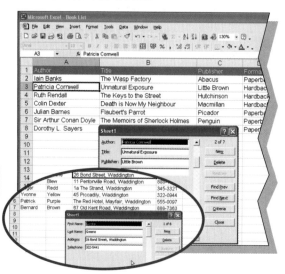

If you have a book collection stored in an Excel database, Form view will show you the complete record you have made for each book — author, title, publisher and format (above). With an address book, Form view will bring up the name and address, plus any other information you have stored (inset).

WHAT IT MEANS

RECORD

A record is one entry in a database. For example, in an address book you would probably have one record for each person. The information within a record is split into fields. In a list of records in an Excel worksheet, these fields are the individual columns you use for separate pieces of information, such as the name, address and telephone number.

Making an address book

A record of names and addresses is useful to have on your computer. Here we show you how to make one.

1 The first task is to choose the headings you want to use. We've started with first names, last names and addresses in the first four columns, adding other headings for telephone numbers or email addresses. You could even put headings for anniversaries such as birthdays, or people to go on your Christmas card list.

2 The next job is to enter all the names, addresses and other details (also see PC Tips). Here we've typed lots of names and addresses straight into the Excel worksheet. However, the worksheet soon becomes a confusing way to look at lots of names and addresses.

3 Let's try a more convenient way of viewing the names and addresses. First, highlight any one of the cells containing information by clicking over it. Now go to the Data menu and select the Form command.

4 This is what Form view looks like. Notice how it displays our list one record at a time, with each piece of data (or field) in its own text box. The buttons on the right let us step backwards and forwards through records, add new ones and delete old ones. To begin, click on Find Next.

5 Now we're looking at the second record in our address book. We can repeat the process by pressing the Find Next button until we reach the last record. We can also work backwards through the records. To go back to the first record, simply click the Find Prev button.

6 To add a new record to our address book, press the New button, type the new information into the text boxes and press the [Enter] key. You will then see the new record appear in the worksheet and an empty Form view, ready for you to add another new record.

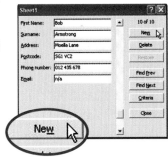

7 Now let's delete an old record we don't need any more. Use the Find Prev and Find Next buttons to locate the right record and click the Delete button.

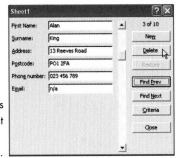

8 As a safety precaution, Excel asks you if you're sure you want to delete the record. Click the OK button to confirm your decision and you will see that the record disappears from the Form and also from the table of information in the worksheet. To close the Form view and return to the worksheet, just click on the Close button. Save your changes as usual, using the Save command in the File menu.

Conditional formatting

We've already seen how you can apply formatting to make cells more noticeable. Excel can also be set up to apply formatting automatically to draw your attention to important developments.

Making cells stand out from the rest of a worksheet – by changing their text style and background colour, for example – is a handy feature of Excel. We know that Excel makes it easy to add such simple formatting (see Stage 1, pages 58–59), but wouldn't it be useful if you could use the formatting to make a cell stand out, depending on the value of the data in it? You can do this by hand, but it is especially valuable to get Excel to do it automatically.

For example, let us imagine you use a worksheet to keep track of the payments in and out of your bank account. Wouldn't it be great if your bank-balance cell automatically turned red whenever you went into overdraft? Well, Excel can do this for you using a process known as conditional formatting.

● Balancing the books

Conditional formatting is so called because it allows you to set a condition at which Excel will automatically format a cell. In the

	A	B	C	D	E	F
1	Item	Date	Payments	Receipts	Balance	
2	January Salary	02/01/03		£800.00		
3	Rent	03/01/03	£220.00			
4	Supermarket	06/01/03	£35.66			
5	Petrol	11/01/03	£15.02			
6	Supermarket	14/01/03	£31.45			
7						
8	Totals		302.13	£800.00	£497.87	
9						
10						

	A	B	C	D	E	F
1	Item	Date	Payments	Receipts	Balance	
2	January Salary	02/01/03		£800.00		
3	Rent	03/01/03	£220.00			
4	Supermarket	06/01/03	£35.66			
5	Petrol	11/01/03	£15.02			
6	Supermarket	14/01/03	£31.45			
7	Holiday Booking	21/01/03	£500.00			
8						
9	Totals		802.13	£800.00	-£2.13	
10						

To start with, our bank-balance in cell E8 is healthy and Excel displays it in black (top). However, as soon as we add our holiday booking payment, the bank account becomes overdrawn (now shown in cell E9). Excel draws our attention to this fact by making the text in the cell turn red.

example (left), the conditional formatting applies only when your bank-balance cell reaches a condition of less than zero.

Every time a new entry is made on your worksheet, Excel automatically checks the bank-balance cell's value to see if the set condition has been reached. Of course, you don't have to set the condition at zero, you can choose any figure you wish and apply it to any cell. For example, you might get Excel to turn the bank-balance cell orange if it falls below £200, to warn you that you could be in danger of becoming overdrawn.

You can use conditional formatting for many different types of worksheet. Supposing you are doing a research project on mountains and you have entered details of the heights of various peaks on your worksheet. Excel can be set up to highlight any mountains that exceed or fall short of your desired conditions. You could get Excel to show all the mountains that are over 7000m in one colour and those that are below 5000m in another.

Applying conditional formatting

We are going to use the example of a worksheet containing a list of the tallest mountains in different countries to show how to apply conditional formatting.

1 Here is a worksheet listing mountains by their country and height. At a glance, it is hard to tell from the worksheet which mountains are over 7000m or under 5000m. However, we can use conditional formatting to pick them out.

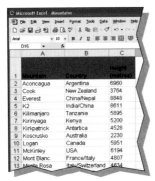

2 Let's start by trying to give the mountains rising to over 7000m a different background colour. Use the mouse to highlight all the cells that contain mountain heights and then go to the Format menu and select the Conditional Formatting option.

PC TIPS

To locate which cells have conditional formats, choose Go To in the Edit menu and click Special in the dialog box. Click Conditional formats and then click OK.

Microsoft® Excel

3 This will bring up the Conditional Formatting dialog box. You set conditions and actions by changing the text in each box and using the Format button.

4 The first box contains 'Cell Value Is', which is OK, so click on the down arrow at the right end of the second drop-down box and select greater than.

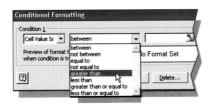

5 The dialog box changes to provide a window in which you enter your condition. Type 7000 into this box. Then click on the Format button.

6 Use the Font tab in the Format Cells dialog box (left) to change the text to yellow and the Patterns tab to change cell shading to red. Click on OK to close. To return to the worksheet, click on OK in the Conditional Formatting dialog box. Heights over 7000m show up as yellow on red (right).

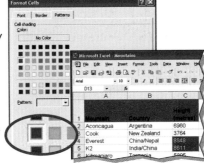

7 While this gets the point across, we'd prefer to emphasize the names of the mountains rather than their heights. To do this, you must first remove the conditional formatting that you originally set up. Highlight the same cells as in Step 2, then bring up the Conditional Formatting dialog box and click on Delete. Excel asks you to confirm your choice. Select the Condition 1 checkbox, click on OK and return to the worksheet.

8 Select the cells containing the mountain names (cells A2 to A15 here) and bring up the Conditional Formatting dialog box. Choose the Formula Is option in the first drop-down box and type =C2>7000 in the new text box. Use the Format button to set the cell format as in Step 6. Click the Add button.

9 The dialog box expands to let you apply another condition. Use the Formula Is option, type in the formula =C2<5000 and use the Format button to set a different format (right). Click on the OK button.

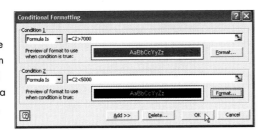

10 You can now see how the worksheet reflects two sets of conditions. By using formulae in conditions, you'll find that you can give your worksheets more built-in intelligence.

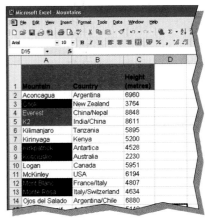

Advanced cell formatting

Detailed entries on a worksheet can take up too much space if they are kept on a single line. Excel includes several tools that help you format text and keep your worksheet neat, tidy and readable.

So far, you have seen how to apply simple formatting effects to worksheet cells in Excel and how to change the background colour of cells and the colour, size and font of text by using the Formatting toolbar (see Stage 1, pages 58–59). Now you'll see how you can add all sorts of text alignment options to your formatting skills to make your worksheets much easier to read and understand.

● When the text won't fit

These options are a great help when you have a few cells that contain very long lines of text. Normally this text overlaps into the cells next to them. If you want to constrain some text to fit the width of the cell it's in, you can get Excel to 'wrap' it. This converts it into a miniature paragraph (bottom left).

Excel even makes it a simple drag-and-drop affair to change the angle of text in a cell (as shown inset right). You can even specify an exact angle for the rotation. Alternatively, you can make text appear in a vertical stack, which is very useful if you need a narrow column.

Another advanced formatting option is Merge cells. By joining adjacent cells into one cell you can make your worksheet easier to use. For example, if you have a three-column table, you can combine the three cells above the table into a single cell for a heading using the alignment commands.

● Formatting cells

While you can carry out some of Excel's alignment options directly from the toolbar, the more powerful commands are only available through the Format Cells dialog box. This has an Alignment tab which includes all the alignment options.

You need only select the cells you want to format and bring up this dialog box to use the commands. After you follow the exercise on the next page, you will soon get the hang of even the most advanced options. Practise with a dummy worksheet if you are worried about accidentally changing or losing your data.

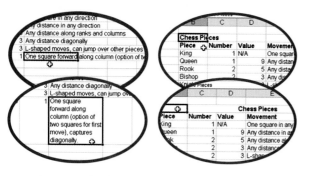

By using Excel's advanced – but simple – formatting options, you can rid yourself of many awkward text problems. You can make a long line of text wrap as a mini-paragraph (above left) and make a table heading sit in the centre of a range of cells (above right).

WHAT IT MEANS

MERGE CELLS

Until now, all our Excel examples have used a regular grid of cells – with all cells in a column the same width and all cells in a row the same height. However, Excel also allows you to merge adjacent cells so one cell spans more than one column or row.

Formatting text in cells

You can use the Cells command from the Format menu to align text in cells and make your worksheets not only more attractive, but also easier to read. Here's an example of a worksheet containing text only. We'll improve its overall legibility by formatting.

Microsoft® Excel

INDENTED LISTS

You may find that for some types of table a small indent helps readability. By using the Indent option you can specify the exact amount. First select the cells you want to indent, bring up the Alignment tab and increase the Indent setting. This is a tidy way to make lists with several sections easier to read – as shown in this example of fruit and vegetables.

1 Enter an easy table like this. We've used simple formatting to widen column E and add colour and emphasis.

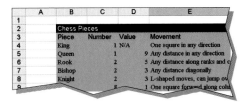

2 We want to make our title 'Chess Pieces' sit across the four columns of our table. Select the four cells, B2 to E2. A simple click of Excel's Merge and Center button will merge these four cells into one and allow us to use the 'Chess Pieces' text as the centred title.

3 Highlight the four sub-headings from B3 to E3. Select Cells from the Format menu (or see PC Tips, below). Click on the Alignment tab in the Format Cells dialog box and use the mouse to rotate the Text pointer below Orientation to 45 degrees. Click the OK button to see the result (inset).

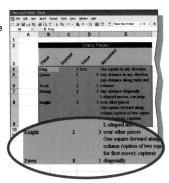

4 Now we want to make sure the long text entries in the Movement column don't run outside our coloured columns. Highlight the cells (E4 to E9 in our example) and go to the Alignment options again. On the left of the dialog box you will see three Text control options: tick the Wrap text checkbox and click the OK button. You'll see the long text lines wrap into paragraphs within the cells.

5 However, where cells have become taller to allow the text to fit, text in the rest of the row stays at the bottom of the cells. This looks a little odd (inset), but it can be altered. First, select all the cells in the table (B4 to E9 here).

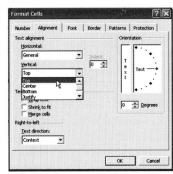

6 Bring up the Alignment tab again. Under the Text alignment section, you will see two drop-down boxes that control the position of text in cells. Click on the drop-down list box under the Vertical label. Select the Top option and click on the OK button to apply this change.

PC TIPS

You can also bring up the Format Cells dialog box by using the right mouse button. Once you're used to it, you'll find this is a lot quicker than using Excel's menu bar. First select the cells you want to format, then click once on the highlighted cells with the right mouse button. You will see a small pop-up menu; one of its options is the Format Cells command. Select this and you will see the usual dialog box.

7 For the final touch, we'll use a simpler alignment option to centre the text in the cells under the Number and Value sub-headings. First, highlight the cells (C4 to D9 in our table on the right), then click on the Center button on Excel's Formatting toolbar.

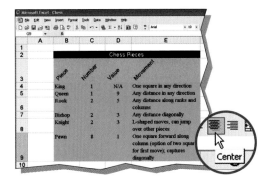

Understanding cell references

We have seen how Excel puts references into formulae so that it can make calculations. It's not essential to know exactly how this works but, as usual, an understanding of the basics helps avoid mistakes.

Performing calculations is incredibly easy when you use Excel. For example, if you want to add the contents of cells A1 and A2, with the result appearing in A3, just type =A1+A2 in cell A3. You can change the numbers in cells A1 and A2 and Excel still updates the result in cell A3.

The key to all this is the way Excel allows you to refer to cells by their column (as a letter) and row (as a number) co-ordinates. These cell references (A1, B3, X86, etc.) are a fundamental part of Excel as it uses them to keep your calculations up-to-date when you move cells around. It's well worth spending some time getting to grips with how cell references work if you want to get the most out of Excel.

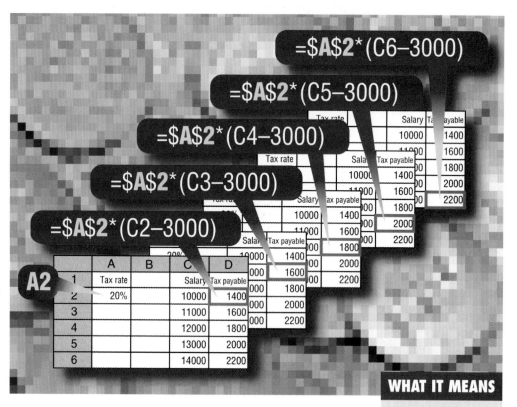

● Automatic updating

Type some numbers into cells A1 and A2 and the formula =A1+A2 into cell A3. Now insert a new row before row 1 by clicking on cell A1 and selecting Rows from the Insert menu: you will see the numbers shift down one row.

The numbers and the sum are still the same, but surely the answer to the sum should be different as A1 and A2 have now both changed? Double-click on cell A4, though, and you will see that Excel has changed your formula to =A2+A3.

Most of the time this automatic updating will prove extremely helpful because it saves time and effort. For example, if you have set up lots of calculations in your worksheet, you don't want to go through manually updating them all just because you have added a new row or column.

● Relative and absolute cell references

In our simple example, Excel changes the formula. This is because the references we originally typed (the 'A1' and 'A2' in =A1+A2) are relative cell references and can change according to the cell in which they appear. As another example, type some numbers into cells B2 and B3. Now select Copy from the Edit menu to copy the formula from cell A4. Paste it into B4 by selecting Paste from the Edit menu. Excel guesses that you want to add the figures in the B column and therefore changes the cell references in the calculation: the formula it puts in cell B4 is =B2+B3.

However, for some calculations, you won't want Excel to change the cell references. In order to do this you need to use an absolute cell reference instead of a relative one. We show you how to do this on the next page.

WHAT IT MEANS

ABSOLUTE CELL REFERENCE
An absolute cell reference in a formula always refers to exactly the same cell co-ordinates. If you copy the formula to other cells, it will always be the same.

Absolute cell references look just like relative cell references, but use $ signs – so you would use A1 instead of A1 and B4 in place of B4 in such references.

Using absolute cell references

Absolute cell references have many uses – especially for constant factors, such as the one set up here. Working through this exercise will pay off in the long run.

1 We'll start with the simple tax calculator. Type the information shown here into a blank worksheet. Unlike our previous worksheet (see Stage 2, pages 66–67), we've brought the tax rate out to a separate cell (B1) so we can take advantage of absolute cell referencing.

This basic layout now allows us to calculate the salary after tax for more than one member of the household, but requires the tax rate to be entered only once. You may want to adjust your column widths to fit names in neatly.

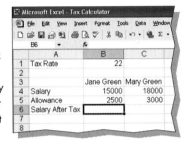

2 The first step is to add a formula to calculate Jane Green's salary after tax. This formula must work out the taxable salary after allowances, calculate the tax payable and deduct it from the salary to produce the salary after tax. It sounds complicated, but a single formula can do it. In cell B6, type =B4-(B4-B5)*B1/100 and press the [Enter] key. Excel calculates the net salary.

3 Now let's see what happens when we copy this formula into cell C6 to calculate Mary Green's salary after tax. Click on cell B6, choose Copy from the Edit menu, move to cell C6 and then select Paste from the Edit menu to paste in the formula.

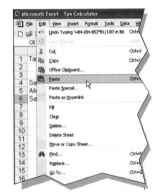

4 Excel has automatically updated the relative cell references in our formula, so the cells B1, B4 and B5 have been replaced with C1, C4 and C5. Unfortunately, in this case it has updated the B1 reference to C1, which is blank, so the calculation is wrong. We need to keep the reference to cell B1.

5 Let's replace the relative reference in the original formula. Click on cell B6, move to the Formula bar and change B1 to B1. When you press the [Enter] key, you'll see the result is still the same. You will see that Excel highlights the cells affected by the formula in different colours (inset).

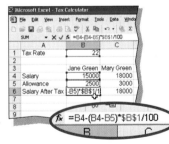

6 Copy the formula from cell B6 into cell C6. You'll notice that Excel now gets the calculation right.

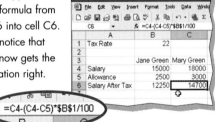

7 Now, let's imagine we want to add another row of information to this worksheet, such as details of another taxation rate. Right-click on the beige square at the left end of row 1 on the worksheet and choose Insert from the menu that appears.

8 Next, type the new tax information into cells A1 and B1. Notice how the formulae in cells B7 and C7 still calculate the correct result. This is because Excel can automatically update absolute cell references as well as relative cell references when you modify a worksheet. Click on cell C7 and look at the formula that's displayed in the Formula Bar. You can see that the absolute references to cell B1 have been updated to those for cell B2.

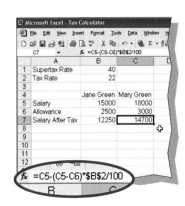

PC TIPS

Cells in other worksheets

We have shown you how to set up workbooks that consist of several worksheets. Excel also lets you create formulae that refer to cells in other worksheets, by using an exclamation mark with the worksheet name and the cell.

All you need to do is include the name of the worksheet as part of the cell reference. For example, to multiply the contents of cell A1 in Sheet1 by cell A2's contents in Sheet2 and have the result placed in a cell in Sheet3, you would type =Sheet1!A1*Sheet2!A2 into any of Sheet3's cells.

What do you do when you don't want to be distracted from important parts of your worksheet by masses of other information? The simple answer is to hide the sections that you don't need.

Hiding rows and columns

A s you become more experienced with Excel, you're likely to start constructing more complex worksheets containing larger tables of information. Sometimes this will make it difficult to pick out important facts and figures – such as annual or monthly totals – from a mass of unwanted detail.

As we've already seen, we can use cell formatting to make important cells stand out in another colour or font (see pages 58–59). But what do you do if you want to see the really important figures on-screen without having to scroll backwards and forwards through a large worksheet?

● **Concealing information**
The solution is to conceal all the detailed information when you aren't using it. Excel lets you do this by hiding complete rows and columns of a worksheet. Don't worry about accessing the data. When you hide a row or column, all the figures and formulae that are contained within its cells are remembered and used by Excel.

All you have to do to hide a row of figures on a worksheet is to select it, click on the Format menu, click on the Row option and select Hide from the sub-menu that appears. You can use the same technique to hide a column, too.

It is just as simple to unhide rows and columns as it is to hide them. You might be

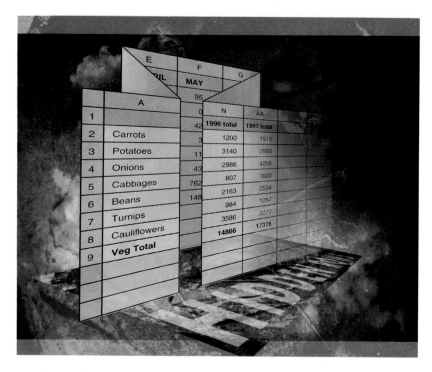

wondering how it's possible to retrieve a row that you might have hidden if you can't see the row to select it. The answer is easy: you just highlight the two rows on either side of the hidden one. Then go to the Format menu, position the mouse pointer on the Row option and choose Unhide from the sub-menu that appears.

Here's a typical table of information (left) relating to a family greengrocery business. The monthly sales totals contain lots of detailed figures for individual items, but it's quite hard to see the 'big picture'. By hiding the rows of individual fruit and vegetable figures (below) it's a lot easier to see how overall fruit and vegetable sales vary from one month to the next.

Show only the main rows or columns in your document by hiding unnecessary text.

WHAT IT MEANS

UNHIDE
The Unhide option is the reverse of the Hide option and is used to make hidden rows or columns visible again. If you want to reveal all the hidden rows and columns in a worksheet at once, click on the beige button in the top left corner of the worksheet to select all and then choose the Unhide option.

Microsoft Excel - Brown's Grocers

File · Edit · View · Insert · Format · Tools · Data · Win

	A	B	C	D	E	F	G
1		Jan	Feb	Mar	Apr	May	Jun
2	Carrots	34	96	22	5	6	11
3	Potatoes	656	56	43	44	95	324
4	Onions	88	34	65	21	0	65
5	Cabbages	78	23	68	11	42	24
6	Beans	23	667	432	43	3	77
7	Turnips	675	35	57	762	11	33
8	Cauliflowers	345	657	9	148	612	668
9	Veg Total	1899	1568	696	1034	769	1202
10	Apples	55	0	67	1	11	88
11	Pears	3	67	53	62	565	45
12	Bananas	21	54	89	41	32	

Microsoft Excel - Brown's Grocers

File · Edit · View · Insert · Format · Tools · Data · Window · Help

	A	B	C	D	E	F	G	H	I	J
1		Jan	Feb	Mar	Apr	May	Jun	Jul	Aug	Sep
9	Veg Total	1899	1568	696	1034	769	1202	1618	1705	319
19	Fruit Total	582	1198	625	285	813	685	672	2876	372
20										
21										

Arial
P44
9 Veg

How to conceal unwanted data

With continued use, a worksheet can grow in size. Hiding the greater part of the information it contains can make it easier to see the overall picture.

1 To illustrate how hiding rows and columns works, we've set up a table of sales figures for a family greengrocery business, but you can use any worksheet for the following steps. In our worksheet, we want to make it easier to see how the overall monthly fruit and vegetable sales compare.

2 Let's hide the row of figures for carrots. Select the Carrots row by clicking on the beige button at the left end of the row. Click on the Format menu and then select Hide from the Row options. You'll see that Row 2 disappears from view, but the row below is unaltered.

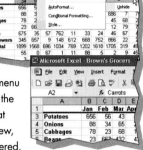

3 Even though Row 2 can't be seen, its data is still present and calculations that include the carrot sales figures are still correct. For example, the totals in the Veg Total row stay the same.

4 Hide the other rows of individual vegetables by selecting them all at once and using the same menu selection as in Step 2. As a result, we then jump from Row 1 to Row 9 (inset).

5 Here's how to restore the hidden rows whenever you want to look at, or update, any of the detailed figures. Use the mouse to highlight the first two rows of the worksheet, where Rows 2 to 8 are hidden. Then go to the Format menu and select Unhide from the Row options.

PC TIPS

A quicker way to hide

There's a quicker way to hide rows and columns than going through the Format menu and sub-menus. Once you've selected your rows or columns by clicking on the beige buttons, simply click the right mouse button and then choose the Hide option from the menu. Unhide works in the same way.

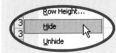

6 You can also hide a column of a worksheet. Let's use this to pick out the February sales figures. Highlight the January column, go to the Format menu and position the mouse pointer on the Column option. Then select Hide from the sub-menu that appears.

7 As with the rows, it's also possible to hide more than one column at a time. Use the mouse to select all the other columns of monthly figures after February. Go to the Format menu and choose Hide from the Column sub-menu.

8 You can restore hidden columns when you want to see the other monthly figures again. Start by highlighting the first three columns of the worksheet with the mouse. Go to the Format menu, position the mouse pointer over the Column option and choose Unhide from the sub-menu.

9 Of course, you can combine hiding columns with hiding rows at the same time. We've used the options on the Row and Column sub-menus of the Format menu so that only the annual totals for the fruit and veg tables are visible.

Make charts look great

Do you want to give your charts and graphs a more professional image?
Here are the secrets of how to make great-looking charts with Excel.

We have already seen how to use Excel to create pie charts from the data stored in your worksheets (see Stage 1, pages 60–61). But, with a little extra effort, you can make your graphs and charts really leap off the page.

Once Excel has created a chart, customizing it is as simple as clicking on the part you want to change with the right mouse button. For example, you can choose to work on the chart's title, its legend (or key) or the data points that make up the actual chart.

You can format a chart element in much the same way as you would a worksheet cell. This means you can apply font, alignment and background-pattern formats to the chart's title, add special effects to the bars or pie segments in your charts, and much more. As you experiment with the techniques shown opposite, you'll find that different options for varying chart elements are available, depending on whether you're editing a pie chart, bar chart or line graph.

● Quick results

You can select individual elements by clicking on them in the chart itself. A right-click will bring up a menu of the formatting tools. For example, if you're working on a segment of a pie chart, you can apply a wide range of colours, patterns and fills. As an even more impressive fill, you can use any photograph or drawing that you have stored as a graphics file. Opposite, we show how to enhance a pie chart comparing school sports by using pictures of the activities themselves.

WHAT IT MEANS

DATA POINTS

A data point is the element of a chart that represents a particular value in your worksheet. For example, in a pie chart each segment is a data point. In a bar chart each bar of the graph is a data point. In a line graph each point plotted on the line is a data point.

We know how to make individual elements of graphs and charts colourful, but with a little extra knowledge, customized colours and pictures can also be incorporated.

Making more attractive pie charts

You can use some of Excel's advanced charting tools to give a simple pie chart a unique and much more impressive look. Below we show you how.

FOR THIS example, we have entered some data and created a pie chart using Excel's Chart Wizard. We have followed the basic method covered in Stage 1, pages 60–61, in order to set up a chart of a school class's favourite sports.

Microsoft® Excel

1 Use the mouse to select the segment of the pie chart that represents football. To do this, slowly click twice on the segment, so that Excel doesn't interpret it as a double-click.

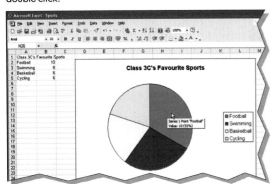

2 Right-click on the segment and then choose Format Data Point from the menu that appears.

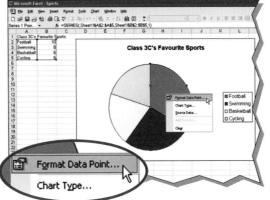

3 In the Format Data Point dialog box, make sure the Patterns tab is selected, then click on the Fill Effects button.

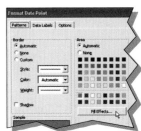

PC TIPS

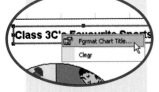

We've used the right mouse button to jazz up the sections of the pie chart here, but you can also use it to customize other elements in the chart. The text can be formatted just like the text in any worksheet cell.

For example, right-click on the chart title. You will see a pop-up menu with a Format Chart Title option. If you select this, you'll see a dialog box that lets you change the typeface, colour and alignment. Try experimenting with other chart objects.

4 The Fill Effects window gives us an impressive choice of ways to fill this slice of the pie chart with colour gradients, patterns and textures. However, we're going to use an image of a footballer – so choose the Picture tab and click on Select Picture.

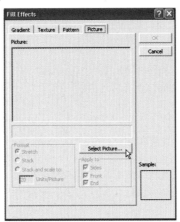

5 Use the Select Picture dialog box to find the picture you want. We have selected this clip-art image from the Microsoft Office CD-ROM. Click on the OK button in the Fill Effects window and then on the OK button to close the Format Data Point dialog box.

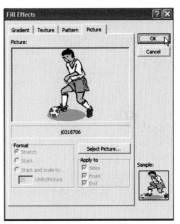

6 The football segment of the pie chart should now look like this.

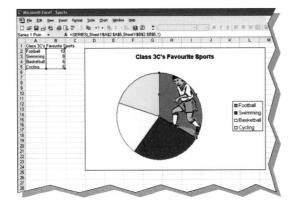

7 Now repeat the process for the remaining three segments to fill them with appropriate pictures. The final result should look as smart as this.

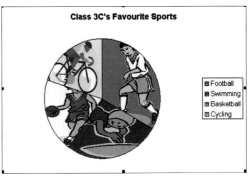

The smart way to fill cells

Creating a useful worksheet can be quite arduous. However, Excel can lend a hand and save time – even when copying and pasting cells isn't appropriate.

Excel provides you with more than one way of filling cells with the same type of data. For example, rather than having to copy and paste the same information repeatedly, Excel allows you to highlight specific cells, which can then be filled from the Edit menu. For adjacent cells, you can even drag the contents of one cell and drop them into another (see Stage 1, pages 56–57).

However, so far we have only used this feature to fill in cells using identical data. Now we are going to discover how to fill a range of cells automatically with, for example, ascending or descending numbers.

● Smart fills

You could fill cells A1 to A5 on a worksheet with the ascending numbers 100, 200, 300, 400 and 500. Excel also provides ways for you to fill cells with successive days, months or years. Most of these automated fills can be accomplished with a simple drag of the mouse. These so-called 'smart fills' are controlled from the Series option on the Fill sub-menu. If you select this, it opens a dialog box that offers you a choice of four fill types: Linear, Growth, Date and AutoFill.

● The four options

The Linear option is used to increase (or decrease) the values between cells by a fixed amount each time.

Growth works in a similar way, but by increasing the values between each cell exponentially – 1, 2, 4, 8, 16 and so on, for example. Date, obviously, refers to date-related data fills, allowing you to choose from day, month and year.

The fourth and final option, AutoFill, will assess the data already keyed into the first few highlighted cells and then automatically decide on which type of fill is necessary for the remaining cells.

Producing labour-intensive documents that incorporate long lists of headings can be made easy with Excel's AutoFill option. This makes preparing a complex workbook, based around a calendar perhaps, far less time-consuming.

PC TIPS

Excel will also let you add your own customized fill options. For example, you can set up a series of atomic elements to help with a science project. To do this, choose Options from the Tools menu and select the Custom Lists tab from the dialog box. Then, all you have to do is type in your list of elements and click on the Add button.

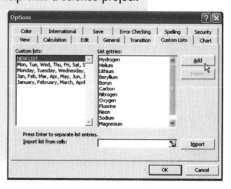

Saving time with smart fills

Here, as an example of how useful smart fills can be, we show you how quickly you can make a calendar for the whole year.

1 Start by consulting a calendar, then type in a few days and dates in January. As you can imagine, it would take ages to finish the calendar if we had to type in everything manually. Instead, we'll use Excel's smart fill tool.

2 First, we will fill in the month names. Highlight the cell containing Jan (cell B2 in our example) and the eleven cells to its right. Now select Fill from the Edit menu and choose Series from the sub-menu. Choose AutoFill from the Type section of the window and click on OK.

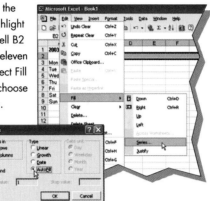

3 The names of the months have appeared in the highlighted cells. Next, we'll add the remaining weekdays of the month. Highlight the cell containing Sun (in our example, cell A9) and the 30 cells below it. Again, select Fill from the Edit menu and choose Series from the sub-menu. As before, choose AutoFill and then click on OK.

4 The next job is to fill in the dates for January. Highlight the 31 cells that will contain the dates and bring up the Series dialog box again. Excel looks at the numbers that were already entered (Step 1) and suggests a linear series with a Step value of one between cells. Click on the OK button.

5 Scroll to the bottom of the January dates. You can see that the 31st falls on a Friday. Scroll back up the worksheet and find the first Saturday in the February column. Type the number 1 and repeat Step 4, selecting this cell and the 27 cells below it (or 28 if it's a leap year).

6 Repeat Step 5 for the remaining months of the year, remembering to change the number of cells you highlight to reflect the number of days in each month.

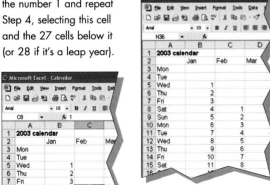

7 Now, apply some cell and text formatting to add the finishing touches to your calendar and make it easier to read. Grey out the weekends and bank holidays and add a coloured fill to indicate the unused days at the top of the calendar.

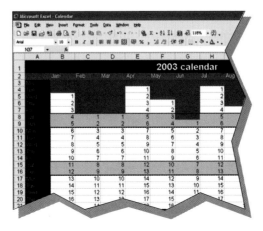

There is a special mouse technique to help you use smart fills more efficiently. Type January into any cell on your spreadsheet. Then select this cell and look for the small black square that appears at the cell's bottom right corner. Click and drag this

square downwards. As you do, Excel guesses that you want to fill these cells with successive months of the year and shows the series in the form of a small yellow tip box. Release the mouse button and Excel will fill the cells. This works for numbers and the days of the week.

Microsoft® Excel

Modifying text styles

With CorelDRAW, you aren't stuck with the basic typefaces that come with Windows. You can create new letters with striking, original shapes – even ones that look as if they are hewn from solid granite.

If you normally work with text using a program such as Word, you might think of type as pretty much a fixed element. Once you have chosen a font, you can change its size, style or colour, but not the basic shape of the characters.

With CorelDRAW, on the other hand, this is anything but the case. Type can be edited like any other object you create. CorelDRAW even goes out of its way to provide tools to help with everything from the basics, such as changing the colour and texture of text, to sophisticated options, such as creating your own customized typefaces.

● **A choice of text styles**
CorelDRAW is able to do this because of the way it handles vector-based images. It still uses ordinary fonts – exactly the same ones as you find in Word – but it allows you to convert them into shapes so that they behave like any other object drawn on the worksheet. From there, you can do with them what you will.

There are two types of text available in CorelDRAW: Paragraph Text and Artistic Text. Paragraph Text works in exactly the same way as in Word: in fact, the text Property bar looks quite similar to Word's Formatting toolbar. It has all the same functions, allowing you to choose the font, alter the size, and add basic formatting commands such as Bold, Italic and Underline. And, of course, you can choose to align your text to the left, centre or middle, or to justify it. To make things easier, CorelDRAW uses the same icon symbols as Word for all these functions.

Artistic Text is most useful when you want to start playing around with text, by doing such things as adding special effects or altering its shape. It is the tool of choice for anyone who wants to create interesting logos, or who would like to produce more imaginative or decorative text effects.

WHAT IT MEANS

ARTISTIC TEXT
This is CorelDRAW's term for text to which you can apply special effects – distortion, extrusion, blending and so on (see Stage 2, pages 84–87). Artistic Text is created using the Text Tool.

CorelDRAW ®

● Creating imaginative effects

When text is first typed in using CorelDRAW's Text Tool, it is a fixed shape which can only be changed in basic ways, such as shrinking, moving and rotating it. However, you can convert the text into curved objects very easily. This adds object nodes to each character, which enables you to change its shape and edit it as if it were a CorelDRAW object.

Once text has been changed into curved objects, you can start applying a number of special effects to the text. Essentially, these are the same as the effects that can be used with any CorelDRAW object, such as distortion, adding a texture or other pictorial effect, and merging with other objects. However, by bringing a little imagination to the special effects you choose, and the way that you apply them, you can create some exciting images.

● First steps with Artistic Text

In the examples shown on the next page, we use the Envelope special effect to distort the text into dramatic shapes, using pre-set envelope designs and your own creations. We also look at how the use of colour effects can suddenly make text appear much more interesting and dynamic, either by using the

CREATING YOUR OWN TYPEFACE

Perhaps the most impressive thing you can do with text in CorelDRAW is to create your own typefaces. This is quite an involved process, but allows you the ultimate freedom when using text.

Instead of changing letters every time you want them to look different, you can define a set of characters for your own alphabet. This can then be saved and used at any time in the future.

Of course, this will take some time, so if you don't fancy creating your own complete typeface from scratch, you can simply alter an existing one, which allows you to edit or replace only the existing letter shapes that you need.

Fountain fills from previous exercises or the amazing clip-art-like fills that come with CorelDRAW.

Finally, if you're really adventurous, you can start experimenting with the shapes of the letters. You've already learnt how to move and use nodes, and this works in exactly the same way.

Some advanced effects

CorelDRAW offers enormous scope for experimenting with Artistic Text. Here we show some of the most popular effects you can achieve in addition to the main examples that are shown in the step-by-step exercises.

AS WELL as the examples on the following pages, you can produce many other effects. These include making text run round a shape or outline, as is often seen on badges and labels. Fitting text to a fixed path or outline (top) is easy, as you simply draw a curved line for the bottom of the letters to follow.

Bevelled text (middle), which looks as though it has been carved out of a solid material, is also easy to create using the built-in Bevelled tool and just a little bit of tweaking to ensure the text stays readable.

Realistic shadows can also be created from a copy of your original shape, which is then distorted and blurred to look as if the letters are solid and the shadow is being cast by a real light source (bottom).

Even features such as large, dropped capitals at the start of paragraphs, or text specially fitted inside irregularly shaped objects are relatively easy to achieve. The only real limit is your imagination.

Using Envelopes and Fills

A number of CorelDRAW's basic graphic effects work particularly well with text, and provide interesting results. Here we take a look at Envelopes and Fills.

1 Select the Text Tool from the toolbox. Click once with the mouse in the drawing area. A vertical bar will appear, which shows you where your text will begin to appear.

2 Before typing anything, use the Property Bar options. We'll start with a bold typeface. Click on the drop-down font list and scroll down to select Arial Black. You can also use the size drop-down box to choose a bigger size (24 point).

3 Now type your text. For the time being, keep the line of text quite short, as we have done here.

4 Select the text box and then click on the Interactive Envelope Tool which appears when you click on the small black arrowhead on the fourth tool from the bottom of the Toolbox.

5 The Envelope toolbar appears. It includes several ready-made shapes for you to use. Click the Add Preset button and a drop-down list of shapes appears. Select one by clicking on it. You'll now see the text change to reflect the shape you chose.

6 We'll now use some colour effects to add more interest. Select the text box again and choose Favorite Fills and Outlines from the Scrapbook sub-menu of the Tools menu.

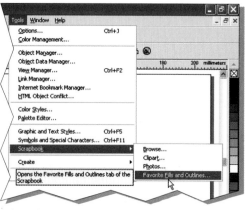

7 A folder containing two more folders appears. Double-click on the Fills folder, then on Texture. Small icons that represent the different texture patterns available appear. Double-click on one of them; we've chosen mineral.

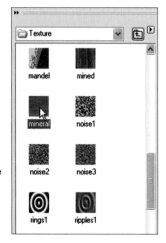

8 You will instantly see your line of text fill with the pattern you selected. If you want a different pattern, click on the Fill Tool, then the Pattern Fill Dialog option to bring up the Pattern Fill dialog box. Locate your bitmap pattern and then click on Load.

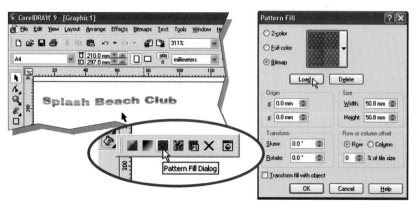

Changing the shapes of letters

We've given these letters a special twist to suit a Halloween party, but you can easily choose an example that will be more useful to you – perhaps using Artistic Text to create a personal logo.

1 Select the Text Tool from the Toolbox. Once again we have chosen Arial Black and set it to 24 point (see Step 2 on the previous page). Click the cursor on the screen and type in your text.

2 In order to edit the letters with the Shape Tool you must first convert them to curves. Select the text with the Pick Tool and click the Convert To Curves button on the Property bar.

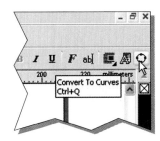

3 At first, the text will look the same as before, but click on the Shape Tool and you'll see a large number of nodes appear around the two words.

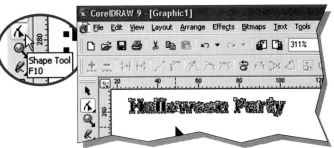

PC TIPS

As you edit the nodes of a character, remember that it is now just like any other CorelDRAW shape. This means you can add and delete nodes as much as you like.

To add a node, click on the outline with the Shape tool where you want the node to appear and then use the large plus button that appears at the far left of the Property bar whenever you have the Shape Tool selected. The minus button (to the right) can be used to remove a selected node.

4 Try altering the shape of some of the letters. Use the Shape Tool as normal to move the nodes (inset). You'll probably have to zoom in using the Zoom Levels drop-down menu on the Toolbar to see them clearly. You can also add or delete nodes to create more flexible shapes (see PC Tips).

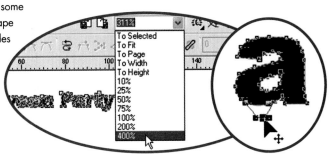

5 Remember, if things go wrong you can use the Undo button (with an arrow curved to the left, see inset) to go back and erase any changes one action at a time. CorelDRAW, unlike Microsoft Paint, remembers all the actions you do, so you can undo your edits all the way back to the initial blank page. You can also reinstate changes if you use Redo – this button's arrow is curved to the right.

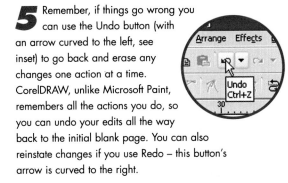

6 Now that the text has been converted to curves, you can use any ordinary object tool to alter it in the same way as the Shape Tool. For example, you can change its colour. Try using a simple fill or, as we have done here, apply a Fountain fill (see Stage 2, page 83) to create the result shown below.

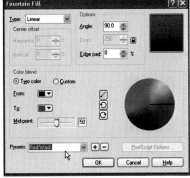

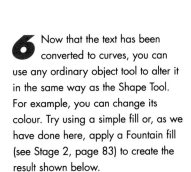

Introducing Corel PHOTO-PAINT

When you buy the CorelDRAW Essentials package, you also get several handy graphics extras. One of the most useful is PHOTO-PAINT.

P HOTO-PAINT is one of the two main programs supplied in the CorelDRAW Essentials package. However, unlike CorelDRAW, which is vector-based, PHOTO-PAINT is a bitmap-based paint package. This means that you work with pictures made up of thousands of dots, much as you do in Microsoft Paint (see Stage 1, pages 62–85). However, PHOTO-PAINT is far more advanced than Microsoft Paint and offers a much wider range of features for creating and editing bitmap pictures.

Menu bar
Nearly all Windows programs share the same basic features, of which the menu bar is one of the most important. PHOTO-PAINT is no exception, although its bar does contain a number of special options.

Standard toolbar
This contains buttons for various common commands, such as File Open and File Save.

Property bar
The basic layout of PHOTO-PAINT is very similar to that of CorelDRAW; in both programs the Property bar changes according to which option or tool has been selected. The default setting shows information relating to the Pick Tool.

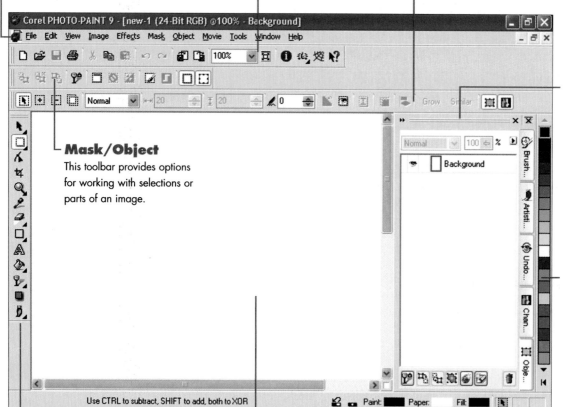

Mask/Object
This toolbar provides options for working with selections or parts of an image.

Docker
PHOTO-PAINT uses a docker window, which can be hidden, to provide access to many different options. You can hide or show parts of images, tweak the paintbrush settings and undo or redo past actions with this docker.

Palette
The palette is extremely versatile, and although it displays only a small number of colours by default, you can pick any colour that the human eye can distinguish, via one of four types of colour picker.

Toolbox
PHOTO-PAINT's Toolbox is in the same position as the one in CorelDRAW, but the tools available here are very different. Most are not object-based, and there is a wide variety of brushes and editing tools.

Canvas
This is where all the actual work and drawing is done. The default canvas size is quite small, but you can change it to any size you choose and to any colour or pattern.

Colours Used
This series of displays indicates the particular colour of paint you are using, the page you are painting on, and the fill, if you choose to use it.

WHAT IT MEANS

OPACITY

The term 'opacity' refers to the degree to which an object or paint is transparent. Paint that is 100% opaque will cover the background completely. Paint that is just 5% opaque is almost transparent.

● **Advantages**

If you've followed the Microsoft Paint exercises, you'll have realized that while it's adequate for simple pictures, even the most accomplished computer artist can create only rather basic and cartoon-like pictures with it. This is because it lacks any advanced tools and relies almost entirely on a few brush strokes, plus the steadiness of the user's hand.

PHOTO-PAINT, however, is much easier to use as it provides a greater degree of accuracy and has many additional features, such as safety nets, colourful fills, more realistic brush strokes and opacity. These tools help you to add more subtlety to your pictures than Microsoft Paint allows. For example, you can use softer, merging shading on a background, rather than having abrupt changes of colour. You can also soften the edges of an object.

● **Realistic pictures**

PHOTO-PAINT comes into its own when you are working with photographic images from a scanner or digital camera. The program enables you to adjust or edit the images in several different and important ways; for example, you can adjust the brightness and contrast to help make the picture clearer.

CorelDRAW ®

Get started with *PHOTO-PAINT*

How to start up PHOTO-PAINT and set up a blank window in which to work.

1 You will find the Corel PHOTO-PAINT program in the CorelDRAW Essentials folder (inset) in the Start menu.

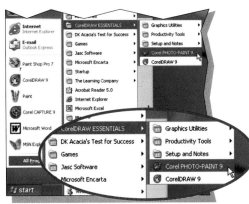

2 When you start PHOTO-PAINT, you will see a welcome screen very similar to that used in CorelDRAW. You have five icons to choose from. For this exercise, click on the one at the top left, which is called New Image.

3 You will see a large dialog box with several sections. The options here control the following:

Color mode: This lets you choose how many colours your image should be displayed in. Usually, 24-bit RGB gives the best display quality.

Paper color: PHOTO-PAINT lets you choose any colour you'd like to work with.

Image Size: Think of this as 'paper size'. You can pick almost any size you wish.

Resolution: This lets you select how many pixels (dots) will be used for each millimetre (or inch) of your painting. The more dots that are used, the finer the detail in the image will be. The final parts include options for very advanced users.

4 For our first exercise we want to choose the exact number of pixels to use in our picture. Click on the box in the Image Size section that currently says 'millimeters' (yours will have 'inches' if your PC is set up to work in imperial units), and select pixels from the drop-down list.

5 Still in the Image Size section, change the numbers used for the width and height to 400 and 300 and then click the OK button.

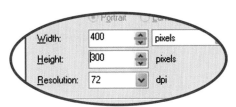

6 You will now see your blank image ready to use (right). PHOTO-PAINT shows your image in its own window inside the main PHOTO-PAINT window. This allows you to work on several pictures at once (unlike Microsoft Paint).

PHOTO-PAINT basics

Start by getting used to the main tools available in PHOTO-PAINT. Other tools can be added later as you become more familiar with the program.

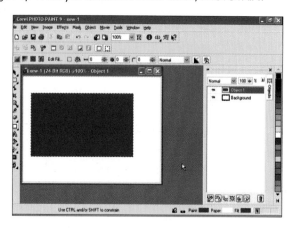

IF THE huge number and variety of tools used in PHOTO-PAINT looks intimidating after the simple appearance of Microsoft Paint, it's worth trying some basic tools to see how they work. If you glance down the Toolbox you will see that some, such as the Rectangle Tool and Eraser, look the same as those in Paint. However, after a few minutes of experimentation, you'll soon find that these tools are much more powerful than Paint's.

1 We'll start by drawing a simple coloured shape on our blank image. First, select the Rectangle Tool from the Toolbox on the left.

2 Now click with the right mouse button on a square in the colour palette on the right side of the screen. You will see the Fill box at the bottom of the screen change to indicate the colour you have chosen.

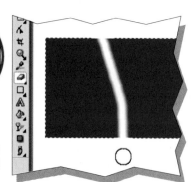

3 Draw a rectangle using the same click-and-drag technique you have used in Microsoft Paint and CorelDRAW (see Stage 1, page 65 and Stage 2, page 71). When you release the mouse button, PHOTO-PAINT immediately draws and fills in the rectangle.

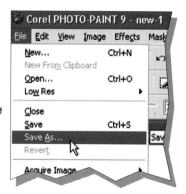

4 Now try the Eraser Tool. Click once on the tool in the Toolbox and then click and drag your mouse through the blue rectangle. As you do so, you'll see that the path it has cleared through the blue rectangle has soft edges. This contrasts with Microsoft Paint's eraser, which leaves hard edges when it erases.

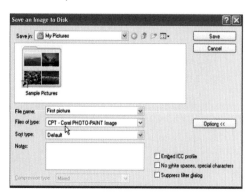

5 Now let's save this example. PHOTO-PAINT saves files in the same way as other Windows programs, so select Save As from the File menu (right).

6 Use the Save In drop-down box to find your PC's My Pictures folder, then type in a name for this picture and click the Save button.

Note: PHOTO-PAINT uses its own file format (with the CPT extension), but it can also export pictures in many different formats for use in other programs (see PC Tips, right).

PC TIPS

Saving in different formats

PHOTO-PAINT can export your images in many formats. Among the most useful is the Bitmap (BMP) format used by several Windows programs, including Microsoft Paint.

PHOTO-PAINT's advanced tools

Extend your graphics capabilities using PHOTO-PAINT's advanced tools.

PHOTO-PAINT has many more advanced tools and options than the Microsoft Paint program. Although the tools are more sophisticated, they are easy to use once you have experimented a little. To give you some idea of how these tools can help you to create better pictures, we'll introduce you to some of the most commonly used ones below.

Brush Types

PHOTO-PAINT has a huge number of brush types and styles – far more than Paint. You can specify just about every aspect of the brush, including its type (airbrush, paintbrush, and many more). You can also choose from several options that affect the way 'paint' is applied to your 'canvas', such as its thickness.

Image Sprayer

This amazing tool paints with images; as you drag the pointer over your blank page, it leaves a trail of mini-pictures. PHOTO-PAINT has several ready-made image brushes: for this picture we've simply drawn an X on a blank screen using the foliage image brush. You can also create your own image brushes.

Fills

PHOTO-PAINT also provides you with many different fill options, just like CorelDRAW. Whereas Microsoft Paint has just one solid fill, PHOTO-PAINT has (clockwise from top left) a solid fill, fountain fills, texture fills and bitmap fills.

Smearing, Smudging and Blending

PHOTO-PAINT has other tools to edit your pictures, once you begin drawing them. The tools are able to smear, smudge or blend parts of your drawings. This helps to give them a more realistic and non-computerized look. You can also use these tools to customize the images stored on the CorelDRAW CD-ROMs for use in your own pictures.

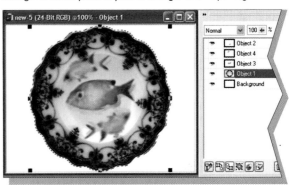

Safety Nets

Where Microsoft Paint can undo only the last three commands, PHOTO-PAINT has a system of 'Safety Nets', which allow you to undo any number of commands. It presents the commands that you have carried out as a list, allowing you to see exactly what has happened in your painting.

Objects

PHOTO-PAINT can also use some of CorelDRAW's object-based drawing capabilities. Objects can be made to 'float' behind or in front of the bitmap image you are painting. You can also make objects transparent to create composite pictures.

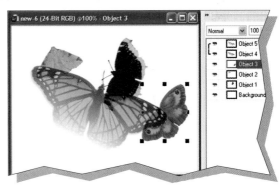

Masks

You can create and edit masks for your pictures. These masks allow you to mark off parts of your picture to protect them from paint – just like masking tape does when you are painting a window frame. The difference is that PHOTO-PAINT masks can be absolutely any shape you like.

Editing Movies

You can even use PHOTO-PAINT to create and edit video movie files that you can play on your computer. You can use any of PHOTO-PAINT's tools on individual frames of a movie and then reassemble them into a complete film of your own making.

As well as having lots of fun with **PHOTO-PAINT** effects, you can also bring old photos – and the memories that they inspire – back to life.

Simple photo editing

Whether you have access to a scanner or not, the ability to alter photographs and other images is extremely useful – and exceedingly easy in Corel PHOTO-PAINT.

We have already seen how photographs and images can be reproduced on letters and documents (see Stage 1, pages 46–49), converted into backgrounds for the Windows Desktop (see Stage 1, pages 70–71) or used in other packages.

But, with the right software, you can do so much more with your images. Once a photo has been scanned and saved on your computer (see page 107), you can use a program such as Corel PHOTO-PAINT to retouch it, to change the brightness and colour, to cut out parts of the picture, or to add 2D and 3D effects.

● A change for the better

There are usually two reasons for making such changes. First, for example, you might want to improve the quality of your photograph before you use it again by enriching the colour and light. Alternatively, you might want to add some effects to alter

the picture – from something as simple and fun as changing the colour of your pet dog, to stretching or squeezing images of famous film stars.

● For greater effect

There is a wide range of effects available and all work in a similar way. Often, all you have to do is select the effect and apply it to your picture. You can even undo the changes you have made if you don't like the effect and want to start again. Once you've learnt how to brighten an image, it's also easy to sharpen or blur it. If the original quality of the photo that was scanned is poor, you can compensate for that as well by revitalizing faded areas or even removing scratch marks and blemishes.

Whatever the task, be it serious or light-hearted, PHOTO-PAINT should be able to help – and without a camera or darkroom in sight. We show you how to make a start on the opposite page.

WHAT IT MEANS

RETOUCH
This term refers to any alteration made to a completed picture, usually a scanned photograph. Retouching can be a minor change, such as making the picture slightly brighter, or a more substantial alteration, such as cutting out part of the picture and replacing it with a new image.

Retouching photographs

Here we show you how easy it is to make a number of amendments to a photograph – from simple contrast changes to more complex two-dimensional special effects.

1 The photo we are going to retouch comes from disk two of CorelDRAW Essentials. We've chosen 815044 from the Birds folder. As you can see, the scan hasn't been done very well and the image is a bit too dark.

2 To change the brightness and contrast, click on the Image menu. Choose the Adjust option and select the Brightness/ Contrast/Intensity option from the list.

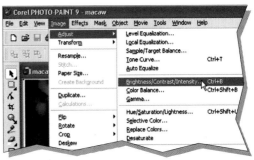

PC TIPS

You don't need a scanner if you want to practise retouching photos. There are plenty of images on the CorelDRAW CD-ROMs that you can use; alternatively import an image from someone else's PC or the Internet.

You will find plenty of photo images on disk two of the CD-ROMs that come with CorelDRAW. Use PHOTO-PAINT's Open command to access the photos from the CD-ROM to get started.

3 A new window appears, containing several controls. The Brightness, Contrast and Intensity slider bars work much like the controls of a television set or PC monitor. To change the brightness, move the slider bar to the left for a darker image or to the right for lighter one. If you click on the Preview button (inset), you can see the effects of your work on the image before deciding whether you'd like to save the changes.

4 You can change the Contrast and Intensity in the same way. Experiment and check your changes with the Preview button. If your changes make the picture worse, simply press the Cancel button or move the sliders to a new position and preview the result. Click on the OK button when you're happy with your changes.

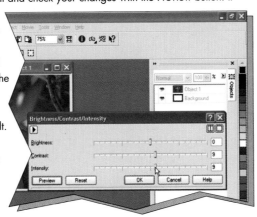

5 If you want to try something more exciting, there are lots of special effects you can apply to the picture. We'll try one of the Distort effects, called Pixelate. This will stylize your picture so that it is composed of much larger blocks of colour. From the Effects menu, select the Distort option and then click on Pixelate.

6 The Pixelate dialog box works similarly to the Brightness/Contrast/Intensity box. You can change the shape of the pixels with Pixelate mode. We've selected Radial, so the colour blocks seem to revolve around the centre of the picture. Use the sliders in the Adjust section to alter their width and height. The smaller the pixels are, the clearer the picture will be. We've chosen 5 to give a blurred effect. Use the Opacity slider to set how much the original picture shows through. When finished, click OK.

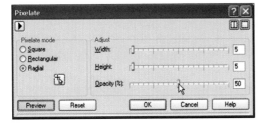

7 You'll now see the difference you can make to any image with just a few mouse clicks. Try some of the other options under the Effects menu to see what other changes you can make. As always, don't be afraid to experiment.

Resizing pictures

You might have found exactly the right picture that you were looking for, but if it is five times larger than your screen or printer paper, you're going to have to learn how to shrink it to fit.

Any computerized picture has its own specific shape and size, which can be measured using a number of different units. Programs such as Corel PHOTO-PAINT can tell you the size of an image in inches, centimetres or even millimetres. When working with computer images, though, it is often more useful to describe their size in pixels. These are dots that make up the images on your PC screen.

The number of pixels that are used to display Windows tells you the resolution of your screen – the more pixels there are, the more detailed the image is on screen. Many home computers are set at a resolution of 800x600; that just means it's 800 pixels wide by 600 pixels tall.

Browse through photos on the CorelDRAW CD-ROMs and you will find that most images are 768x512 and fit the screen quite comfortably. However, if you are scanning your own images, you are likely to create much larger images; it's possible to get a computerized image of 1800x1200 by scanning just a postcard-sized photograph.

Whether it's for a special effect or just to make a picture the exact size you want, it's easy to fit a computerized picture into any space!

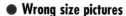

Distorting pictures can be fun to experiment with and will add impact to page designs.

● Wrong size pictures

You may want to display a picture on your Desktop background but if you're using an 800x600 display and you find a 1024x768 pixel picture, it will not fit on the screen. In this case, you'll need to change the size of the picture. Programs such as PHOTO-PAINT can solve this type of problem in several ways. You could use the selection tool to choose an 800x600 pixel area of the picture and then get PHOTO-PAINT to cut everything outside this area out of the picture.

Alternatively, you can resize a picture to match your exact requirements, by stretching or squeezing it from the edges. You can change a picture to almost any shape with PHOTO-PAINT, although this can result in distortion, as shown above and left.

If you start with a portrait photo of 400x600 pixels and change it to 800x600 pixels, the subject's face will be stretched to twice its width. This can be fun to use for special effects. Opposite, we'll show you how to resize a picture that's too big so that it fits neatly on to the background of your own customized Desktop.

Fitting a picture to the Desktop

We've looked at different ways of customizing the Desktop (Stage 2, pages 12–13). Now we'll make it unique by using our own choice of picture as a Desktop background.

1 You can change the size of any image, from the sample photos on disk two of CorelDRAW Essentials CD-ROMs to photos you've taken on a digital camera. Here we are using a photograph that has been scanned on a flatbed scanner (see page 107). Start PHOTO-PAINT and use the File menu's Open command to open the image.

2 If you open one of Corel's sample photos, you see a dialog box reminding you that you cannot save the picture to the CD-ROM. However, you can save it to your hard disk. Press the OK button.

3 It's best to save the file with a new name as soon as possible. Select Save As from the File menu and use the dialog box to rename the image. It's a good idea to use the My Pictures folder to store your images. The default suggestion for the Files of type box is JPG – this is perfect for Windows Desktop images.

4 The first thing you'll notice is that the photo is quite large – certainly larger than your computer screen. If you were to use it as a Desktop background, you wouldn't be able to see it all. But this is where PHOTO-PAINT's ability to change the size of a picture comes into effect. From the Image menu choose the Resample option.

5 From the Resample dialog box that appears you'll see that you are able to choose the exact size of the picture. Click on the units drop-down list at the top right of the Image size selection boxes. Select pixels from the list of options.

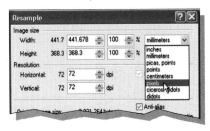

WHAT IT MEANS

ASPECT RATIO
The aspect ratio is the ratio of a picture's width to its height. When resizing an image, it will look distorted (squeezed or stretched) if the aspect ratio changes.

6 First, type 800 into the Width box. As you do so, the Height box below will automatically change to read 667 (the exact figure depends on the dimensions of your original picture – if you chose another photo, it might be different).

7 If you now try to type 600 into the Height box (the other dimension we want for this picture), you'll notice that the Width changes (it becomes 720 in our example). PHOTO-PAINT always tries to keep pictures in proportion when changing their size. This is because the Maintain **aspect ratio** box is ticked, but you can change the proportions if you want to make the picture exactly 800x600. First you will have to untick this box, then type in the correct Height and Width. PHOTO-PAINT will squeeze your image to fit the new dimensions. In our example, a beach landscape, this is fine as the minor distortions won't be noticeable. Just click on the OK button. Save the picture and exit CorelDRAW.

8 To make this picture your Desktop background, right-click anywhere on the Desktop to bring up the Desktop pop-up menu. Select Properties.

9 We've already used the Display Properties dialog box for changing the number of colours Windows uses (see page 13), but you can also use it to choose pictures for the background. First click on the Desktop tab. This will show you a picture of what your display looks like. Click on the Browse button and use the dialog box to find the file you saved in Step 3. Select it and click OK. Then click on OK again to close the Display Properties dialog box.

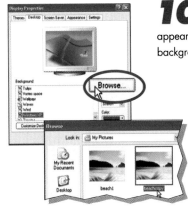

10 The picture will instantly appear as your Desktop background.

PHOTO-PAINT's different brushes

Artists who work with acrylic or water-based paints have a variety of different brush styles available to them. With PHOTO-PAINT, computer artists have just as much choice.

O ne of the major benefits that CorelDRAW PHOTO-PAINT has over simple paint programs is the amount of control it gives you over brush types. You can choose from a huge range of brushes, brush nib shapes, and the type of 'paint' that is used.

You're not restricted to painting on perfectly smooth paper, either. You can choose the type of surface on which you are painting – such as cartridge paper or an expensive cotton canvas, as used by real artists to heighten the reality of the paint surface.

● Choosing your brushes

When you click on the Paint Tool button in the Toolbox, you will see PHOTO-PAINT's Property Bar change to reflect the options available (below). These options let you choose the type of brush – from conventional brushes to pencils, airbrushes and even

specialist brushes that mimic famous painting styles, such as Impressionism and Pointillism. Some of the other popular options available include quick access to choice of brush size and nib shape (whether circular or square) directly from the Property bar.

For full control over the huge variety of available brushes, you use the program's Docker windows. Like CorelDRAW, PHOTO-PAINT brings together related options into a single window. Corel calls these options Dockers because they 'dock' into position at the side of the PHOTO-PAINT window.

● Brushes and nibs

Select Brush Settings from the Window menu's Dockers sub-menu. At the far right is the usual X button for closing the window, and

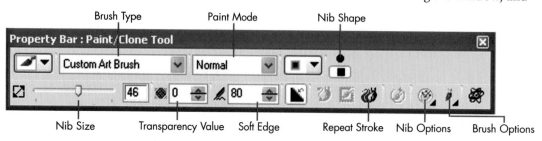

When you are using the Paint Tool, the Property Bar changes to give you quick access to many brush choices.

The canvas effect can be used to make a photograph (top) look as though it's been painted on one of the materials used by artists, such as cotton (above), wood, paper or canvas.

on the left is the Collapse Dockers button. Click on this to make the contents of the window appear or disappear.

The main part of the Brush Settings Docker menu lets you choose from a wide variety of ready-made nib shapes and sizes. Here you'll find more than the simple circular and square options offered on the Property bar. For example, there are stars, swirls, and even a collection of unusual shapes for a paintbrush, such as lions, birds and human figures. When you click on one of these, painting becomes as simple as choosing a colour and clicking on the painting area you wish to fill in.

If you can't find the nib shape you want, you can easily create your own design. Any shape you can draw with the mouse can be made into a nib. This is one area of painting that is easier to do on a computer than with a real brush.

● Effects

As well as changing the properties of the brush, you can also change the type of paint you use, just as if you were using a palette. This is achieved via the Effects menu, which allows you to alter the thickness, 'wetness' and texture of the paint.

Effects work slightly differently from brush options. When you alter the type of brush and nib, it affects the shapes you paint subsequently. When you use Effects, however, these will only affect your existing painting. For example, if you select part of your picture and use the Effects menu to add a wet paint look, it will affect only the selected area and will not apply to any subsequent changes you make.

● Canvas effects

With all the options available for brushes and paint, it's no surprise that PHOTO-PAINT also allows you to alter the background of your 'paper' as well. This is done by using canvas filters, which can be added at any stage of your drawing to give a texture to the background. Experiment to see what looks best with your picture.

If you want to give your picture the look of a painting created on canvas, for example, you simply apply a linen-type texture to the whole painting area. You can have lots of fun with your existing pictures by applying effects to them. For example, if you have a photograph of a relative, it's simple to make it look like a painted image just by making use of a canvas effect. No extra painting work is necessary and when printed out on high-quality paper, you have an ideal gift!

Advanced Paint Tool Settings

IN ADDITION to changing the nib and brush types, you can also make a number of alterations to the way the brush strokes are applied to the page.

At first, these will seem like minor changes, mostly because you simply have to change a percentage or move a slider bar. But they can have a profound effect on how your brush appears on the page.

You can access the brush options through the different sections of the Brush Settings Docker. The top part lets you change the angle of the brush and its size.

By clicking on the small black arrows next to each section name, you reveal extra settings for the Paint Tool.

The Brush Texture section includes options for the way brush strokes bleed in a painting. For example, you can simulate watercolour painting by tweaking the Bleed and Sustain Color settings so that as you paint in one colour, it blends with the colours of paint already there underneath.

The Dab Attributes option lets you control the way successive dabs of the brush are applied. You can change the spacing – making brushstrokes closer together or further apart, depending on your specific needs – and you can also add some subtle (and not so subtle) colour variations by moving the Hue, Saturation and Lightness sliders away from their normal '0' settings.

Choosing brushes and paint effects

To get the best out of your own abilities (and those of your computer) try using the different brush styles PHOTO-PAINT has on offer. We look at some here.

1 Start a new picture and then click on the Paint Tool in the Toolbox on the left of the PHOTO-PAINT screen.

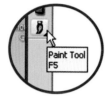

2 Select Brush Settings (right) from the Dockers sub-menu on the Window menu (far right).

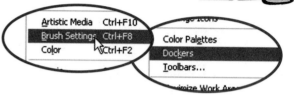

3 Use the pop-up window's scroll bar to look through the different nibs. Pick one that would be useful for drawing a tree and single-click on it.

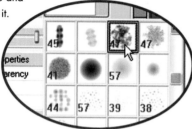

4 Now select a shade of green from the colour palette on the right and start to paint a tree. Feel free to experiment with different nibs for the trunk – you can see the nib here gives an uneven edge.

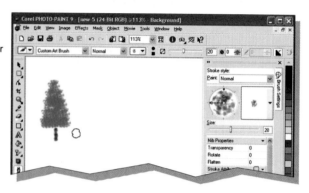

5 For the second tree we shall use the same nib, but alter the texture of the paint so that it looks as if it has been applied wet. Paint another tree, ready to apply the texture.

6 Select the Rectangular Mask Tool from the Toolbox (inset, below) and drag a rectangle over the second tree so that it completely encompasses it.

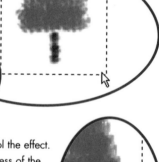

7 From the Effects menu, select Distort and then choose the Wet Paint option.

8 A dialog box appears, with two sliders to control the effect. Alter the size of the drips (Percent) and the wetness of the paint (Wetness), and you can see your picture change to show the effects. Click on the OK button when you are happy with it.

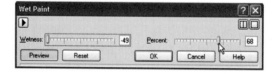

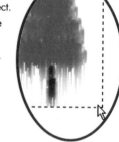

9 For the final tree, try one of the pre-set brush types. Click on the Art Brush button (inset below) on the far left of the Property bar and select the last brush. Then select Pointillism from the drop-down list box just to its right.

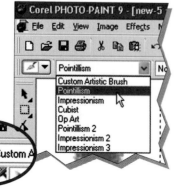

10 Now, as you paint your tree, you will find that it is built up from many small dots. However, the great thing is that you don't have to draw the individual dots yourself, as PHOTO-PAINT does it for you.

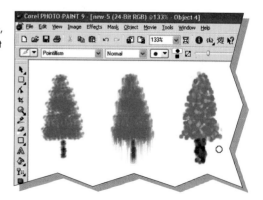

Making your own brush nibs

As you can see, there are many different ways you can alter your chosen brush in PHOTO-PAINT. If you still can't find exactly what you want, you can make your own.

AS WELL as customizing the brushes by using pre-set commands, you can also create a custom nib completely from scratch. In fact, the pre-set nibs are really just simple bitmap pictures, so you can easily create your own and specify it as a nib. Below we do just that by drawing a picture of a leaf and then using it to paint a tree.

When drawing a new nib bitmap, you should remember that it will generally be used with one colour at a time. Any holes you wish to include in the nib bitmap drawing will also have to be carefully drawn to ensure they have no gaps in them through which the brush fill colour might seep.

When making any customization alterations to the nibs, it is best to do it at a high zoom magnification because most brush nibs are, by necessity, fairly small when they appear on-screen.

1 Start a new painting and create a simple shape with the Paint Tool. You'll need your Property Bar and Brush Settings Docker in view (see pages 82–83). Take extra care to make sure the shape is clear and distinct. In our example we've used a leaf.

2 Draw a Rectangle Mask around your design. Now select Create from Contents of Mask from the drop-down menu that appears when you click on the Nib Options button.

Add Current Nib
Delete Current Nib
Create from Contents of Mask…
Nib Load
Save As

3 Click on OK in the box that appears (below) and the shape you want to use will immediately become a nib.

Create a Custom Brush
Nib size: 44 pixels
OK
Cancel
Help

4 Use your new nib to paint a picture. Notice how the black and white areas of your original nib control where the paint is applied.

5 Go to the Brush Settings Docker window and click on the Brush Texture heading. Change the Bleed setting to 50 (far right). Now select the star-shaped brush from the drop-down window (inset, centre). Drag it to create some fireworks (inset, right)

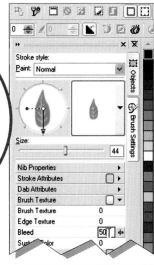

6 Use the Dab Attributes section to adjust the way successive dabs appear. Experiment with the Spacing and Spread settings and see how the star brush paints differently.

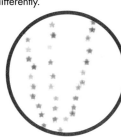

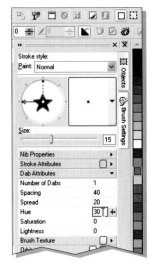

7 By using these settings wisely, with just a single stroke you can come up with many excellent effects that would otherwise take a long time to create, such as flocks of birds.

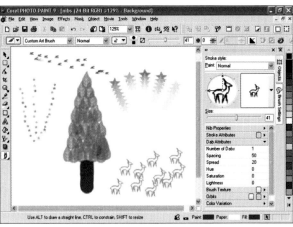

Being creative with PHOTO-PAINT's filters

Even if you're no good at painting with the mouse, you can use PHOTO-PAINT's many filters to edit and customize existing images so that you can create your own works of art.

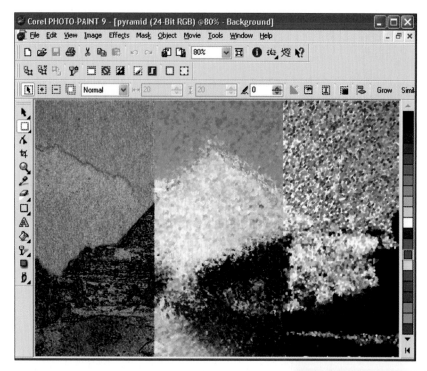

CorelDRAW's filters can turn your photograph into a Pointillist 'masterpiece' or a shimmering reflection.

Despite having the help of PHOTO-PAINT's huge number of brushes and nibs, not everyone is cut out to be a computer artist. Painting with a mouse needs just the same creative and compositional skills as painting with real brushes and genuine oils or watercolours. The mouse and PHOTO-PAINT's many powerful features are no substitute for talent.

However, the companies that make graphics programs know that not everyone is a latent Van Gogh, so they pack plenty of features into their products to help make PC art easier. In fact, many of the professional computer artists who buy advanced art programs, such as PHOTO-PAINT, don't intend to paint images from scratch. Instead they want to apply their programs' image-editing features to work on existing images.

● Filter features

By being creative with the dozens of powerful filters built into PHOTO-PAINT, you can manipulate any type of picture. Photo-retouching filters (see pages 78–79) let you adjust brightness, contrast and the amount of highlights, mid-tones and shadows in an image. Every media art department in the world uses such filters to make photos as clear as possible before publication.

Other filters have much more dramatic effects. You can apply PHOTO-PAINT's Squizz filter to warp a picture (see page 88): the effect is like looking through a distorting glass lens. As with all the filters, you can add as much distortion as you like and control which parts of the picture are changed.

These filters are a great way to get youngsters interested in the world of computer image editing. It's fun to take photos of your favourite people and stretch their faces into silly shapes. You can save the photo and print it out on a colour printer to make a unique personalized greetings card.

● Instant artist

If you want to create the illusion of a painted image, PHOTO-PAINT's filters can help out. There is a special set called Art Strokes that can adapt any photo using a painting style of your choice (see opposite).

At first glance, the Art Strokes seem similar to the texture effects that PHOTO-PAINT can apply to an image (see page 83). By adding a texture to a photo, you can give the impression that it is printed on a surface, such as canvas, linen or even concrete. It's a great effect, but the image still

looks like a photo. By contrast, the Art Strokes filters are much more sophisticated and much more flexible. They actually repaint the whole picture by applying brush strokes to a plain background.

The idea behind filter software is that it looks at the colours of the pixels in the original photo and uses them to choose paint colours. It then repaints the picture in a variety of different styles. For example, it can redraw the picture as if it were created with watercolours: the filter picks up the main colours from the photo, but when it creates the new picture, it simulates the delicacy of watercolour brush strokes to give the typical wash effect of watercolour pictures. The original picture is hardly recognizable, as all the tiny details are washed out, leaving a more artistic version of the image (see Painting made easy box, opposite page).

● Customizing tools

There's almost always a lot more subtlety and flexibility in these effects than in the simpler texture ones. You can see just how the filter will affect your image and fine tune it in many different ways. For example, in the Palette Knife filter, you can change the size of the knife itself, alter its angle or soften the edge of the paint stroke laid down by the knife.

Combining filters

PHOTO-PAINT's filters needn't be used in isolation – you can combine them to get even better effects.

To create a particularly realistic painting effect from a photograph, you can combine several filters in succession. For example, if you use the Impressionist Art Stroke filter (see page 89) and then the Canvas texture, you can turn a flat photograph into an image that looks like it has been painted on coarse fabric.

You're not restricted to realistic images – there are plenty of weird and wacky filters that can help you to create out-of-this-world images from your photos. For example, the Psychedelic command (in the Color Transform sub-menu) lets you create the wild colour changes that you often see in pop videos. You can then use this with other filters to change the original picture beyond all recognition.

You can also use different filters on different parts of your image. Just select an area before choosing a filter from the Effects menu. Applying different filters to separate areas of an image is perfect for creating a composite look. You could, for example, create a 'painting' done half in oils and half in watercolours.

The starting point for many a graphic adventure using PHOTO-PAINT's filters is an ordinary photograph.

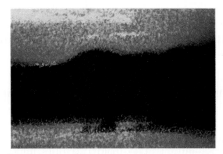

Use the Impressionist Art Strokes filter and you can turn the photo into an Impressionist-style painting.

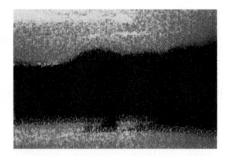

Next, use the Canvas texture to make the picture look even more like a real painting.

This beach-side photo has had the Psychedelic filter applied to it, brightening its contrasts and colours.

Next, use the Ripple filter to add a watery look to the psychedelic beach-side graphic.

Turn a single photo into an amazing composite painting, using as many filters as you need.

Fun with photos and filters

Have fun with PHOTO-PAINT. Here we attack a picture with the Squizz filter.

1 Start PHOTO-PAINT and open a suitable image. We've opted for 66060 from Animals, Farm, in the Photos folder on disk two of CorelDRAW's CD-ROMs, but you can use any image you have to hand.

2 Click the Effects menu and then select SQUIZZ 1.5 from the HSoft sub-menu. When the Squizz welcome screen appears, click the BRUSH button at the bottom of the screen.

3 Your picture now appears on the left of the dialog box, with settings on the right. As your mouse passes over the picture, a circular outline shows the Squizz brush. If necessary, you can change the size of this brush in the Brush Properties section of the dialog box.

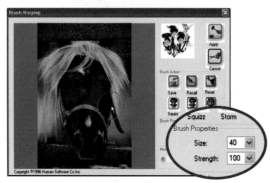

4 To start Squizzing, drag the brush over any part of the image. Squizz drags the paint around as if it is made of elastic. Notice how the colours are still as smoothly blended as in the original photo.

5 When you've finished distorting your image, click the Apply button on the right to make these changes to your photo (or click Cancel to leave the photo as it is).

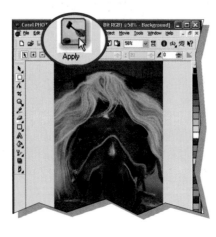

6 Squizz has two modes of working. The first is the brush you've already been using. The second is the Grid option, which helps create regular distortions. Open another photo and bring up Squizz again, this time clicking the Grid button when the welcome screen appears. The image appears with a rectangular grid overlying the picture (inset).

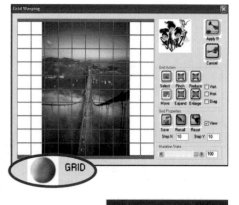

7 Click and drag the corners where the lines intersect. When you release the mouse button, Squizz squeezes and stretches the pixels in the image to match the new shape of the grid.

8 You can move as many of the corners as you like, gradually warping the image into a new shape. When you click the Apply button, PHOTO-PAINT makes the changes to your image. It's a great way to see a new slant on familiar images.

PC TIPS

If you know what sort of distorting shape you want to make with the grid, you can drag as many of the corners as quickly as you like. Once you stop, PHOTO-PAINT will catch up and redraw the preview with your changes shown.

Paintings from photographs

Create a painting by using PHOTO-PAINT's Art Strokes on a photograph.

1 Open an existing photograph in PHOTO-PAINT. Select a picture that has very distinct shapes and outlines, such as this image of a pyramid. Click on Art Strokes in the Effects menu and select the Sketch Pad command from the sub-menu.

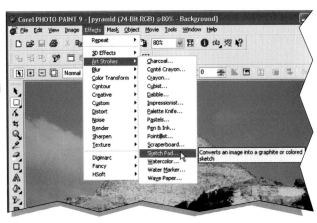

2 As soon as the dialog box appears, PHOTO-PAINT applies the Sketch Pad filter to the image. It uses the default settings for this particular filter. In a few moments you see a black-and-white shaded sketch of your photograph.

3 The Sketch Pad dialogue box shows the settings that give you control over the virtual pencil. Try dragging the Style slider right to the Fine end and do the same with the Outline slider.

4 Your sketched photo is redrawn, with lots more detail added by the pencil. This shows the rough texture of the pyramid more clearly than the original Sketch Pad settings.

5 PHOTO-PAINT also has a virtual set of coloured pencils up its sleeve: click on the Color option in the dialog box to access them. Make the sketch, then click on the OK button when you are happy with the effect.

6 PHOTO-PAINT is packed with great instant-art filters: open the photo again and try the Impressionist filter, listed in the Art Strokes menu. You get a superb result within a few seconds; painting this from scratch would challenge even the best computer artist's abilities.

PC TIPS

To view both the original photo and the altered picture, click the button with the two rectangles that appears near the top right in a filter's dialog box. This will show the images side by side.

7 To achieve a different Impressionist effect, select the Dabs option in the Impressionist dialog box. You can add more colours to the Impressionist palette by dragging the Coloration setting to the right.

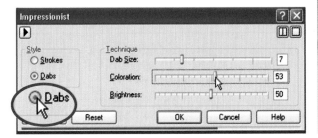

Using CorelDRAW to combine photographs and drawings is lots of fun and very easy. It's a great chance to be really creative and makes use of the advanced facilities of this program.

Adding photos to drawings

The real beauty of the CorelDRAW package is that it contains programs for creating and editing both bitmap images (such as photos and paintings) and vector images (such as drawings and illustrations). You'll be able to get even more out of the program, however, once you learn how to combine these two types of images. CorelDRAW makes it easy.

CorelDRAW itself is a drawing program (see Stage 2, pages 68–69) and Corel PHOTO-PAINT is a bitmap editor (see pages 74–77). So far, we've kept the two areas separate, but CorelDRAW can use bitmap images created in other programs. It also lets you use bitmap pictures as patterns to fill objects in your drawings.

● More realism
Although you can create accurate pictures with CorelDRAW, nothing is as realistic as a photograph. And there are many occasions when using a bitmap image is preferable to using vectors, as CorelDRAW does.

Greetings cards, for example, can benefit from the personal touch. While you could simply use a photo editor to create and print

a bitmap picture, by using the picture in a drawing, you can add words and shapes in a manner that is not possible when you are using a photo editor.

The added benefit of importing bitmaps into your drawings is that you can edit them in the same way as vector objects. You can change the appearance of the picture and add special 2D and 3D effects. The possibilities are limited only by your imagination.

● Adding a bitmap to your drawing
The actual process of adding a bitmap picture to a drawing is easy. Browse through the CD-ROMs that came with CorelDRAW. One of them contains thousands of photographs that you can use for any purpose. Remember, the manual shows small preview pictures of the images on the CD-ROM to help you find what you're looking for.

Once you've found a suitable picture, you can simply drag and drop it on to your drawing. In the following example, we'll create a composite picture using a photograph and some CorelDRAW shapes. We'll also show how to use a bitmap pattern to fill a CorelDRAW shape.

Making a composite image

CorelDRAW can combine drawings with photos. Here we use some of the images from the CorelDRAW CD-ROM.

1 Adding a photo to a vector drawing is very simple in CorelDRAW. For this example, we'll cheer up a clip-art image of a desk blotter by adding a scenic photograph. We'll start by clicking on the Tools menu and selecting the Clipart option from the Scrapbook sub-menu.

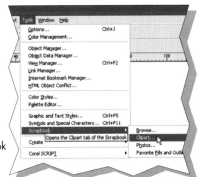

2 Select equip018 from the Equipment folder within Office in the Clip Art folder. You can insert the image by dragging and dropping it on to the work area.

3 You'll see the desk blotter appear on your page. You can now add a photo to use in the white area. Choose Photos from the Scrapbook sub-menu.

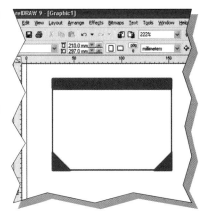

4 Naturally the choice of photo is up to you. Here, we've used 647058, which is in the Leisure folder within the Photos folder. Drag and drop the photo on to the desk blotter.

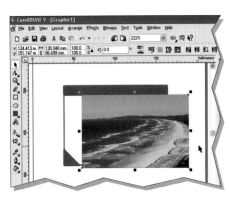

5 To put the photograph behind the clip-art image, click on it with the right mouse button, click on the Order option and select the To Back command. In this respect, the photograph you have added works just like any other object you would add to a picture.

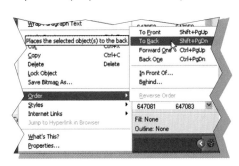

6 The photo is a little large for the border, so we need to make it fit into the frame correctly. Now that it's behind the frame, we can use the Shape Tool (inset) to grab each corner of the picture and take it to the inside corner of the blotter frame.

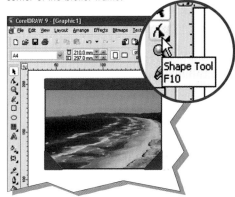

Filling shapes with bitmap patterns

1 You can add bitmap patterns to any shape in your drawings. For this example, just start with a new shape. We've used the Polygon Tool to draw a simple pentagon. Click on the newly drawn shape with the right mouse button and select Properties from the pop-up menu that appears.

2 Click on the Fill tab of the dialog box that appears. From the line of six buttons, click the third from the left and select Bitmap from the list of Pattern fill options.

3 Click on the drop-down palette of bitmaps and choose one of the patterns. Press the Apply button and the bitmap pattern will fill the entire polygon.

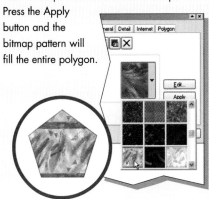

Hardware

Monitor choices

If you're thinking about getting a new monitor for your PC, it's worth looking at the alternatives before splashing out. In the past, most people have upgraded their monitors mainly to get higher resolutions than their current monitor is capable of producing but, in recent years, flat-screen monitors have become cheap enough for home PC users to consider – saving lots of desk space and effort if you need to move your monitor.

● Benefits of upgrading

The typical monitor supplied with PCs is a 15-inch model with a CRT – or cathode ray tube – screen (see How a conventional monitor works box, below). Together with the graphics adaptor fitted inside your PC, the screen's electronics dictate how much detail you can see. The higher the resolution – the number of dots used to create the screen image – the more detail you get.

There are many benefits to using a screen with these higher resolutions. Text is easier to read because each letter shape is made up of more dots. This is less tiring for the user as the brain has to do less work. You can also see more of your documents without scrolling (see screengrab, below). It also becomes possible to use two programs side-by-side on the screen if you need to do so.

When you decide to upgrade your PC's monitor, there are several options open to you, from low-cost high-resolution monitors to space-saving slim screens.

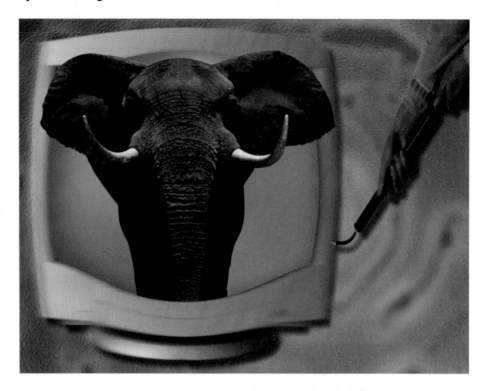

● Avoiding eyestrain

On a typical 15-inch monitor, resolutions higher than 800x600 are often possible but the result is that Windows icons, menus, buttons and text become too small for many people to use easily. By upgrading your monitor to a larger size, you can set your PC to these higher resolutions, getting all of the benefits outlined above without having to strain your eyes.

There's a very healthy market in larger screen monitors, which means that you can upgrade

This image shows the area of a document when viewed on a typical 15-inch CRT monitor, and the shaded area reveals how much more is visible on a 19-inch monitor.

HOW A CONVENTIONAL MONITOR WORKS

Almost all home PCs come with a CRT (cathode ray tube) monitor. These work just like conventional TV screens: a beam of electrons scans the screen from top to bottom, shining on red, green and blue phosphor dots that have been coated on the inside of the screen. The image is then created by switching the electron beam on and off in sychronization with the scan running from top to bottom.

On a TV, the switching of the beam is controlled by the aerial or set-top box. On a PC, the beam is controlled by the PC's graphics adaptor. Although there have been minor space-saving improvements in CRT technology in recent years, CRTs remain bulky – as deep as they are wide – and heavy. As such, the larger CRT monitors can be inconvenient for use in the home.

Different monitor resolutions explained

Here you can see just how much extra working area you get when you upgrade to a monitor that can run at a higher resolution than the 800 x 600 that a typical 15-inch monitor displays. The extra space means that there's much less scrolling to do to move around your document, and you can also work on two pages much more easily.

For other programs there are other useful benefits. For example, in Excel you can read long lines of data very easily and there's no risk of accidentally misreading along the lines of data as there is when you

have to scroll to see other cells. For desktop publishing and other graphics software the extra pixels allow you to see more detail in your designs.

High resolutions can also help to reduce the fatigue that can set in when working with text on smaller screens. Because there are more dots available to form each letter, the letter's shape is more clearly defined – which means that the brain has less work to do when you are reading from the screen.

The expense of a flat monitor can be more than justified by the saving in space it provides.

If you have the desk space, a 19-inch CRT monitor is a cost-effective way to get a bigger Windows Desktop.

without breaking the bank. Monitors range in price from £125–£200 for a 17-inch monitor, and from about £180–£300 for one that is 19 inches. Larger monitors are available, but these are generally aimed at the graphics professionals.

● Comparing CRT and LCD

The biggest problem with larger CRT monitors is their bulk, but this is also the main advantage for their chief rival, the LCD – or liquid crystal display – monitor. For each inch you add to the viewable screen of a CRT monitor you also add an inch to the depth. Larger CRTs take up an alarming amount of desk space, and can often look out of place in the

home. However, an LCD monitor need never be more than a few centimetres thick – no matter how big its viewable screen.

In addition to the difference in size, LCD monitors consume a fraction of the electricity that a CRT monitor uses. In recent years, there has also been concern that CRT monitors emit harmful radiation. While these health concerns have not been proved, LCD monitors do not emit the same type of rays.

That said, CRT monitors do have some benefits over LCDs. One is the viewing angle. If you need to sit at an angle to your PC screen, a CRT monitor could give you a better view of the whole screen. This is because

LCD screens need to be viewed 'face on'. When seen from an angle, colours can be distorted and you may not be able to see the image on the whole screen.

Another consideration is colours. Most CRT monitors can display unlimited colours, but some LCDs are only capable of displaying hundreds or thousands of colours – although an increasing number of LCDs do now feature unlimited colours. If colour display is an important factor, check the capability of the monitor before you decide to buy.

● Making your choice

Five years ago, even the smallest LCD monitor would have cost well over £1,000, but you can now upgrade for under £300. Like CRT monitors, they are available in a range of sizes, but it's important to note that LCDs and CRTs are measured differently. As the table below shows, the screen image on a 17-inch CRT is equivalent to that on a 15-inch LCD.

You should bear in mind that the 19- and 21-inch CRT monitors are very heavy – you must take care when moving them.

It is also important to compare warranties when buying monitors. Many now come with three-year guarantees at no extra cost, so it is a good idea to shop around for the best deal.

Monitor size	Typical viewable diagonal	Best screen resolution	Increase in detail over a 15-inch CRT
15-inch CRT	13.5 inches	800x600	n/a
15-inch LCD	15 inches	1024x768	63%
17-inch CRT	15.5 inches	1024x768	63%
17-inch LCD	17 inches	1280x1024	173%
19-inch CRT	18 inches	1280x1024	173%
21-inch CRT	20 inches	1600x1200	300%

The amount of extra detail you get when upgrading your monitor size and screen resolution is astounding, and it's the reason that no-one who has used a large screen ever wants to go back to a small screen.

MEASURING MONITORS

Like TVs, monitors are measured across the screen diagonally. That said, it is usual for CRT monitors to have a maximum viewable area that's an inch or so shorter than the claimed measurement. The difference in display size is due to the fact that some of the CRT's glass screen is hidden behind a plastic bezel, while the manufacturing process for LCD screens ensures that the whole screen is visible.

Upgrading to an LCD monitor

If you want to regain desk space from a bulky computer monitor, an LCD is the perfect choice – and you'll get fantastic image quality, too.

If you're still persevering with a 14- or 15-inch monitor, upgrading your PC monitor is a smart move (see pages 94–95). Upgrades such as adding better speakers or extra games hardware can enhance a few computing activities but because you use your monitor all the time this really is one of the best value-for-money upgrades available.

● **High resolution advantages**

By opting for a bigger monitor you can take advantage of higher resolutions for the Windows Desktop (see pages 12–13). Much as a larger desk lets you spread out your papers and physical documents, a larger Windows Desktop gives you more space for your virtual documents. Not everyone upgrades just for more Windows Desktop space, however. An increasing number of people prefer to regain the space that a CRT monitor takes up on their desk. Large CRT monitors are bulky and rarely fit in well with home décor styles. In contrast, an LCD monitor consumes a fraction of the space.

● **Inside an LCD monitor**

Whereas a CRT monitor uses an electron beam to create the image on the inside of the screen, an LCD monitor uses a rigid grill of cells placed in front of a bright white light. Each cell represents a pixel in the

image, so a 1024x768 screen has almost 800,000 cells. Each cell has red, green and blue filters; by controlling the amount of white light that passes through each filter, the LCD's electronics can create colours of any shade and hue for any of the pixels in the screen.

These cells are only a few millimetres thick, and the white light panel is also very thin. In total, the whole assembly only needs to be a centimetre or so thick. Some LCD monitors can even be hung on the wall, which frees up yet more space on your desk.

● **DIY option**

Unlike many PC upgrades, upgrading a monitor is a simple DIY job – even for the most nervous novice. This is because there are only two connections to make and there's no

need to open up the PC's system unit. It should only take a couple of minutes and Windows automatically detects the new monitor, so there's very little set-up work required.

GAMER ALERT!

Although LCD screens are better than CRTs in many respects, they don't suit all computer users. Game players, in particular, should think carefully before upgrading to an LCD monitor. The reason is that it takes an LCD screen slighly longer than a CRT monitor to switch individual pixels on and off. Although the time difference is only a fraction of a second, it means that the movement in some fast-paced games can appear a little blurred. LCD technology is constantly improving, however, so if you're a keen gamer, ask for a demonstration before buying.

Installing an LCD monitor

Adding a new monitor to your PC takes just a few moments and, with a little tweaking of the Windows Desktop, all of your programs benefit.

1 The first thing to do when installing a new monitor is to remove the old one. Before doing so, make sure that both the monitor and computer are turned off and the power cord is unplugged. That done, unplug the signal cable from the socket on the back of your computer. The cable might be screwed into place, so you will need to unscrew it before removing the cable.

2 Here are the new and old monitors, showing just how little space the thin LCD monitor on the left takes compared to the old CRT monitor. Remove the old monitor and position the new LCD monitor in its place.

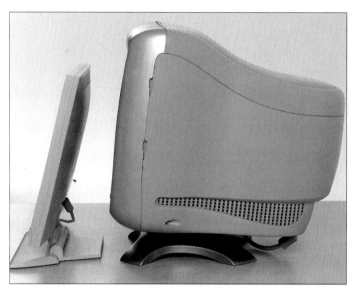

3 Connect the new cables in exactly the same way as the ones on the old monitor were connected. Remember to use the screws that secure the signal cable to the graphics card socket to ensure a firm and reliable connection. You can now plug in the power cable and turn on your computer and monitor.

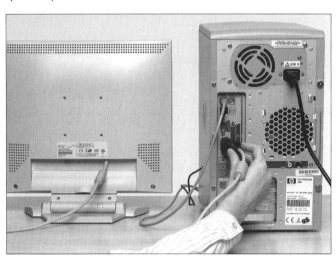

4 Most new monitors are automatically detected by Windows and, as a result, messages appear on screen. You now need to tell Windows to use a higher resolution. Click on the right-hand mouse button on an empty part of the Desktop and select Properties from the pop-up menu.

5 With an LCD monitor you must make sure that the screen resolution of the Desktop exactly matches the number of pixel cells in the LCD itself. Check the new monitor's manual for the figure. In this case, it's 1024x768, so we have adjusted the Screen resolution slider on the Settings tab accordingly. Click on the OK button to apply the screen settings.

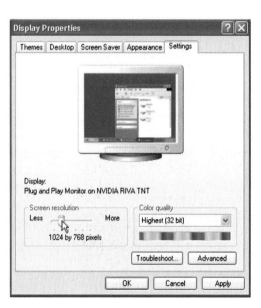

PC TIPS

Although monitors are designed to work with all operating systems, it pays to ask about compatibility with Windows XP before you buy. If there is any room for doubt, ask for a 'no quibble' refund should your Windows XP computer and new monitor fail to work together.

The procedure for monitor upgrades is much the same whichever size and type of monitor you buy. If you decide to opt for a larger CRT monitor rather than the type of LCD screen that we've used, you can still follow the same steps as those shown here.

Adding a Zip drive

If your computer is starting to fill up with files, or you're worried about losing data, why not add a Zip drive? For a small outlay and very little bother, you'll instantly gain lots of extra storage.

Zip drives have been around for only a few years but they are now firmly established as a popular form of computer storage – and it's easy to see why.

Zip disks resemble a chunky floppy disk but they can take up to 100MB or 250MB of information – 70 to 170 times more than an ordinary floppy. The drives cost between £60 and £130, while a 250MB disk costs around £11 when bought in a pack of four. The disks are also reusable, which means you can save and erase data as many times as you wish, just as you would with a regular floppy disk.

● Convenient storage

Zip disks are conveniently portable, too. You can easily fit two or three into a shirt pocket or bag, and the drive itself isn't a great deal bigger (no bigger than a small paperback).

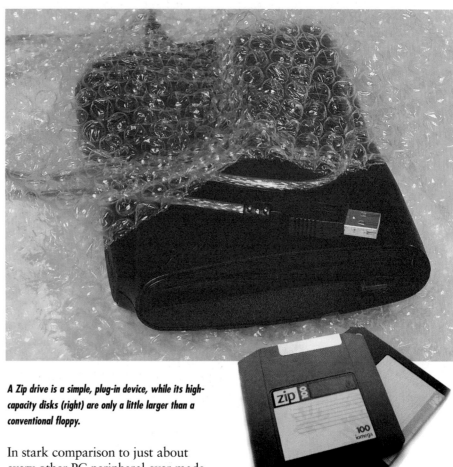

A Zip drive is a simple, plug-in device, while its high-capacity disks (right) are only a little larger than a conventional floppy.

ZIP DISK BACKUPS

While transferring data between computers might be the most common use of Zip disks, they also work extremely well as backup disks. Using Microsoft Backup, you simply work your way through the Wizard-style interface, choose the files, folders or entire drives you want to back up, and then select your Zip drive as the destination.

If you're backing up a large amount of data, the software will simply prompt you to insert another disk when the disk is full (although Backup confusingly calls each disk a 'Tape'). The software automatically splits large files across a number of disks (see below), so the process requires very little intervention.

It's so quick and easy that anyone with a Zip-equipped PC has no excuse for not performing regular backups.

In stark comparison to just about every other PC peripheral ever made, the Zip drive is quite a stylish addition to your desktop. Add all that up and you have a very affordable, handy and desirable computer add-on.

In office use, the main function of Zip disks is to send big files from one place to another; at 100MB or 250MB each, they can take a lot of data – the text of several lengthy books, for example. But Zip disks have plenty of appeal for home computer users, too. They are very effective for backing up data (see box, left), being far bigger and far faster than the now old-fashioned floppies. Also, Zip disks are far more physically robust and less prone to magnetic corruption.

● A choice of drives

Zip drives come in various formats. The best type to buy as an add-on is an external type, which is connected to the computer by a cable. External Zip drives come in three versions.

The USB Zip drive plugs into your PC's USB (Universal Serial Bus) socket. A parallel port Zip drive connects to any PC via the parallel port socket. The SCSI (pronounced 'scuzzy') version needs a special SCSI connector, which typically takes the form of a card that plugs into a spare slot inside your PC and gives you a new socket at the back.

When you've connected the drive and started the PC, the Zip drive icon will appear in the My Computer window. Its drive letter will depend on the devices fitted.

DVD Drive (D:)

Iomega Zip 100 (F:)

The main advantages of external Zip drives, whether parallel, SCSI or USB, are that they are a cinch to install and very portable. If you want to transfer big files to another computer which doesn't have a Zip, you can just take the drive along as well as the disk.

The USB drive has the advantage of being 'hot-pluggable' – you can connect it without switching off your PC. You can also buy an internal Zip drive, which occupies a 3½-inch bay at the front of your PC – the same size as a floppy drive. These tend to be a bit cheaper and will reduce the clutter on your desktop, but they aren't portable and can be quite tricky to install. You really need to get a professional to fit an internal drive – which, of course, negates the saving over an external model.

● Using a Zip drive

After you have attached the Zip drive and installed its software, the drive works much like the floppy disk and CD drives. The Zip drive icon will appear inside your My Computer folder, where it will automatically be assigned the next letter of the alphabet (following those used by devices such as your hard disk and CD-ROM drive) as its drive letter.

The Zip software also includes utilities to help back up important documents and settings. Check the user guide for more information.

USB POWER

One extra benefit of using the internal or external USB version of the Zip drive is that both take their power from the PC itself. This means that once you shut down your PC, the power to the Zip drive is also switched off.

With the parallel or SCSI external versions, you must remember to switch off the Zip drive's power supply after shutting down your PC.

Installing a Zip drive with a USB connector

Connecting this type of Zip drive to your PC is easy and takes just a few moments, so it's the ideal solution for home PC users.

1 The first step in adding the USB version of the Zip drive is to locate the USB sockets on your PC. On most PCs these are tucked around the back near the keyboard and mouse sockets. A few PCs have USB sockets on the front panel, and you can use these if you prefer. Plug the USB lead into one of the vacant USB sockets.

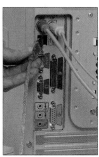

2 Now position the Zip drive close to your PC – on top of a tower case is perfect. Insert the other end of the USB lead into the socket on the back of the Zip drive.

3 Windows automatically detects the new hardware and a message box appears on screen to alert you.

4 Install the Zip drive software, following the instructions in the Zip drive manual. This makes the necessary adjustments so that Windows can recognize the drive.

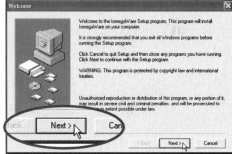

5 Next, look in the My Computer window, and you'll see an icon for the drive. Insert a blank Zip disk and double-click on the drive. You can test that it's working properly by dragging some documents from your hard disk to the Zip disk window.

6 When you have finished working on a Zip disk, you must eject it from the drive. Right-click on the Zip disk icon in the My Computer window and select Eject from the pop-up menu. After a second or two, the disk pops out of the drive.

Introducing digital cameras

Imagine a camera that requires no film, has no processing costs, lets you send photographs around the world within a few minutes of taking the shot and even allows you to re-touch a photograph using your computer. All this is possible with a digital camera.

Digital cameras are the latest computer accessories to find their way into people's pockets. A few years ago digital cameras cost more than £1,000, but a basic model now sells at less than £100. So what do you get for your money?

A digital camera is similar to a traditional film-based camera, except that it stores your pictures electronically – that is, in a digital format that your PC can then use. Both traditional and digital cameras use a lens to focus the picture, an aperture to control how much light enters the camera, and a shutter to control how long the light comes into the camera. That's where the similarities end, however.

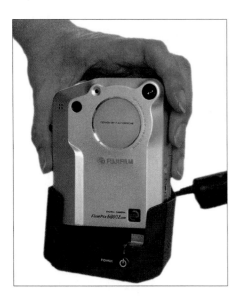

A few digital cameras come with cradles that the camera slots into. Because you can leave the cradle plugged into your PC, it makes downloading images quick and easy.

In a film-based camera, the picture is projected onto a piece of plastic film with a light-sensitive coating. In a digital camera though, the picture is projected onto an electronic component called a charge-coupled device (CCD) that scans and converts the image into an electronic data file.

● **Colour by numbers**
The file consists of numbers that represent the colour and brightness of all the spots that make up the picture. This information is then stored in memory – like the memory in your PC – inside the camera.

Photographic film needs to be processed and developed. First, the film is chemically 'fixed' so that light does not affect it any further. Second, the pictures on the film are stored as

negatives and are then printed onto special photographic paper. Although this can be done in as little as an hour, it's not cheap and it requires a fully equipped laboratory.

With a digital camera, you simply connect it to your PC and 'download' the digital pictures. Transferring the pictures to your computer is quick and costs nothing, although if you print them with your colour printer, you have to pay for the paper and coloured inks.

● **Private view**
Many digital cameras include a built-in liquid crystal display (LCD) that allows you to view a picture as soon as you take it. This means that if you don't like it, you can erase it from the camera's memory and shoot it again.

Later, with the appropriate software, you can view the pictures instantly on your computer monitor.

For example, let's say you want to send a favourite aunt in Australia the latest family photos. Simply point your camera at the clan and shoot – within a fraction of a second, the picture is taken.

● Automatic settings

Like most 35mm cameras, everything is automatic, but it can take a little time for a digital camera to work out the light settings and automatically adjust the aperture size and shutter speed. Then there may be a wait of

CHECKPOINT ✔

Here are some of the key features of digital cameras that you should consider before buying one:

☑ Resolution: the number of dots making up the image. The higher the resolution, the better. Very cheap (approximately £100) digital cameras may have a resolution of less than a million pixels (or 1 megapixel), while for mid-range, pricier models you should be looking for two to three mgapixels as a minimum resolution.

☑ Image storage: the number of pictures the camera will store. On many cameras you can store more images if you choose a lower quality resolution. Standard storage ranges are around 50–200 pictures at low resolution (640x480 or thereabouts) and 5–20 pictures at maximum resolution.

☑ Memory cards: nearly all digital cameras let you plug in a tiny memory card to store extra images. Check the capacity and price of these additional cards as they can vary widely.

☑ Monitor: almost all digital cameras feature an LCD panel where you can check if the picture has come out correctly and select camera options from an on-screen menu.

If your digital camera has a viewing screen, you can check the picture as soon as you have taken it. If you don't like the result, you can simply erase it.

After installing the software supplied, the pictures can be downloaded onto a PC for viewing or printing. Each of them can be viewed in 'thumbnail' form (above). You can zoom in on any individual frame to see it in more detail (right). Some programs include extensive features for display, editing and printing as well as for changing the camera settings.

a few seconds before the image is saved into the camera's memory (more advanced and expensive cameras are quicker). During this brief period, the camera's processor chip compresses the data to squeeze as many images into the camera's memory as possible – usually far more than the 24 or 36 you get on a roll of film.

● Downloading

When you've taken your quota of photos, or the camera's memory is full, it's time to transfer your snaps to your PC. To do this, simply plug the lead supplied into the camera, then plug the other end into your computer (see pages 102–103). You can then run the software supplied and transfer the photos.

Once the photos are copied to your computer, you can erase the files from the camera and start shooting again.

ARE THEY AS GOOD AS THE REAL THING?

If you're looking for award-winning, high-quality printed photographs, then today's affordable digital cameras cannot quite meet the same standards as a film-based camera. First, photographic film can record much more detail than even £1,000 cameras. Digital pictures from low-cost cameras often appear rather 'fuzzy' when studied closely.

Second, the type of lens used for most digital cameras tends not to be as good as that on a conventional camera, which can result in a poorer image. This degrades the final image. Only the most sophisticated digital cameras have lenses as good as those on film-based cameras. But if you're looking for photos that are adequate for a range of jobs, perhaps for a newsletter, advertisement, photo-ID or to send a picture by email to a family member or friend, then a digital camera is ideal. There are no film or development costs, and you can duplicate the photographs by copying a file on your computer.

egypt [1:2] (Background)

In the meantime, the photographs can be viewed on your computer. If you have a colour printer, you will be able to print copies – remember that the higher the resolution of the printer, the better the quality of the printout.

Because the pictures are digital, you can even edit them with a graphics package. For example, you could brush out that spot on your nose or even copy the spot to a less-deserving family member!

Plus, of course, if you have access to the Internet, your email software will let you attach a photograph to your message and send it to your friends and family.

Adding a digital camera

A digital camera can be a useful peripheral or just a great gadget to play with. Either way, connecting it to your PC means you can view, edit and print your own pictures.

During the past couple of years the digital camera has exploded onto the market, offering the user error-free photography and much, much more. The ability to take a picture, check it on a built-in LCD screen, and then either save or retake it is quite a draw for gadget-loving computer users. Add to that the ability to transfer pictures on to your PC – to include in a document, Web page or email – and they become almost essential buys.

In fact, for the would-be digital photographer, the only potential complication comes in the different ways that digital cameras connect to the computer. Most include all the cables and software CD-ROMs or

Connecting a digital camera to your computer is easy. You will then be able to download your own pictures and work on them with your favourite art package.

disks that you will need, but you must still check that you can connect it to your computer with the minimal amount of fuss before deciding which one to buy.

● Latest technology
Digital cameras are evolving rapidly, but the most common way of connecting one to a PC is by means of a USB cable. This is simple, as we show opposite, and you do not need to switch off your PC to make the connection. All modern PCs have USB capability, but an older PC might require a different connection approach. For example, you can

choose a digital camera that uses memory cards to store its photos and also buy a card reader for your PC. This attaches to the PC and can read the memory card in much the same way as a floppy disk.

In the exercise opposite, we show how straightforward it is to connect the camera to your computer by using a USB cable. When your digital camera or card reader is plugged in, you can use the camera's software to see thumbnail-sized previews of the photos you have taken and decide which ones to transfer to your

With a digital camera, an inkjet printer and good quality paper, quite astonishing results can be achieved almost instantly.

computer's hard disk, and which ones you don't want to keep. Most cameras also come with photo-editing programs. Depending on the make and model of your camera, you might find that such software varies widely in capability. The simplest software allows you to vary the brightness and contrast in your photographs, but others include special effects which make it possible for you to twist and distort the photos in weird and wonderful ways – great for creating your own greetings cards.

It's also important to note that if you simply want to print out your photographs, then you can bypass the connection process and buy a simple photograph printer, such as the HP photosmart series of printers, from £100–£350. This allows you to connect your camera directly to the printer and print out high-quality prints at traditional photograph sizes.

Connecting a camera to your PC

Taking pictures with a digital camera is one thing – making the connection and downloading them to your computer is another. Here we show you exactly how to do this.

1 Because digital cameras tend to consume power from their batteries quickly, it's important not to use the batteries unless absolutely necessary. The first step is to plug the mains power adaptor/charger into the socket on your digital camera.

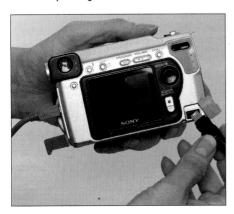

2 Now plug one end of the USB cable into the USB socket on the camera. Only one end of the cable fits into this socket, so you can't accidentally get it wrong.

THE MOVING IMAGE OPTION

Some digital cameras allow you to capture video clips in addition to photos. However, these cameras have only enough memory to store a few seconds of video, so they're not the best choice if you really want to try digital video too.

Instead, take a look at digital video cameras. These use similar sensor chips but the digital image data is stored on videotape instead of memory chips. Most can also capture still photos, giving you the best of both worlds.

3 The other end of the USB cable fits into a vacant USB socket on your PC. These are usually located on the back panel, although some modern PCs also have USB sockets on the front panel.

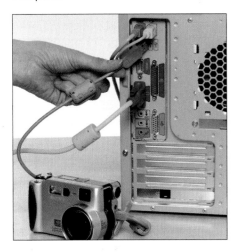

4 Within a few seconds your PC automatically detects the camera. If this is the first time you have used it with your PC, you may need to install the camera's software from the CD-ROM. Read the camera's user guide for information on the full range of software features. In some instances you double-click on My Digital Camera to view the pictures. Here, you double-click on the Sony Memory Stick icon which holds the picture files.

5 Digital camera software varies, but all include a program that can download thumbnail images from the digital camera. Choose the ones you want to view full-size and your PC copies them from the camera's memory to the PC. You can edit and save the photos and, importantly, delete them from the camera to free up memory for more photos.

Understanding scanners

VIVITRON 15

A scanner is one of the most useful and exciting tools you can add to your computer. It enables you to copy pictures and photographs and incorporate them into your letters and documents.

A scanner works rather like a photocopier but, instead of copying a picture onto another sheet of paper, it copies it onto your computer.

Scanners work by passing a bright light over your original page. The light that is reflected back is picked up by the scanner's sensor. The brighter areas of the picture reflect lots of light and the darker areas reflect less.

The scanner converts the picture into data that your PC can understand and sends it down the cable to your computer. The scanning software running on your computer rebuilds the data into a picture you can see on your screen. You can then save the picture onto your computer's hard disk and incorporate it into other documents on your PC.

● What could I use a scanner for?
Scanners have many uses. You can use them to copy photos, drawings, graphs or pages of text. Once you have scanned in your pictures, you can use software to do all sorts of useful and fun things to them, from changing their brightness and

The C Pen manual scanner is really a mini-digital camera. You pass it over the text to be scanned and the image is transferred to your PC via an infra-red connection.

contrast to using special effects to liven them up. If you have access to the Internet, you can send your scanned pictures across the world in seconds via email (see Stage 1, pages 154–156).

● Flatbed scanners
There are several varieties of scanner for the business and professional user, ranging from the tiny C Pen manual scanner to drum scanners for the print industry. For the home or small office user the flatbed scanner is the obvious and sensible choice. It is versatile, scans at high quality and is reasonably priced. The flatbed scanner looks and works in much the same way as a small photocopier. You simply lift the lid, place your original on a sheet of glass and the light sensor moves under the page. The flatbed scanner can also be used to scan books, magazines and mounted photographs.

Once found only in commercial offices, the flatbed scanner has now become a popular piece of kit for many home PC owners.

● Flatbed software
Most flatbed scanners are also supplied with a number of software packages that help you get the most out of the hardware. The software makes it easier to use the scanner and provides you with easy access to special effects for use in all kinds of documents.

Flatbed scanners were once so expensive that they were beyond the means of all but the graphics professional. However, prices have

All-in-one devices like this Hewlett Packard LJ 3100 combine scanner, printer and fax/copier in the same box. You can save a lot of space and minimize wire tangling with such hardware.

fallen dramatically in recent years – to the extent that you can now buy a good flatbed scanner for as little as £60 and a superior, high-quality one for between £125 and £200.

● All-in-ones

Space is always at a premium in the home or office. A flatbed scanner is relatively small but it still takes up desk space – as do your printer and your fax/copier.

However, if you combine all three devices in one box, you can give yourself some much-needed elbow room. A wide range of such all-in-one devices are now available from leading manufacturers, such as Hewlett-Packard and Xerox. They cost between £200 and £400 – the quality rising with the price.

OPTICAL CHARACTER RECOGNITION

This is the phrase, often shortened to OCR, given to software that can look at a page of text, 'read' it and convert it into text that you can edit in your word processor. This software can save lots of time-consuming re-typing when text isn't available on disk.

It works by looking at the shape of the letters on the page and trying to match them against shapes it knows. This means that if the document it is reading is of poor quality, the OCR software often can't recognize the letter at all, or it makes a guess. For example, OCR software can easily confuse a slightly blurred 'cl' with a 'd'.

The versatile scanner

You may find that a scanner proves to be the best addition you've ever made to your computer system. Everyone in the family will find a way to use it – here are just a few ideas to get you started.

School essays

Adding an illustration can make a world of difference to all sorts of documents, from school essays to business reports.

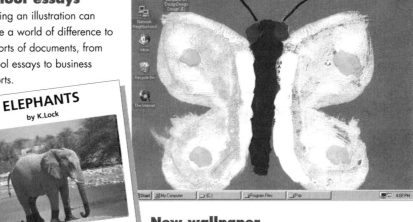

New wallpaper

Use your scanner to copy one of your child's drawings and you can use it as your Desktop background – it makes a change from sticking the picture to the fridge!

Newsletters

If you help publish a club newsletter, a parish magazine or fanzine, you can use your scanner to bring it to life. 'Published' photos of a club's events always prove popular.

Personalized greetings cards

Scan family photos and print your own greetings cards; you'll find that a scanner is the ideal partner for a colour ink jet printer.

Digitizing your signature

If you send faxes direct from your PC, you can scan a copy of your signature and add it to your letters.

Adding a scanner

In order to get the most out of your scanner it is important to choose the right one to fit your needs. And of course you need to connect it correctly.

Having established on the previous pages what a versatile addition to your PC the scanner is, the next steps are to decide what kind of tasks you want to achieve with it and which type of scanner is best suited to your needs.

The most popular type of scanner is the flatbed scanner. This has a flat sheet of glass – typically just bigger than A4 in size – under a plastic lid. You can scan anything that you can place face-down on this glass surface – under the glass a light-sensitive scan head moves from top to bottom to capture the image.

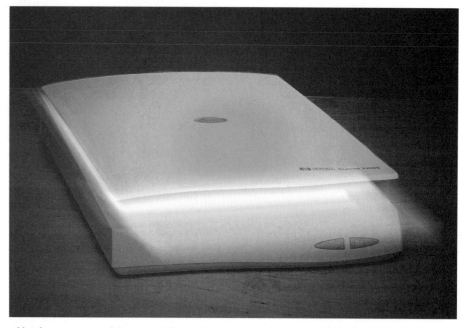

Although scanners are available in many different shapes and sizes, the best overall choice for home computer users is the simple flatbed scanner which is usually very easy to fit.

CHECKPOINT ✔

BUYING A SCANNER

✔ Unless you're sure you need portability, opt for a flatbed scanner. No other types offer the same all-round scanning flexibility.

✔ All scanners can scan black-and-white pages or photos, colour images and so on. If you need to scan slides or negatives, take some along to the shop before you buy. Many low-cost scanners have only very basic slide and negative scanning capabilities, and some have none at all. Ask for a demonstration before making your choice.

✔ Scanner resolution is important, but don't be overly swayed by very high resolutions. Many scanners can produce images at more than 1,000 dots per inch (dpi), but this yields very large files that are slow to edit. Few people scan at more than 300dpi.

✔ Check for useful software bundles. Most scanners include basic image-editing software, but some include an optical character recognition program which can detect words and letters and turn them into text for editing.

● Other types of scanner

There are other types of scanner, most of which operate in different ways. For example, some come in the form of an over-sized pen with a large LCD display. You swipe the pen over a line of printed text and the scanner recognizes the letter shapes and converts the image into words that you later download to a computer. Other portable scanners have a motorized sheet feeder – instead of the flatbed technique where a scan head moves down a stationary page, a motorized scanner pulls the page through the scanner and past the scan head. These scanners can be much smaller than A4 in size.

● Scanner connections

Most scanners attach to the PC via the Universal Serial Bus (USB) or the parallel port. You may come across some that connect via SCSI. This is an efficient but older standard that

requires a SCSI card to be fitted inside the PC. It's not a good choice for home computer users as you may need an expert to fit the SCSI card.

● Ready to go

Fitting a scanner that connects to an existing port is by far the easiest. This is shown opposite with a typical flatbed scanner, in this case one that connects via a USB connection, although parallel port scanners are also easy to install (see Parallel port connection box, opposite). In fact, the only difficult aspect of adding a flatbed scanner to your PC is finding space for it on your desk.

To install scanner software, follow the on-screen instructions. As soon as this is done, you can use the software to capture photographs. Software will vary – the example opposite will give you an idea of the steps, but follow the instructions for your own scanner.

Connecting and using a scanner

Choose a USB flatbed scanner and you'll soon be turning your favourite photos, kids' finger-painting and all manner of artwork into digital images to edit on screen.

1 Clear enough space to place the scanner on your desk. You need to arrange the scanner alongside your monitor and computer so that it's easy to reach and close enough for all the cables to connect.

2 Plug the scanner's power supply into the mains and the power connector into the socket on the back of the scanner. Then plug the USB cable that came with the scanner into the USB connection on the scanner.

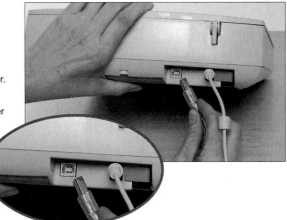

3 Now you can plug the other end of the USB cable into an unused USB socket on the back of your PC.

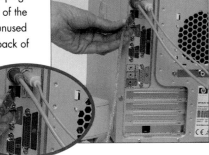

4 Windows will automatically detect the scanner and starts to set it up. Follow the installation instructions for your scanner, using the manual as a guide and inserting the scanner software CD-ROM when prompted.

5 Now you're ready to scan. Lift the scanner lid and place a photo face down on the glass surface. Push it against the corner so that it's sure to be perfectly straight. Lower the scanner lid gently so that you don't accidentally disturb the photo.

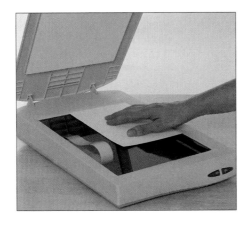

6 This scanner has a push-button to start the scanning process. If your scanner lacks this, you must start the scan by using the scanner's software. Look for a Scan command in the menus or amongst the toolbar buttons.

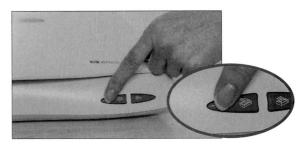

7 Your photo appears on the screen. Many scanners do a draft scan first, allowing you to select an area of the photo and an image quality setting for the final scan.

PARALLEL PORT CONNECTION

If you opt for a scanner that uses the parallel port, the installation process is almost identical to that shown above. However, you should switch your PC off before making the connection between the PC and scanner (Step 3). When you switch it on again, Windows should automatically detect your scanner – if it doesn't, insert the software CD-ROM that came with your scanner and follow the on-screen instructions.

The scanning process is exactly the same as that shown above, with only minor differences from program to program.

Making music

Connecting a simple piano-type keyboard to your computer can turn it into a sophisticated music-maker.

Nearly all modern music has been influenced by computers in some way. Musicians such as the Pet Shop Boys and Jean-Michel Jarre used computers to generate almost every type of sound, but even acoustic music has benefited, as computers are now used extensively during record production to mix and process music tracks.

However, the most common musical use of computers has been to link them to a piano- or synthesizer-type keyboard. The PC can then be used to store a whole series of notes and play them back later – a technique called sequencing.

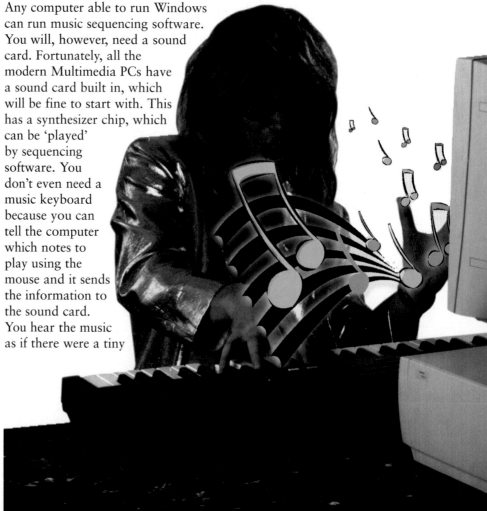

Controller keyboards, such as the Roland ED PC-180A, don't have any built-in sound synthesizer of their own. Instead, you use them to input notes to your computer, which can then play music through its sound card's synthesizer chip.

● A one-man band

Sequencing means that a single musician can record parts for several different instruments and play them back all at the same time so that it sounds like a whole band. It also means that a would-be musician no longer has to have the manual dexterity to play lots of different instruments. Once the basic notes have been entered, the computer can be used to edit the music (taking out any wrong notes, for example), then play it back fluently and at any speed. This has opened up enormous possibilities for home music-making. With a moderate grasp of the principles, even an inability to carry a tune need no longer be a barrier to having fun with music-making.

● Computer requirements

Any computer able to run Windows can run music sequencing software. You will, however, need a sound card. Fortunately, all the modern Multimedia PCs have a sound card built in, which will be fine to start with. This has a synthesizer chip, which can be 'played' by sequencing software. You don't even need a music keyboard because you can tell the computer which notes to play using the mouse and it sends the information to the sound card. You hear the music as if there were a tiny

– and perfect – musician inside. For creating music, however, this approach is not really practical. A music keyboard lets you input notes more naturally. The computer can also record the key you've hit, how hard you've hit it and for how long. You can then replay this information using any sound available on your sound card, such as a guitar, trumpet or even a barking dog.

Once it's on the computer, you can edit it, perhaps changing the tempo or transposing the melody up an octave. The key to all this is a system called MIDI, which is what makes music on a computer so flexible and efficient. The important thing to remember when you play a MIDI file, is that the sound quality depends on

---

WHAT IT MEANS

MIDI

Standing for Music Instrument Digital Interface, MIDI is really two things: a standard way of connecting one MIDI instrument to another, and a type of computer file that stores the notes of a piece of music.

A MIDI file stores details of which note is being played and its sound characteristics – such as how strongly it is being played. You could think of it, if you wish, as the electronic equivalent of a musical score.

Your computer sound card is a MIDI instrument in its own right. With the correct cable, you can connect it to any other MIDI-compatible instrument.

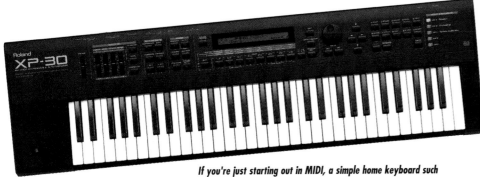

If you're just starting out in MIDI, a simple home keyboard such as this Roland XP-30 might be the best first step.

HOW BIG ARE MIDI FILES?

Because they record instructions rather than sounds, MIDI files take up very little space. A MIDI file for an entire CD's worth of an orchestral composition can actually be stored on a floppy disk.

the calibre of the synthesizer. If you are unhappy with the sound quality of your MIDI synthesizer you can get your PC to send the MIDI information down a cable to a MIDI music keyboard for a better sound.

● Keyboard types

You can choose from a wide range of keyboards to suit all budgets and aspirations.

Cheapest of the options is the controller keyboard, which doesn't actually make a sound itself – it is the computer that makes the sound. The controller keyboard plugs directly into your computer and allows you to play the notes on the keyboard and then edit them on the computer screen. When you

have finished, you can play the notes through the sound card's synthesizer chip and out of your computer's audio speakers.

A controller keyboard is basically all you need to get started, although you can buy several extra components to increase the sounds available. The

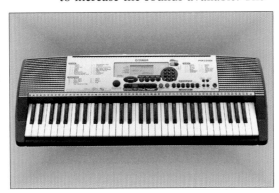

This mid-priced Yamaha keyboard is programmed with sounds suited to a wide range of music, from classical to pop.

next step up is a music keyboard that has synthesized sounds and effects built-in. This type is very popular for home use. However, many low-cost models don't work with MIDI. For computer use, it's essential to have a MIDI keyboard.

You will find a wide variety of MIDI keyboards available in high street stores. When buying, remember to tell the sales assistant that you will need a cable to connect it to your computer. Some music keyboards that are designed for home use plug straight into the sound card's joystick port and come with a suitable cable, but many are sold without a cable so it's best to check.

● Built-in sounds

MIDI keyboards differ widely in price, depending on the quality of the sounds inside. The cheapest have a limited range of sounds – more akin to the home organ – and might not sound much better than the synthesizer chip on your sound card.

At the top of the range are professional and semi-professional keyboards. These often have almost unlimited sound possibilities, as you can tweak the built-in settings in many different ways.

You can also buy add-on hardware called MIDI expanders. These devices connect to the PC in just the same way, but don't have a keyboard of their own. They are mostly used when you simply want to increase the number, or quality, of sounds that you can create on your PC.

MUSIC SOFTWARE

The most important piece of software for the computer musician is a MIDI sequencer. This program is used to record the notes you play on the music keyboard, edit them to correct any mistakes, and then to save the MIDI file on your hard disk. If you're not comfortable with the idea of playing a piano keyboard, most sequencers also let you create music by placing notes on a musical stave on screen.

You also use the MIDI sequencer to play the MIDI files you create, which it does by directing the notes through your sound card's synthesizer chip or out through a MIDI cable to a music keyboard.

You can move and/or copy the notes around at any time, so if you write a song, you need only write the chorus once and then copy and paste it as many times as you need.

The best aspect of a MIDI sequencer is that you can record different parts to build up a piece of music one instrument at a time. For example, you can record a bass part first, and then replay it through the synthesizer, while recording a string section at the same time. What's more, the MIDI sequencer will always play back the music perfectly.

A sequencer screen can look confusing at first. All the on-screen tools act just like the facilities available in a real recording studio.

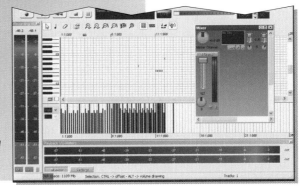

Once you have bought a MIDI keyboard, it takes only a matter of minutes to connect it to your computer. You can then install the software and be ready to make beautiful music.

Connecting a MIDI keyboard

On the previous pages, we have shown how adding a MIDI music keyboard to your computer can open up a new world of sound. However, before you start exploring the joys of creating music on your PC, using music composer programs and sequencing software, the MIDI keyboard and computer must be connected up.

● Types of connection
Some MIDI keyboards are connected to your computer via a cable that is permanently wired into the back of the keyboard itself. More commonly, a special cable (called a MIDI lead) is used. This has a pair of round 5-pin plugs on one end that fit into the music keyboard's MIDI sockets.

The lead from the keyboard plugs into your PC's joystick socket, which is internally connected to the sound card. Once connected to each other, MIDI music information – including which notes you play, how long you hold the keys down and how hard you hit them – is able to pass along the MIDI cable between the sound card and the keyboard.

THE SOFTWARE

The software you choose will play an important part in making sure that your computer and the music keyboard work properly together.

You will need to tell the software – usually a sequencer – that you have a MIDI music keyboard attached. You will almost certainly need some of the information from the music keyboard's manual to set up the software so that it knows how to get the most from your music keyboard.

Connecting the keyboard to your PC is a relatively simple plug-in process, as shown in the step-by-step guide opposite. You then need to install the music software that you intend to use – either a program that came with the keyboard or a separately purchased MIDI sequencer.

● Software set-up
All Multimedia computers have a sound card that is suitable for use with a MIDI keyboard. If the sound card has been properly set up under Windows, and is working with other applications, it will be ready to work with your music keyboard. However, you will still need to set up the computer using the software and instructions that were supplied with the keyboard.

Once your new keyboard is set up, and with a sequencing program to organize the notes you enter, you'll soon be composing your own music, laying it down instrument by instrument, and then combining it all together using the power of your PC.

Making the keyboard connections

Thanks to MIDI connectors being standardized, plugging in a music keyboard is simple and takes just moments.

YOUR FIRST step should be to read the instruction manuals that came with the keyboard and sound card (or the section of your computer's manual that covers the sound card). The physical connections (shown below) are quite simple to make – and even easier for those keyboards which have a cable permanently attached, as you can then skip Steps 2 and 3 in the connection sequence.

You will also need to read the instructions for your choice of music sequencing software, making sure the computer knows where data is being input. Again, music keyboards specifically made for connection to a computer often come bundled with music software and have more detailed instructions about getting started once the connections are made. Just follow the instructions and then let it flow!

1 Because most keyboards ignore USB and use the joystick port, it's necessary to switch the PC off before you plug in the keyboard. Make sure everything is properly closed down and switched off before trying to connect any leads. Unplug, to be sure, as this will avoid the risk of damage, not only to yourself but also to your PC.

2 Most MIDI keyboards use a cable that's specifically made to connect the keyboards to PCs (you may have to buy one as it isn't usually included with MIDI keyboards – expect to pay around £15). It has a chunky PC-type plug at one end and a pair of smaller, round plugs on the other.

3 Locate the MIDI sockets on the back of your music keyboard. There will be two or three close together, marked MIDI IN, MIDI OUT and – if there's a third – MIDI THRU. MIDI THRU is used only for connecting extra MIDI devices. IN and OUT refer to signals passing into and out of the keyboard (see box below).

4 Fit the plug marked MIDI IN into the socket marked MIDI OUT, and the MIDI OUT plug into the MIDI IN socket. This might seem confusing, but there's a way of understanding it to make it seem quite simple (see MIDI IN to MIDI OUT box).

5 Look at the back of your computer and locate the joystick socket. It will be close to where the speakers connect. The chunky end of the cable plugs into this socket.

If you already have a joystick connected to your computer, remove it. Some MIDI cables have a pass-through socket which allows you to plug the joystick into it. If not, you'll have to swap between the two plugs manually.

MIDI IN TO MIDI OUT

At first glance, the way MIDI cables and sockets connect may seem a little confusing. You connect the MIDI IN plug from the computer's sound card to the MIDI OUT socket on the music keyboard, and vice versa.

It will help to think of the MIDI connections as a flow of musical notes: the notes you play on the music keyboard flow out of its MIDI OUT socket into the MIDI IN plug of the sound card cable and then into the computer. Likewise, when using the computer to 'play' the keyboard with a musical composition program, notes flow from the computer, along the sound card cable and out of its MIDI OUT plug into the keyboard's MIDI IN socket.

Home Learning & Leisure

Computing in shops

When you get to a shop's checkout, the chances are that the job of totting up your bill and printing out a receipt falls to a computer that's a very close relation of the PC on your desk at home.

Go into virtually any shop, whether it's a corner newsagent or a huge supermarket, and you can almost guarantee that your purchase will be logged on an electronic till. Although, with all its extra appendages, the electronic till might look like a completely different machine, it is essentially a PC, with many of the same components as the computer in your home or office. It has the same type of microprocessor, and an operating system which is likely to be a variant of MS-DOS and Windows.

● Looks aren't everything

Despite their different appearance, such till systems use familiar computer components and have familiar input and display devices:

the keyboard and the monitor. But in this case the keyboard might be built into the PC itself and be fitted with a credit/debit card reader. There might also be an additional mini-monitor, which can be rotated to face the customer so that he or she can see the cost and total of the items bought. A printer, or even two, outputs receipts and this too might be built into the system unit. But, perhaps the most significant difference from a home system, is the bar code reader.

● Instant information

Bar codes are essential to modern point of sale (POS) systems. A bar code is a printed series of parallel bars and lines, usually black on white, used to represent the binary digits that computers deal in. As such, a bar code can be read instantly by an optical scanner (the bar code reader) connected to the PC till. There's a bar code on the back cover of this book.

● Processing the data

How the till deals with the data from the bar code is central to the computing process in the retail industry. In the supermarket, the checkout operator passes your jar of coffee across the scanner and the item and price are registered. These details are added to the bill, which is totalled up and printed when your basket is empty. You offer payment (cash or a credit/debit card, whose magnetic strip is read by the computer), and you are given your receipt. The obvious benefits are speed and accuracy – there's no laborious keying in of prices, so there's less chance for the operator to make mistakes.

The amount of work that goes on behind the scenes in a busy shop is vast. Without computers to help, it would be extremely time consuming to run such a business.

The retailers reap these benefits, but the scope of POS goes much further than simplifying the checkout process. The data captured simply by reading the bar code on a purchase is valuable in all sorts of ways. The retail POS computer is merely one link in what can be a vast, networked chain of computer technology. The POS is constantly feeding information – items sold, cash taken and so on – into this wider system so that the retailer can manage the business more effectively.

● Point of sale

POS systems have led to enormous improvements in the efficiency of stock control. Before such systems were introduced, a store's stock had to be monitored manually. Inevitably, this was not as accurate and the store suffered loss of sales during periods when it was closed for stock-taking. With POS systems, however, the bar code of an item is read into the till

The Beetle 20 from Wincor Nixdorf is a typical electronic shop till. It uses familiar computer technology, but also includes a customer monitor, card reader and receipt printer.

computer, which sends that information to a database monitoring the shop's stock. This database is programmed to send requests to a much larger, central database, which decides how much stock needs replenishing at that branch.

The result is that the store maintains a steady level of stock and the customer is rarely disappointed by finding that an item is unavailable. There are clear benefits from such systems, even at the independent corner shop. A small retailer with an electronic POS till can tell instantly with each individual purchase just how much of any one item is in stock, and can re-order if necessary.

● The burden of data

The types of POS systems employed by large retailers require massive investment in hardware and software. A supermarket chain might have, for example, 400 stores, each with 15 checkouts; that amounts to 6,000 tills, each of which has to be networked to the store's back office computers, see Back office box, right. These, in turn, have to be connected to larger computers at head office and at the warehouses. The amount of data to be processed and transmitted is enormous. As a result, companies tend to rely both on specialist software and network systems.

● Specific software

The software comes in the form of programs written to manage a specific task, such as IBM's Supermarket Application. Alternatively, companies use modified back office software, which tailors a standard package to their particular requirements.

● What next?

Soon we'll see more supermarkets introducing self-checkout systems, where you take a hand-held bar code scanner around with you and 'swipe' each item you select as it goes into your trolley. You'll be able to pay for the goods by

swiping your debit/credit card through a reader. This system, it is claimed, should finally put an end to queues at the checkout.

Retail chains are also becoming more and more sophisticated in terms of what they do with the data they extract from POS systems. The boom in customer loyalty cards means that retailers know more and more about your shopping patterns and can target you with increasingly focused offers and promotions.

A thermal or impact receipt printer is built into the terminal.

A monitor is included, with the option of an additional, two-line customer monitor.

There are eight ports for peripherals and networking.

A credit card reader is included.

A battery inside the chassis backs up the till in case of power failure.

A standard QWERTY keyboard controls the computer.

IBM's SureOne is a POS terminal designed for use by independent retailers. As well as a computer and printer, it provides a credit card reader and receipt printer.

BACK OFFICE

As a customer, you only see a tiny amount of what goes on in the retail business. What you don't see is the back office operation: the activities that ensure goods are in the shops at the right time and right price, and reordered and restocked, discounted or discontinued when appropriate. In chain stores, this side of retailing involves massive amounts of data.

A large supermarket might have as many as 400 outlets and stock several thousand different lines of goods. Massive amounts of data are generated and analyzed. Stock must be ordered and kept at the optimum level, and management must have detailed reports to help them make strategic decisions. To cope with all of this, the software has to be sophisticated and yet robust, and is often written from scratch to suit a particular kind of business.

If you don't often get the chance to visit the world's best art galleries, you can take advantage of the wonders of computer technology to bring the great masterpieces right to your desktop.

Modern art

Appreciation of art can be a time-consuming and expensive pursuit. You may have to travel great distances – possibly to different countries – to view the masterpieces and, when you arrive at the gallery, there are often hefty entrance fees and long queues ahead.

Furthermore, many of the world's most famous paintings are protected by glass screens and there is rarely the necessary amount of information accompanying the paintings to satisfy your curiosity about the artists' inspirations and intentions.

Fortunately, there's another way to indulge your passion for paintings – you can have the exhibition brought to you by your computer.

Although viewing the work of a great master on your PC isn't the same as seeing the real picture, there are many advantages – the costs are low and you can take your time to absorb the many facets of a great work of art.

● Art on CD

There are many places to find information on art. You'll find entries for most of the world's great artists

Browse a comprehensive data repository of van Gogh's 2,200 art works with Vincent van Gogh: The Complete Works. The most extensive CD-based art catalogue of its type, this title was the result of years of research.

on CD-ROM encyclopedias, such as Microsoft's *Encarta* series and the Hutchinson *Multimedia Encyclopedia*, and there are also several CD-ROMs dedicated to the appreciation of art. After an initial flurry in the 1990s of CD-ROMs aimed at the home user with only a casual interest in fine arts, the latest batch of Windows XP-compatible titles are very much focused on the proper art student, or at least the serious amateur.

Vincent van Gogh: The Complete Works, for example, provides an in-depth and comprehensive catalogue of all 2,200 works from the master. This labour of love was compiled by David Brooks using information taken from the Van Gogh Gallery Web site. Every detail concerning the paintings is included, from exhibition lists to

information on the art's origin and history ('provenance'), as required by historians, dealers and collectors. The entries are clearly presented in a searchable database which is easily

School and university students can obtain a good grounding in modern art history with specialist educational CD-ROM titles from AVP such as Impressionism to the Twentieth Century.

accessible and the title includes a full set of high-quality photographs of the works themselves.

If you'd like to become familiar with the work of Spanish artist Joan Miró, the CD-ROM *Joan Miró – The Colour of Dreams* provides a thorough investigation into the life and works of the artist. Navigated from a graphical interface based on a beach scene, you can do a lot more than simply view his art: the CD-ROM features original music, games, an hour of animation and several hours of narrative audio, not to mention plenty of fully searchable textual information.

The most comprehensive collection of up-to-date art CD-ROMs, however, is available from Multimedia specialist AVP. One of the best is *Impressionism to the Twentieth Century*, a unique introduction to the works of Impressionist and Post-Impressionist masters such as Cézanne, Gauguin, Seurat and, of course, van Gogh. The CD-ROM encompasses artists such as Monet and Degas and extends right up to the early work of Picasso and Matisse.

Another good example of AVP's specialist titles is *Art in the National*

The Picasso Web site at www.picasso.com gives a fascinating insight into his life and works.

The Grove Dictionary of Art Online is an indispensible Web-based resource for the serious art student.

Links from the Grove Dictionary take you directly to samples of art works located all over the Internet.

Curriculum, a bestseller which has been revised to keep in step with the ever-shifting goalposts of the school syllabus. This CD-ROM looks beyond the great painters of western Europe to cover the wider world of art, including textiles, sculpture and ceramics. It takes students on a grand journey across continents, ancient civilisations and modern culture.

● Art on the Web
The Internet offers art lovers an increasingly rich and effortless way of exploring both the world's great collections and the lives and works of individual artists. A starting point for exploring the variety of contemporary art is www.art.net, where you can check out the work of all kinds of artists from all over the world.

In fact, many of the world's most famous artists have their own dedicated Web sites, from the likes of Picasso (www.picasso.com) to Cézanne (www.expo-cezanne.com) and Magritte (www.magritte.com).

Even the famous *Grove Dictionary of Art* has been re-incarnated as an expensive, but worthwhile, subscription-based Web site, an essential addition to any serious art-lover's

Joan Miró – The Colour of Dreams is a comprehensive CD-ROM covering the life and works of the 20th-century Spanish artist.

electronic library. This massive database has information on every significant artist known to man and now also includes links to external Web sites of official galleries and museums where relevant samples of the artists' works can be found.

But even if you just want to browse for free, it's a near certainty that any artist you can't find on a CD-ROM, you'll find on the Internet.

CONTACT POINTS

**Vincent van Gogh:
The Complete Works**
Price: £30.00*
Email: brooks@vangoghgallery.com
www.vangoghgallery.com

Joan Miró – The Colour of Dreams
Price: 42 euros (approx £28)
Joan Miró Foundation, Barcelona
Email: fjmiro@bcn.fjmiro.es

Impressionism to the Twentieth Century
Price: £39.99*
Art in the National Curriculum
Price: £39.99*
AVP
Tel: 01291 625439

The Grove Dictionary of Art Online
Price: £195 per year* (single user)
Macmillan
Tel: 020 7843 4612
www.groveart.com

*UK prices

Designing your home

If you've grown tired of the way your home looks, why not give your rooms a face-lift by changing their layouts? Your computer, as always, can help.

Have you ever spent a day moving all your furniture around to see if the sideboard looks better in an alcove or against the wall? Everything probably ended up back where it started and all you had to show for your efforts were a strained back and aching muscles.

A far better way of rearranging a room is not to move the furniture at all, but to draw a scale plan of the room and position scale drawings of the furniture on it. This way you can try out all the possible arrangements to find the one you like the best.

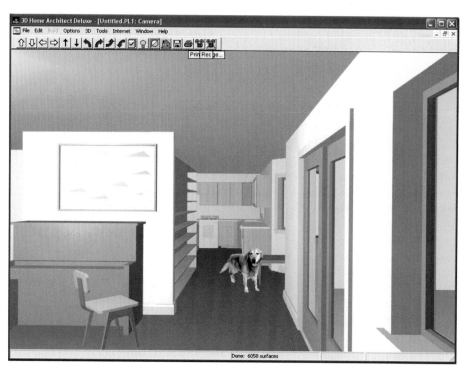

Once you've got the structure and layout right in 3D Home Architect Deluxe 4.0, you can furnish your home and even add pets before taking a virtual walk through to check that it delivers the effect you want.

WHAT IT MEANS

JAVA

Java is a programming language specifically designed for creating highly compact programs. Because of their small size, Java programs can be used to add advanced interactive features to Web sites even when accessed by a standard modem.

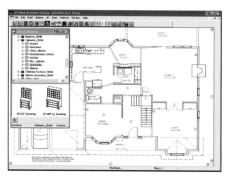

3D Home Architect Deluxe 4.0 *starts with floorplans: you can either create your own or customise one of the ready-made templates.*

● No drawing skills required

While it might seem like a great idea, for most of us drawing a scale plan is about as easy as performing brain surgery. This is where your PC can help. There are computer programs that allow you to create scale room plans, letting you see what a room would look like with your furniture in different places. The software will also add different colour schemes and even produce a three-dimensional design that you can 'walk' through.

● Drawing floor plans

One of the most popular CDs of this type is *3D Home Architect Deluxe 4.0* from Broderbund. This gives you many of the tools used by professional interior designers, but in a simplified form. You can draw floor plans from scratch using the set of easy tools provided, trace around manual sketches you have scanned in, or you could take one of

the 1,650 sample plans and modify it to your own taste.

The floor plan shows the outer walls, doors, windows, and the internal dividing walls. To add

DON'T FORGET THE KITCHEN

There is one room in the house where there is no scope for trial and error when creating virual 3D designs – the kitchen. Since all the units in a kitchen must fit together with precision and be fastened into the fabric of your house, the safest option is to create a 'virtual' kitchen.

Some packages include a specialist 3D kitchen designer, complete with colours, textures and detailed fittings. America's popular television DIY presenter Bob Vila even provides an online kitchen designer on the Web. The software is **Java**-based and is offered as a free service to site visitors.

Professional Home Design Suite isn't content with letting you create just the house, but comes with utilities for landscaping the garden and visualising outdoor details from decks and gazebos to swimming pools.

features, you simply select from a floating library browser window and then place the desired element – such as a window or fireplace – into position. Complex features such as staircases can be accommodated once you have selected dimensions from a dialog box. To see what your dream home looks like in real life, *3D Home Architect Deluxe 4.0* creates three-dimensional views simply by clicking and dragging the

Bob Vila's Kitchen Designer has moved away from CD-ROM to become a Java-based program on the Web.

FloorPlan 3D Home Design Suite 7 allows you to view each floor from above as a solid 3D image...

camera tool anywhere in a floorplan. You can also take a tour through the interior, viewing the rooms with their furniture in position. *3D Home Architect Deluxe 4.0* is a great way to judge the effects, for example, of demolishing an internal wall. There's no mess or expense and you can rebuild everything, instantly.

● **Designing like a professional**
Professional Home Design Suite, from Punch Software, concentrates more on detailed finishing touches than attempting to offer vast numbers of floorplan templates. It comprises a dozen programs which cover a wide variety of home design-related tasks, from creating the house itself to laying out the patio and gardens. For example, there are separate utilities for planning the electrics and plumbing to incorporate into the floorplans, and a 'home estimator' keeps tabs on how much it's all

...or as a wireframe, so you can see internal structures and quickly check what's hiding behind those walls.

costing you as you go along. You can even be very precise about such things as the internal roof structure and designing foundations according to the layout of your plot of land.

The star feature of *Professional Home Design Suite* is its high quality three-dimensional renderings of your virtual property, both inside and out. These also feature in the cheaper Punch package, *Super Home Suite*, which concentrates on the home design essentials.

● **Homing in on virtual reality**
Another key package in this field is *FloorPlan 3D Home Design Suite 7* from IMSI. Like its competitors, this software takes you from floorplan to three-dimensional walkthrough, and comes with a library of ready-made furniture and fittings objects.

As with the Punch products, *FloorPlan 3D Home Design Suite 7* makes it possible to work on outdoor constructions as well as the house itself. But it also uniquely features the advanced *TurboCAD Designer 8* program for drawing up precision blueprints which are used by most architects and contractors.

Inevitably, designing your own home requires considerable effort, but with these Desktop suites you can do the job like a professional.

CONTACT POINTS

3D Home Architect Deluxe 4.0
Price: £20*
Broderbund, distributed by Mindscape
Tel: 01293 651300

Professional Home Design Suite
Price: £49.99*
Super Home Suite
Price: £29.99*
Punch Software, distributed by FastTrack
Tel: 01923 495496

FloorPlan 3D Home Design Suite 7
Price: £39.99*
IMSI Software, distributed by Mediagold
Tel: 020 7221 4600

Bob Vila's Kitchen Designer
www.bobvila.com
*UK prices

Movie games

Straight from the silver screen to your computer screen – these games enable you to get involved with all the action and adventure of the movies.

The connection between your PC and the cinema can be traced back to the very first few games that were written for the earliest home computers.

A *Star Trek* game was released even before the first *Star Trek* feature film was made. Based on the TV series, it was one of the first examples of a computer game picking up on popular culture. However, with its tiny asterisk-like character representing the spaceship, it could not look more basic when compared with today's CD-ROM Multimedia spectaculars.

● **Computer-generated Hollywood**
The link between PC gaming and feature films is growing stronger each year. It's not just due to the increasing

use of computer-generated special effects employed in Hollywood, either. Rather, as the quality of 3D-rendered visuals and hi-fi audio on the home PC has improved, games themselves have become more cinematic. The game player can now

Indiana Jones and the Emperor's Tomb from LucasArts marks Dr Jones' sixth outing on the PC.

enjoy the feeling of actually taking part in a blockbuster adventure.

● **Essential merchandise**
When a film has been released, a spin-off game can become a major part of the merchandising throughout – and even beyond – the shelf-life of the film. Even if the film had nothing whatsoever to do with computers or the Internet, by the time it is released it will almost certainly have added to the increasing number of PC games based on Hollywood's latest blockbuster movies.

● **Games based on films**
The science fiction genre, of course, seems to lend itself to the medium of computer games particularly well, but you will also find other types of film on your PC. When the graphic adventure *Indiana Jones and the Fate of Atlantis* appeared, based around a plot yet to be explored on celluloid, rumours started that it was going to be turned into a fourth *Indiana Jones* film. But while the fans wait on tenterhooks, the LucasArts game development team has already moved on, with *Indiana Jones and the Emperor's Tomb*.

Other film series have struggled to produce games that do them justice. Although several attempts have been made over the years, there has never been a truly satisfying game based on the *Jurassic Park* or *James Bond* films. In part this seems to be because some films, no matter how action-orientated they may be, just don't translate well to the PC screen; even the longest of films tends to have only three or four unique action scenes and this just isn't enough to fill even the shallowest of PC games.

The most successful movie-based games are those set within the

HOW MOVIES INFLUENCE GAMES

For every game which is officially licensed from a motion picture there are a dozen that are unofficially 'influenced'. In fact, there is scarcely a science fiction game in existence that hasn't been influenced by classic films such as *Star Wars*, *Alien* and *The Terminator*. Other types of films have also influenced some recent titles. *Resident Evil* seems to owe most of its plot to George Romero's series of zombie movies, and the classic *Driver* game appears to be based on the car chases in the Steve McQueen film *Bullitt*, even down to the San Francisco setting and cars used.

'universe' of a film, but which aren't strictly based on the movie's plot. The original *Star Trek* games, which have the freedom to create a plot better suited to a computer game, always tend to be more successful than those trying to translate a two-hour film script into a game with more than 40 hours of gameplay. The *Star Trek* game, *Bridge Commander*, is a great example that takes full advantage of your PC's Multimedia abilities.

● The right connections

Your PC has movie connections in more ways than just game playing, though. There are interactive film guides available on CD-ROM; you'll find movie Web sites that are run by both film companies and devoted fans; and powerful computers have been used by movie studios to create entire films, with only the voices being provided by real actors and actresses.

Film itself may be on the way out. Some films – such as Disney's Toy Story – have been made almost entirely on large banks of powerful computers.

When games inspire movies

ROLE REVERSAL is more common than you might think when it comes to the franchise connection between Hollywood and computer gaming. Ever since the console boom began in the late 1980s, movie moguls have been queuing up to transfer popular small-screen games to the cinema. It's easy to be judgemental about the quality and success of early attempts such as 1993's *Super Mario Brothers* (starring Bob Hoskins, Lance Henriksen and Dennis Hopper) and 1995's *Streetfighter* (starring Jean-Claude van Damme) but 'Siliwood' has since grown into an industry to be reckoned with.

As well as the considerably more successful game-inspired movies shown here, future franchises on the cards include the robot battler *Tekken*, psycho horror *Alice*, action horror *Alone in the Dark*, and plain action *Max Payne*.

Lara Croft: Tomb Raider

If one movie above all proved that money could be made from a reverse game tie-in, this was it. But despite the phenomenal success of Eidos' *Tomb Raider* games, it was the iconic character Lara Croft which sold the film, hence her name inserted into the title. The plot follows the general theme of the game series, featuring mysterious locations, secret agents and undiscovered treasure.

Resident Evil

A secret experiment... a deadly virus... a fatal mistake. As in the original Capcom game, it's up to Alice and a group of commandos to locate the antidote to a virus which is turning people into the undead. And everyone gets to shoot lots of zombies on the way through the maze-like Hive. It may not be art, but the action mystery of the original lends itself to a big-screen treatment.

Check out the games which made it onto the big screen.

Mortal Kombat

Contrary to critics' expectations, this 1995 film was successful enough to spawn a sequel two years later. Characters from the one-on-one fighting game do what they do best in a variety of scenes, just like in the game itself.

Final Fantasy

As well as taking advantage of the highly immersive scenario of the long-running *Final Fantasy* game series, this movie was the world's first full-length entirely computer-animated feature aimed at grown-ups.

From film reels to CD-ROM

There have been film licences since the earliest days of video gaming. Here are some of the more recent offerings.

IN THE early days of video games, film licences had a poor reputation. Often the licence was added at a late stage in a title's development, simply to bolster the appeal of an otherwise lacklustre product.

Nowadays games companies are more in tune with the movies, although many titles do still fall into the trap of featuring too many game styles in a vain attempt to simulate every action scene in a film. Over the next two pages we'll look at some classic examples of movie-licensed games. Most of them are successful games in their own right and, rather than being afterthoughts, are produced with help from the original movie crew and actors.

Star Wars: Galactic Battlegrounds

As if there weren't enough *Star Wars* games already, George Lucas' own company LucasArts has released a game based not so much on the plot of the films as on their universe. The game is a departure from many of the previous *Star Wars* games in that it is a sprawling strategy title rather than fast-paced action adventure, albeit featuring real-time armed clashes.

You can enter the *Star Wars* universe as the Galactic Empire, Rebel Alliance, Trade Federation or any of a number of civilisations, from Wookies and Gungans to Royal Naboo. You build armies and win campaigns with the help of storm-troopers, bounty hunters, Jedi knights…in fact, whatever it takes to survive the Galactic Civil War.

Harry Potter

It was inevitable that the Harry Potter books and the first feature film, *The Philosopher's Stone*, would lead to a game, much in demand at its Christmas launch. But with the second movie complete and further instalments on their way, Electronic Arts has already released its second

tie-in title, *Harry Potter and the Chamber of Secrets* – guaranteed to be at the top of kids' must-have list.

The latest release, with its self-explanatory subtitle 'Dare to return to Hogwarts', involves learning more spells, making new friends and challenging further adversaries as you navigate your way around the mysterious school corridors.

Lord of the Rings

Every bit as beautiful to behold as the record-breaking fantasy film it is based on, *Lord of the Rings: The Fellowship of the Ring* follows the fantastic journey taken by Frodo, Aragorn and Gandalf through Middle Earth. You will encounter elves, escape dragons and do battle with rampaging Orcs in your quest to take the Ring ever closer to its ultimate fate in Tolkien's classic fantasy.

CONTACT POINTS

Star Wars: Galactic Battlegrounds
Price: £29.99*
LucasArts, distributed by Activision
Tel: 0870 241 2148

Harry Potter
Price: £29.99*
Electronic Arts
Tel: 01932 450890

Lord of the Rings
Price: £29.99*
Universal Interactive
www.universalinteractive.com

Spider-Man: The Movie
Price: £34.99*
Activision
Tel: 0870 241 2148

E.T. Phone Home
Price: £19.99*
UbiSoft
www.ubi.com

Aliens vs. Predator 2
Price: £29.99*
Sierra, distributed by Vivendi Universal
Tel: 01268 531245

Emperor: Battle for Dune
Price: £9.99*
Westwood, distributed by Electronic Arts
Tel: 01932 450890

*UK prices

Spider-Man: The Movie

Undoubtedly the Hollywood hit of summer 2002, Sam Raimi's fresh treatment of the webbed Marvel comic hero was begging to be given a 3D action game treatment. This is more than just a tie-in stapled over an existing game engine though: the title benefits from some superb animated graphics and spectacular scenes of 'fantasy violence'. The game will have you on the edge of your seat – tackling villains, duelling with the Green Goblin, and swinging between skyscrapers.

E.T. Phone Home

When Steven Spielberg re-released his classic sci-fi tale *E.T.* as a 20th anniversary edition with CGI-modified scenes, a string of children's gaming titles joined the bandwagon. These currently range from the strategy-based *E.T. Interplanetary Mission* to the PC board game *E.T. Away From Home*. One of the most popular for the kids is *E.T. Phone Home*, a graphic adventure in which you follow the movie plot to help the little alien rejoin his spaceship.

Aliens vs. Predator 2

There has, as yet, been no such movie as *Aliens vs. Predator*. But the idea of these two modern-day movie monsters fighting it out has long ago been explored in a series of comic books, from which an unfilmed movie script was derived. However, where cinema fears to tread, video games rush in, and this is already the second successful game title from the concept. *Aliens vs. Predator 2* is essentially a 3D shoot-'em-up with the twist that you can take the role of either a monster or a human marine. The game does an excellent job of portraying all the protagonists.

Emperor: Battle for Dune

Ever since David Lynch's bewildering gallop through Frank Herbert's mighty *Dune* novels, the film has sparked a long line of strategy titles, right from the early days of home PC and console gaming. The latest, *Emperor: Battle for Dune*, follows the same theme, based in the year 10190 and involving a mix of statesmanship and treachery in order to take control of planet Arrakis, where the spice Melange is found. Whoever controls the spice controls the universe, so you must win armed and diplomatic battles to achieve Dune's conquest.

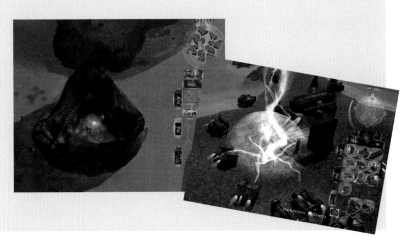

Star Trek games

Star Trek games were once scoffed at by PC gamers. In recent years, however, the TV and film series have become the basis of some excellent games, featuring popular genres.

Star Trek has been a licensing bonanza for all sorts of products as it has evolved over the many years of its existence. For PC gamers the programme's fertility hasn't always been welcome; it resulted in a head-spinning range of mediocre games across a variety of genres from a host of different publishers. Game-playing devotees of *Star Trek* just didn't know where to turn.

Recently, the situation has become much clearer, and the quality of the games somewhat better. Activision now owns most rights in the *Star Trek* licence, and so has the fullest catalogue and most up-to-date releases in terms of Windows XP-compatible titles. The good news is that there are plenty of improved *Star Trek* games out there, covering a wide range of game genres.

At last, the Star Trek games are beginning to match the exciting involvement of the original TV series and films.

Activision's most recent title, released just in time for Christmas 2002, is *Star Trek: Elite Force II*, the second game to be based on the *Star Trek Voyager* universe. It's a moderately violent, first-person shooter (the first release was given an 11+ rating), powered by the *Quake III: Team Arena* game engine.

After a brief prologue on the *USS Voyager* and a short stint at Starfleet Academy, *Elite Force*'s Hazard Team is assigned its toughest mission yet: duty on board the Federation's renowned flagship, the *USS Enterprise*. During the course of the game you get to fight against some of the classic *Star Trek* antagonists plus several never-before-seen alien species who visit your dreams,

including a mysterious nightmare race. To even up the odds, you can arm yourself with 13 different weapons from the humble phaser up to a Romulan disruptor.

Most interesting is the way the *Quake* engine allows you to break out of the confines of ship bulkheads and space station corridors, and undertake team missions in open environments such as expansive alien landscapes, the void of space and deadly swamps. You'll also have to master zero-gravity if you want to do battle on the hull of a starship.

● **Fleeting glimpse**
Activision's earlier release at the end of 2001 was set in the Next Generation universe and based on a

Back on the bridge in Star Trek: Bridge Commander, *Kiska (below) takes control of a knife-edge situation.*

Star Trek: Bridge Commander aims to be as impressive as possible, featuring beautifully rendered ships (above).

very different genre of real-time 3D strategy. In *Star Trek: Armada II,* you are still picking up the pieces from a Borg incursion into Alpha Quadrant, but now the Federation Council has directed Starfleet to find out how and where the Borg were getting in.

This sets the scene for 30 complex missions in which you must command ships and infrastructure of not just the Federation fleet but also those of the

Starfleet Command Volume III lets multiple players join forces for combatting other fleets online in real time.

Gather your ships and plan each move in Star Trek: Armada II, as you plot planets and battle Borgs.

Klingon Empire and Borg Collective. You explore new planetary systems, engage with up to seven other Internet or network-connected players, and generally tread the fine line between peace and war in the known universe.

● Naughty Romulans

Star Trek: Bridge Commander is a space simulation set in the Star Trek Next Generation era. Neither a 3D shoot-'em-up nor a straight strategy game, you command a large starship from a detailed 3D bridge with lots of firepower and configurable defence systems at your fingertips.

You play the part of Jean Luc Picard, commanding a skeleton crew of four, each with specialist know-how. Helmswoman Kiska handles all space flight, while the tactical officer has the full arsenal of the Enterprise's weapons at his disposal. A science officer and engineer provide extra backup – especially by using the shields if your defence doesn't quite go to plan. However, if you find giving orders hard work, there's a mode which lets you do everything yourself.

To assist the immersive feel of the simulation, the game features stunning ship models, generous special effects such as a 3D battlefield planner, and on-screen information which is highly detailed.

A very different title is *Star Trek: Starfleet Command III*, based on a long-standing, turn-based board game

called *Star Fleet Battles*. Over three versions it has grown into an immense 3D real-time PC game in its own right for single and multiple players.

In single-player mode, you must take part in three campaigns, playing as Klingons, Romulans and the Federation. Over the course of the game, you accrue prestige points to spend on better ships and upgrades to give you a better chance of success.

In multiplayer 'skirmish' mode, you engage other players in combat as an action-style free-for-all. There's also a Dynaverse 3 multiplayer environment in which players can join together in the same fleet and battle alongside one another for galactic dominance.

● Great communicator

Looking ahead, expect to see some forthcoming Star Trek games extending to Internet-connected mobile phones, thanks to a deal between Activision and Digital Bridges. Imagine sitting in a meeting at work when suddenly you receive a phone message to say your ship is under attack. That's one call you simply can't fail to answer.

The Internet

Internet chat

Internet chat systems offer the opportunity to communicate live online with other computer users all round the world.

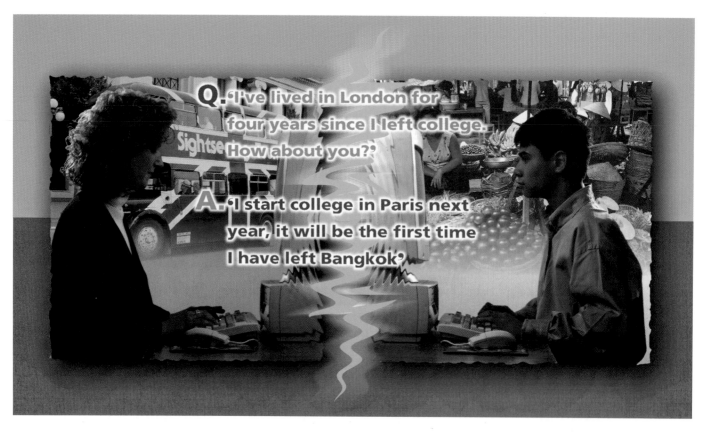

Q. 'I've lived in London for four years since I left college. How about you?'

A. 'I start college in Paris next year, it will be the first time I have left Bangkok'

Sending messages to people all over the world via email has long been, and is still, the main reason why people use the Internet. But email does not happen in 'real time': it's more like sending a letter than making a phone call. However, it's actually very easy to talk, or 'chat', to other people on the Internet in real time, and not just to a single person, but to a host of participants all over the world. In fact, Internet chat is so easy that it has become one of the fastest growing areas of use.

In the earlier days of the Internet, real-time chat was an extremely complicated business; you had to download substantial programs which could be confusing to use. And finding the 'chat rooms' where people gather was no easy business. Nowadays, the whole thing has become much simpler, largely because the software that powers the chat system downloads in a matter of seconds. That, together with the massive and growing number of people online, means that Internet chat has never been easier. Just log on to the home page of any major ISP (Internet Service Provider) and you'll find a link taking you directly to chat areas. We show how, and what is available, over the next three pages.

● **People and topics**
Chat rooms cover every conceivable interest. There are rooms dedicated to dealing on the stock market, to soaps, to football and to pop music, to name but a few. There are also many rooms created specifically for certain age groups, such as teens, 40-somethings and so on. And, of course, there are many rooms – with names such as Love Shack, Singles Bar and the like – where the chat often takes the form of more flirtatious conversation.

Whatever the room or the ISP, the format is very similar and easy to use. The screen generally presents a main window showing the participants' contributions. A narrow window at the bottom is where you type your own, before clicking on Send or hitting [Enter] to send it to the chat room. On the right you will nearly always find a list of the users currently active: in many services you can click on these to get personal details (if supplied) and to send mail to or chat one-to-one with other users, away from the main chat room.

A WORD OF WARNING

Although some chat rooms – such as those on AOL – are monitored by a guardian, the general rule is that they are a free forum. People can, and do, say just about anything, sometimes in very salty language. So you need to exercise caution about which chat rooms you, and especially your children, enter. Fortunately, potentially unsavoury ones are nearly always easily identifiable by their names.

Using Yahoo! Chat

Yahoo! is one of the Internet's most popular sites. It offers a range of services, including numerous different chat rooms which are easy to access and use.

1 Go to the Yahoo! UK site (www.yahoo.co.uk) and click on the Chat link near the top of the page.

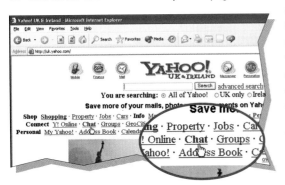

2 As a first-time visitor, you'll have to register in order to get a user ID and a password. Remember that you don't need to use your real name – and it's probably advisable to use a pseudonym if you value your anonymity. Just type in your chosen ID and password in the boxes at the top of the page. You'll also be asked to provide some personal details so that Yahoo! can help out should you forget your details.

3 Once that's done, you are taken to the home page of the Chat area (see below) where you'll see links to Featured Rooms and the Complete Room List. Click on the Complete Rooms List link to see links to all of the Chat Categories and Chat Rooms (see right). Simply click on the one you want to visit.

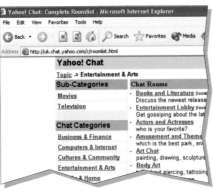

4 Before you can actually enter the chat room, you may have to install the Yahoo! Chat software. All you need to do is click on the Yes button in the dialog box that appears and the software will download almost instantly.

CHAT TOPICS

The front page of the Yahoo! Chat area offers several featured rooms that you can jump straight in to. If you're new to Chat then it's probably a good idea to check these out first. But these are far from being your only choices. The UK version of Yahoo! Chat offers well over 200 categories of chat room, covering just about everything from business and computing to romance and religion. And there are dozens of rooms dedicated to local chatting, so you can check out folk from your very own area.

The vast majority of these rooms are safe and welcoming places, where people go to interact with others and benefit from their advice and experience. The one category you should be wary of, particularly if children or teenagers are going to be online, is romance. There is a wide variety of chat rooms within this category, and generally they are pretty safe. But rogue chatters can and do make appearances, sometimes with pretty offensive material. Enter these rooms at your own risk, and monitor them carefully if your children are going to use them.

5 Now you're ready to chat. The main screen window shows who is entering and who is leaving the room, and the sender and text of any messages. To join in, all you do is type your contribution in the narrow Chat: box at the bottom of the screen and click on the Send button. On the right is the Chatters window showing a full list of those in the Chat room.

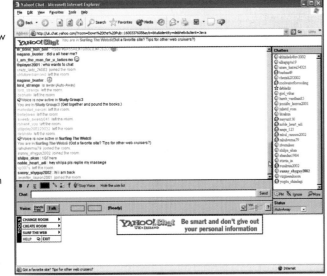

Chatting on AOL

If you are a member of AOL (see Stage 1, pages 146–149), you'll probably find a topic to talk about in one of its chat rooms.

1 Getting into the chat areas on AOL is extremely straightforward. Once you've logged on, just click the Chat & Community channel on the AOL contents window.

2 The AOL Chat & Community page appears. From here you have a variety of options. Click on the chat times link under Hosted Chats where you will find a list of what's available. We've chosen to view Mystic Gardens; simply double-click on the link to enter the room.

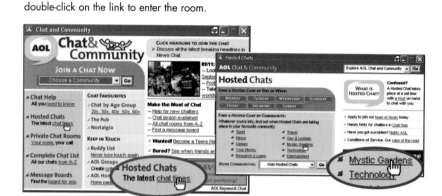

3 To join in, select Go to Chat. The next window informs you that Mystic Gardens has two chat rooms – select your preferred option.

4 The list of members in the room is displayed on the left of the screen. To join in, just type in your message in the long box at the bottom and click Send or hit the [Enter] key.

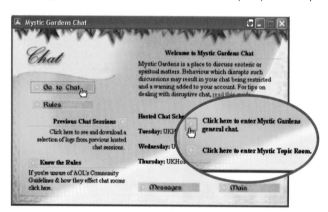

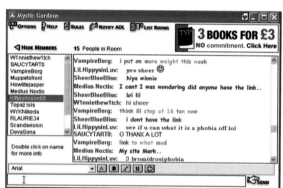

5 Because AOL is a worldwide service, chat rooms are not limited to the UK. Select the Complete Chat List from the AOL Chat & Community page (see Step 2), then just click on International Chat Rooms, then the option 'Have a look around the International channel' and you could soon be chattering away to some new friends in a foreign language.

6 AOL also gives you the opportunity to participate in live celebrity chat sessions. Click on the 'from A-Z' link under the Complete Chat List heading on the Chat & Community page. Now scroll down and click on Celebrity Chat UK in the list. Make a note of the times of any future chat sessions you're interested in so you can log on later and join in.

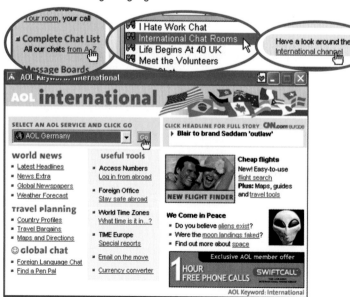

CHAT ROOM SHORTHAND

New chatters will find plenty of shorthand used in chat rooms on the Web. One of the most frequently used abbreviations is 'lol', which is a little bemusing at first. It means 'laugh out loud' and is added to the end of your comment if you mean it as an ironic joke, as in: 'Yes, my other car is a Ferrari, lol'. Another popular one is 'ROTFL' – rolling on the floor laughing – used only when you find the comment extremely unfunny.

Freeserve Chat

Freeserve's chat rooms reflect the interests of its more than 2 million members – and you can even chat without subscribing to Freeserve.

FREESERVE HAS BECOME much more than a simple ISP connecting people to the Internet (see Stage 1, pages 142–145). Its wide range of services mean that it is more of a 'portal', offering a one-stop way of satisfying the need of its users for news, entertainment, listings and Web searching. As such, online chat is an integral part of the offering and one that Freeserve has tried to make as simple to use as possible.

1 To sample Freeserve Chat, go to its chat page (www. freeserve.com/chat/). Four sections allow you to make your choice of chat room. Select one of them to get going.

2 If you are a new user you will need to register a nickname by clicking the New Member link.

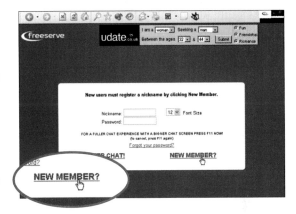

3 Fill in your nickname and email address. If your nickname is successfully registered then your password will be emailed to you almost instantly.

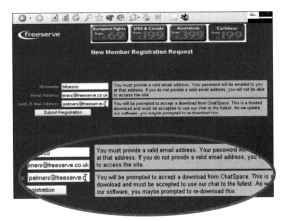

4 You will need to download ChatSpace. This small program downloads in just a couple of minutes. Once you have received your email and downloaded the program, you are ready to go.

5 When you enter, you have the option of chatting in the Lobby which is for general chat with unlimited members or you can select one of the many Rooms – the topics under discussion are listed. As with Yahoo! Chat, to have your say you simply type in the message in the box at the bottom of the screen and click Send or press [Enter]. Users' comments appear in the main panel in different colours. In the right-hand panel, you will see a list of other members who are in the room.

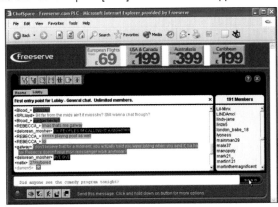

6 The buttons at the top give you various options you might like to explore, for example, chat options and room options, and a member profile button where you can add your own information. There are also some nifty buttons along the bottom with which you can add sound, emotion and actions to your messages, and two for adding colour to your text.

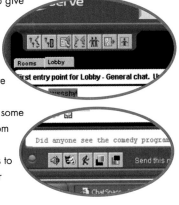

Creating your own Web site

One of the great pleasures of the Internet comes from creating your very own site and having people access it. You don't even need any special software – Windows includes everything you need to learn the basics.

If you have an account with one of the well-established ISPs, then you almost certainly have some free Web space as part of your package deal. By taking advantage of this space, you have the ability to create your own Web site for other Internet users to see.

You could use this space to set up a site for your hobbies, a site to advertise your business if you're self-employed or even a site that simply says 'Hello world' and contains details about you and your life.

Most ISPs provide at least 5MB of space free of charge. Additional space is available at extra cost, but 5MB should give you plenty of scope to make an interesting site.

● It's just another document

Just like the documents you create in Word or Excel, the pages you make for a Web site take up disk space. Similarly, when you create the pages, you store them on your computer's hard disk. The difference is that to make the Web pages visible to all Internet users, you copy (or upload) them to your ISP.

Your ISP has powerful computers, called Web servers, which are dedicated to storing hundreds or even thousands of Web pages for its customers. Anytime someone wants to see your Web site, your Web pages are retrieved from the server.

● An address for your site

Once your Web pages are copied to your ISP's computer, Internet users can see them by typing the address of the pages into their Web browsers. This address will usually be based on the ISP's own address. For example,

AOL users store their Web sites in hometown.aol.com. If you use a different ISP, check your sign-up documents for information on free Web space and addresses. If you visit the Hometown area of the AOL site, you'll be able to see huge categorized lists of people's Web sites and their contents (some are shown opposite). Although the space given to each site might be similar, the contents

are as diverse and unique as the people who made them.

Subjects can range from *Star Trek* trivia to how to look after unusual pets; from needlework to the fuel consumption of a 1940s roadster;

The Internet is great at giving us the opportunity to find people all over the world with similar interests. With a Web site of your own you can announce your own interests – and people will be able to find you!

or from technical PC information to Elvis' inside leg measurement.

● HTML – the Web language

The one thing that deters many people from creating a Web site is that it uses a programming language called HTML (HyperText Mark-up Language). But don't worry – HTML is one of the simplest languages in the computing world and the basics are no more complicated than typing normal text sprinkled with a few special commands.

There's no denying the fact that a page of HTML code can look complicated, but as soon as you start learning what a few of the commands mean, you'll see that everything is quite logical.

● Breaking the code

You might wonder what this odd-looking code has to do with the pictures and text you see when you type an address into your Web browser. After all, you don't see a single piece of HTML code.

What happens is that your browser strips out the HTML commands, which it uses to work out how to display the real content. The browser reads the code to work out where to place the images, words and links and then displays them for the user, who need never see the underlying code that makes it possible.

The following exercises will show you how to create some simple HTML pages. When you've worked through both of these exercises, you'll

be able to put centred text on the screen, as well as pictures and even links – which are all you need to produce a perfectly usable page. In fact, many slow-loading pages are caused by their creator trying to use too many fancy commands.

● Begin with the basics

Learning to take full advantage of the basic HTML commands is important, not only from a technical standpoint, but also for design reasons. However, once you've learnt how basic HTML works, you can use a Web-editing program, such as Microsoft FrontPage Express or Sierra's WebStudio. These easy-to-use programs create all the HTML code for you.

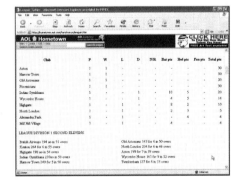

A page on the Web is a great way to let people know what's going on in a society or club, as with this page detailing the season's results in a cricket league.

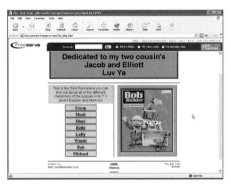

Many Web sites are created by kids; it's a fun way to get young children interested in technology and give them a head start for more serious computing education.

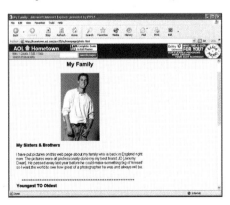

Web sites can allow a family to introduce themselves to the world and tell other people what they are interested in. It's by no means necessary to have a complex site.

Some personal sites have a stylish, smart appearance that differs little from the results achieved on a professional or commercial site.

Making your own Web page

It's easy to make your presence known to the world. Here, we show you how to make a start at constructing your own Web site.

1 The first thing to do with any Web page is to type the simple commands that identify it as an HTML document – we're using Notepad to do this. Type <HTML> on the first line and then </HTML> on the next line. The second command will let the browser know the Web page is finished. The rest of our page will be typed between these commands.

2 Now we'll create a heading for the page. Between our two lines, type another: <H1>My First Web Page</H1>. The <H1> and </H1> commands tell the browser that the text between them is going to be the heading; it will use a bigger and bolder typeface when it displays the page.

3 Finally, type <CENTER> in front of the <H1> command and </CENTER> after </H1>. Now your text will be centred when it appears in your browser window.

4 You can now type in the main text for your Web page. Start by typing a few sentences. Begin on a new line under the heading and type as if you were typing into a word processor. However, when you get to the edge of the Notepad window press the [Enter] key to move on to a new line. Since these words come after the </H1> and </CENTER> they won't be centred or in the style of a heading.

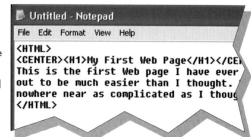

5 To finish off this simple text page, we'd like a line across the bottom of the page. We could add lots of underline characters, by pressing [Shift]+[-]. But there are better and more powerful options built into the HTML language. Create a new line just before the </HTML> line which finishes the page. On this new line type <HR>. This is one of the few HTML commands that doesn't need a </HR> command to switch it off.

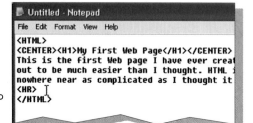

6 Now we'll save the Web page. Select Save As from the File menu, and locate a suitable folder in the Save in drop-down list. Type a simple name into the File name text box, and use a .htm extension (see inset). This file extension identifies it as an HTML file. Make sure you don't forget the full stop beforehand. Click on the Save button.

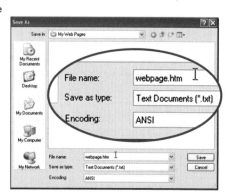

7 Now we want to see the page as it would appear on the Worldwide Web. The easiest way to load the page into your Web browser is to open My Computer through the Start menu and locate the folder on your hard disk. Find your file and double-click on it. After a few seconds your page will load into your browser and you'll see it on screen (far right). Depending on the way your browser is set up, a dialog box might appear before the page loads, asking if you want to log onto your ISP – just click on the Cancel button.

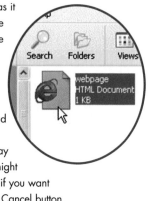

Adding a picture that's a link

As well as telling people all over the world about yourself, you can also show them what you look like. All you need is a picture – the rest is easy!

1 We're going to add a picture between the title and the main text on our Web page. You'll need to find a picture but you might also need to convert it first to Web format (see Pictures for Web sites box, below). Copy the picture into the same folder you used for your Web page.

2 Start Notepad to edit your HTML file. Click on the File menu and select Open. Use the Look in section of the Open dialog box to locate the relevant folder. You won't see the .htm file at first as Notepad looks for files that end in .txt. Click on the Files of type drop-down list and select All Files. You will see your file appear, along with any others in the folder. Select the file and click on the Open button.

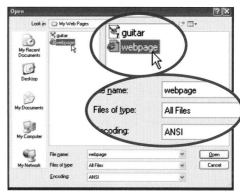

3 Now you can edit the file. First we'll add our picture. Insert a new line under the heading and type <IMG SRC="guitar.jpg">, with the name of your picture in inverted commas.

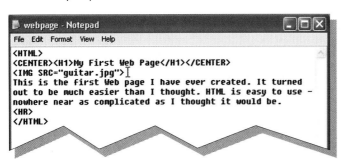

4 As it is, this picture will appear at the left of the page, directly before the paragraph text. To tidy things up, place a <CENTER> command before it and </CENTER> after it. After that, create a new line and add a <BR>. This will place a space between the picture and the text.

5 We can also make the picture a clickable link. This means that when the mouse pointer of the person viewing the page moves over the picture, it will turn into a hand informing the person they can click on the picture to go to a new page. First, though, we need a second page to switch to. That's easy: we'll just edit this page and save it under a new name. Change the page to read as shown here. When you save the file in the same folder, name it link.htm.

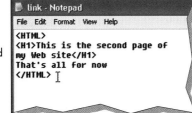

6 Now repeat Step 2 to open the first page of your Web site again. To create the link for the picture, type <A HREF="link.htm"> before the picture command (it doesn't matter if it is before or after <CENTER>) and then type </A> after the picture. Select Save from the File menu to save these changes.

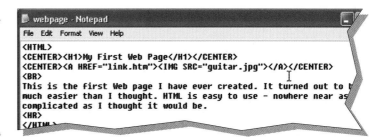

7 View your Web page by double-clicking on the first Web page you created (see Step 7, previous page). Your page will load with the picture in place. Click once on the picture and you'll see the second page appear. This is the principle on which the whole Web works. While there are some Web design techniques that are hard to work out, about 90 per cent of all Web sites are created with commands as simple as these.

PICTURES FOR WEB SITES

Most pictures on Web sites are in GIF or JPG format. These are special formats that are suitable for use over the Internet, since they are compact and are quick to download. Other types of pictures, such as the Windows format, BMP, will need to be converted before being used in your Web pages. Do this with a graphics program, such as Corel PHOTO-PAINT (see page 76).

ADSL superhighway

An Internet connection around 10 times faster than a 56Kbps modem is available in most parts of Britain and other countries. Find out how it can change the way you use the Internet.

From its initial trials in the late 1990s, ADSL (Asymmetric Digital Subscriber Line) has proved to be a Web surfer's dream come true. Anyone who is fed up with dial-up Internet access via a modem will be tempted by the prospect of a permanent 512Kbps connection (around 10 times faster than current 56Kbps modems), allowing almost instant download of Web sites, not to mention access to movies and other content-rich Multimedia. The only problem with ADSL is that, until recently, relatively few people have been able to sign up for it. BT was slow to add the ADSL hardware at telephone exchanges across the country, and the initially high costs made many consumers think twice (see Prices in the UK box, right).

● The technology

ADSL is one of a number of digital technologies that transform the existing copper phone wires into high-speed digital lines for fast Internet access. It's known as 'asymmetric' because it transfers data at different rates 'downstream' (from a site to your PC) and 'upstream' (from your PC). ADSL uses special compression techniques and the unused frequencies of copper wire get as much as 99 per cent more capacity out of the telephone line.

This allows you to surf the Net or download a large file at the same time as having a voice call, and all on just one telephone line. ADSL is

A car repairer sends pictures of crashed vehicles to insurance companies via ADSL links to speed up work-authorization orders.

potentially incredibly fast, with speeds of up to 6.1Mbps downstream (around 200 times faster than a 56Kbps modem) and 640Kbps upstream. In practice, however, these speeds are not currently attainable, with 512Kbps upstream the quoted rate for home use, and 2Mbps available for business users.

Naturally this much faster speed offers all sorts of possibilities for the consumer user and for Web businesses. It allows easy delivery of video and Multimedia content, enabling you to buy or rent and then download all your business and games software, as well as movies, via the Web. It offers consumers choice and convenience and, for businesses, considerable savings in both time and money (in terms of physical outlets, packaging, post and so on). In addition, since the connection can be permanently maintained, you can download enormous files overnight, and email or messaging become instant services. The possibilities of high-speed access are virtually limitless.

PRICES IN THE UK

When ADSL prices were £150 for installation plus £40 per month for Internet access, it wasn't surprising that many home computer users persevered with their modems. However, increased pressure from the telecoms regulator has forced BT to lower the cost at which it offers ADSL to other telecoms companies. Typical monthly fees are just under £30 – lower than many families' dial-up costs.

Installation charges are now lower, too. BT's DIY option removes the engineer call-out fee and costs £85. Before signing up, bear in mind that you have to sign a one-year contract, and you're unlikely to get a refund if you move house after a few months. In addition, you may need a new modem which can cost more than £100.

● The hardware

In terms of hardware, ADSL installation requires a reasonable PC, although any PC able to run Windows 98, Me or XP and that has a vacant USB socket will certainly be up to the job. You then need a special ADSL modem and ADSL line filter. You can fit these yourself, or pay extra for a BT engineer to come and fit them. The filter splits your phone line into two bands, one for data and the other for voice.

However, not everyone can get ADSL. In the UK, the first hurdle is the distance from the local telephone exchange; if you're more than 3.5–4km away, the signals won't travel. So ADSL is primarily an urban phenomenon, as there are more exchanges in towns and cities than there are in rural areas. You can easily find out if you are in range by using the availability checker on the BT Openworld site, the sector of BT responsible for ADSL development and installation; the site address is www.btopenworld.com. Just enter your phone number to find out.

On the other hand, even if you do live in an ADSL-enabled area you won't necessarily be able to receive the service. Poor quality lines between your home and the exchange can interfere with the ADSL signal. Very few lines are affected, but BT will check each line before connecting the service.

Type your phone number into BT Openworld's availability line check page to find out if ADSL is available in your area.

● The local loop

For years, BT jealously guarded its monopoly of the local loop – the last few kilometres of phone line that reaches your home from the exchange – but these days it is obliged to open access to other ISPs. For your own ISP to supply you with ADSL, it has to gain access to the telephone exchange and install its own equipment.

For many, this simply hasn't happened fast enough. Large ISPs such as Freeserve and AOL became so angry that they threatened to sue BT, who countered by saying that some exchanges may be over 50 years old and have very limited space for any additional equipment.

Whatever the rights and wrongs of the case, the roll-out is far behind the schedule envisaged several years ago. ISPs such as BT Openworld, AOL and Freeserve all let you sign up online, although the technicalities mean that you can't get ADSL Internet access instantly. When you choose the DIY installation (the most cost effective option), for example, your line is ASDL-enabled at the local telephone exchange and a package sent to you. Because of this there is a short waiting time – ISPs quote 10 to 28 days. If you select an engineer to do your installation, you may have to wait longer depending on local demands.

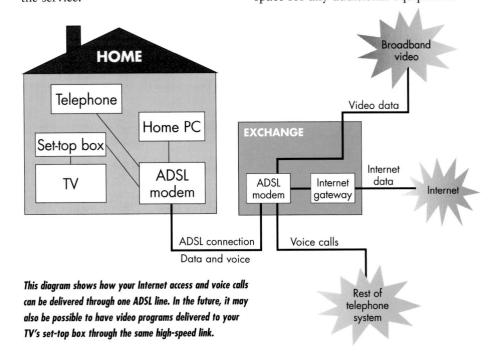

This diagram shows how your Internet access and voice calls can be delivered through one ADSL line. In the future, it may also be possible to have video programs delivered to your TV's set-top box through the same high-speed link.

ALTERNATIVES

If your telephone line doesn't meet the ADSL criteria there may be other options. First of all, if you live in a cabled area you may be able to get cable modem access from the supplier. Cable modems don't offer quite the speed of ADSL, but they can sometimes reach 512Kbps.

Second, BT has trialled 'rate adaptive' ADSL modems. These are capable of supplying a modified (slower) ADSL service to people living more than four kilometres from an exchange. The upstream speed will vary between 64Kbps and 288Kbps, but it's thought that you should be able to download at speeds of up to 512Kbps.

Buying books and CDs from Web sites

Are you having trouble finding that out-of-print book or unstocked CD in your local high street? Broaden your horizons – and chances of success – by shopping on the Internet.

The Amazon.com Web site claims to be the world's largest bookstore with 'Earth's Biggest Selection™ of products'. It would be hard to find a high street shop that is as well stocked. Buying books and other items, such as music and software CDs, via the Internet is really the only way to gain access to an almost limitless amount of choice. Because Internet stores have lower overheads than high street chains, they are also often able to offer their goods at competitive prices.

● Shop until you drop

Buying items from Web sites is very much like buying from a catalogue. As well as the increased range of items on offer, the sites also allow you to use the power of your Web browser and its own search engines to look for specific books or CDs (or any other item you are after). These site-specific search engines enable you to look for books by a particular author, search for books when you know only a portion of the title, or just look for those that cover a specific subject or were published during a certain period.

Most sites organize their wares into useful categories, such as thrillers and non-fiction for books,

or modern jazz and heavy metal for music CDs. Some of the larger sites go even further and offer reviews of their products (often written by members of the public who have bought the item previously), buyer's guides, author/band biographies, links to related fan sites and much more.

Now that e-commerce has really taken off, the breadth and depth of what's on offer has increased. So you won't just find the bestselling books and the top 10 CDs. Instead, you can explore just about any interest you have, from audio books to rare 16th-century music.

Over the next few pages we describe some of the most popular sites around. If your own particular interest isn't featured, however, don't

despair. Simply use the powers of your favourite search engine (see Stage 2, pages 136–137) to seek it out; the chances are that there will be a choice of sites out there that can deliver the goods.

LANGUAGE BARRIER

Thanks to the Internet, getting hold of foreign books or CDs has never been easier. You'll pay more in postage to have a book sent from France, of course, but the online stores offer such a wealth of stock that you probably won't mind the extra cost. It's easy to find the sites as well. Books On Line (see opposite), for example, has a drop-down menu giving access to their sites in Europe. Amazon also has sites worldwide.

Books and CDs on the Web

Here's a selection of Internet sites from all over the world, where you can browse through millions of books, videos or CD-ROMs.

BOOKS AND CDs were the goods that kick-started the Web as a way of doing your shopping. Now these online stores offer not just a massive range of stock and discounted prices, but, in many cases, extremely sophisticated Web sites packed with information about the goods on offer.

All the sites mentioned here use secure online ordering, and most of them allow you to use an ordinary debit card as well as a credit card. If you can bear to wait for a few days to get your hands on what you want, these sites are a great way to buy both your music and your reading matter.

Online bookselling giants

Amazon – the 'first mover' of online bookselling – has been in business for years. It has now been joined by other excellent sites, developed both by media giants and innovative specialist organizations.

Amazon

www.amazon.co.uk

Amazon is an online behemoth, with a presence on the Web you can't escape; its adverts seem to be on just about every site you visit. It's one of the biggest e-businesses and worth an absolute fortune. It's not hard to see why investors are excited; Amazon was the first to launch online bookselling, did it very well, and keeps getting better. It has a massive stock of books – around 1.5 million titles – and offers substantial discounts on popular ones, with smaller discounts on other books. It also supplies plenty of content, from features and reviews to readers' own comments about their purchases. The site now covers a variety of other areas, including music.

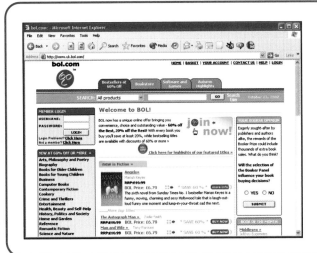

BOL

www.uk.bol.com

Although Amazon had a head start in online bookselling, it doesn't have things all its own way. Books On Line (BOL) is another giant of cybershopping. It's the online outpost of the Multimedia company Bertelsmann, which owns the Barnes and Noble bookstores in the US, among other companies. The BOL site offers a database of 1.5 million books, plus many other goodies to make a visit to the site worthwhile. There are plenty of features, including reviews and interviews, and you can create your own visitor profile of tastes so that recommendations will be waiting for you when you revisit the site. In addition, it's all attractively presented.

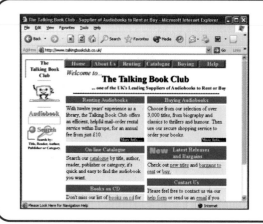

The Talking Book Club

www.talkingbookclub.co.uk

In the modern era you don't even have to read a book to enjoy it: you can listen to it instead, in the shape of an audio book on cassette or audio CD. There's a surprisingly wide range of these, and this site gives you access to around 3,000 titles, covering everything from new releases to unabridged readings of classic novels, such as Marcel Proust's *Swann's Way*, which will keep you occupied for a number of days, to say the least. The service provided by The Talking Book Club started out purely as a lending library of such titles, but now you can borrow or buy as you wish.

HMV

www.hmv.co.uk

It didn't take long for the high-street book and music retailers to realize that they needed an online presence, and all the major chains now have a place on the Internet. In terms of music, the HMV site offers one of the better shopping experiences. It has a comprehensive range of titles, with all the special offers and great titles that you would find on the high street. It has a neat and attractive layout, while a search for an artist or title brings up not just the item itself but also track listings, notes and often reviews. Ordering is quick and easy, and they even send you an email to let you know your order is logged and then another when it's on its way to you.

Map-guides

www.map-guides.com

If you love to go a-wandering, you'll probably need a map or two to help you find your way. If you want an unusual or particularly detailed map, it can be difficult to find unless you have access to a big city. Map-guides can provide an easy solution, however. The online store for Footprint Maps Ltd keeps a massive stock of maps and guidebooks, including large-scale and rare maps that would normally only be available in a specialist bookstore. If you're off walking or climbing in France, for example, it's good to know that they have the entire range of large-scale maps from the official government mapping agency. The rest of the world is similarly well served.

Virgin

www.virgin.com

This is the one-stop site for everything in the Virgin empire, from banking and travel to mobile phones and wine. However, as you'd expect from the company with roots in music, there are also links to Virgin books, and music sites such as Virgin Megastores, v-shop and V2 Music. You'll find music news, reviews, gig guides and charts within these sites. There are also pages for many of the bands on the Virgin record label, from where you can view the latest pictures, hear the newest sounds and see up-to-the-minute videos. Booklovers are equally well catered for with reviews of hundreds of Virgin publishing titles, ranging from biography and sport to new age and crime.

The Book Pl@ce
www.bookplace.co.uk

This British online bookstore has the same range of stock as the multinational giants, but has a number of extras that make it worth a look. For instance, it offers two different magazine-style areas, Bookends (www.bookends.co.uk) and The Book Monster (www.thebookmonster.co.uk), aimed at adults and children respectively. These give more detail on what's happening in the book world and are worth looking at, even if you're not actually thinking of buying a particular book. You can get to the sites either by typing in their Web addresses or via the links on the Book Pl@ce home page.

CDNOW
www.cdnow.com

This is a giant American music store, with European distribution centres, that offers to ship any size of order worldwide. Add what seem to be extremely competitive prices on the CDs themselves, and you need to check CDNOW out before buying elsewhere. In addition, the site is full of useful information, and contains excellent introductions to various genres, such as jazz and classical music. If you decide to add CDNOW's recommended basic collections to your CD rack, you'll not only be enjoying the music but also, within a short while, you'll be able to chat on equal terms with music experts.

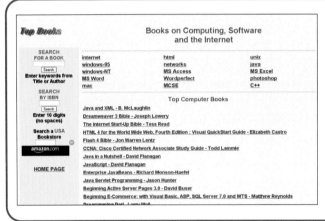

Computer Bookshops
www.ukbookshop.com/compbooks

This giant distributor of books, boasting 1.5 million titles overall, is not a stunningly attractive site. Nevertheless, it's certainly functional, with an easily searchable database, and they'll keep you up to date with new books by email if you want. This site is just the place to go if you want heavyweight computer manuals and related DIY material. Furthermore, if you've mislaid the manuals that came with either your hardware or your software, the site offers to provide what you need to get the best from your computer set-up. It's an excellent place to get help if you're stuck.

Coda
www.codamusic.co.uk

Specializing in folk, world and blues music, this Scottish online retailer boasts a large stock on its site, which is easily searchable by artist or title, and it offers to find an album for you if it doesn't already have it. Post and packaging is included in the quoted prices, so you don't get any nasty surprises when it comes to the virtual checkout. There is no doubt that this is a great resource if the music genres on offer are what turn you on. As well as CDs and cassettes, the site sells music, song books and even traditional musical instruments, such as bodhrans (one-sided drums) and whistles. The site lives up to the statement on its home page: 'Traditional by name, traditional by nature'.

Planning a holiday

One time when you're sure to need plenty of information is when you are planning a trip. So why not use the Internet to discover a wealth of up-to-the-minute travel data and holiday bargains online?

Travel and holiday sites were one of the first categories to make it big on the Internet, for obvious reasons: anyone choosing a holiday – whether a package or a DIY trip – wants as much information as they can get prior to booking it.

However, in the early days of the Internet, finding this information could be something of a hit-and-miss affair, throwing up personal-view snippets from individuals, as well as the more useful, credible, researched sites. There was little in the way of solid information or online booking facilities from airlines or major holiday companies. That has all changed radically now – you can do just about everything on the Internet that used to be done on the telephone, or sitting in the travel agent's shop in your local high street.

● No-frills flights

The major worldwide airlines have been on the Web for quite some time, offering flight information and online booking. However, these outfits have been premium brands charging premium prices; there hasn't been much going cheap. But a significant development in the late 1990s was the boom in bargain-basement airlines offering no-frills flights at low-cost prices.

Online booking is an integral part of the strategy for such companies. It's much cheaper for them than using phone operators, and it can be much easier for the consumer. That said, as these services become more popular, you sometimes find the sites are busy. You also need to be careful when entering booking details – if you make a mistake, for example, by typing the wrong date, it may not be possible to rectify and refunds are rare.

The world of the Internet has a vast array of holiday information and travel destination choices just waiting for your browser to open. Booking tickets, checking flights and viewing hotels before you arrive are just a few Web facilities.

● Package tours

Although the major package holiday companies were fairly late to get on the Internet bandwagon, they are now out there in force. Many of them have bold, attractive and easily accessible Web sites, although the quality and depth of the information available varies widely.

There's a good range of sites, from the cheaper end of the market to the á la carte types – and many sites offer the chance to take advantage of tempting last-minute bargains. However, unless you have a free Internet connection, don't get too carried away browsing. You'll probably still want to pick up the brochures and spend a few hours studying them – although these can usually be ordered online too.

● DIY travel

Many people prefer to organize their own holidays and the Internet caters for them, too. There are plenty of sites that can help you hire a car and find somewhere to stay in almost any country. Generally, typing in a search of the town and country you want to visit, together with the word 'accommodation' or 'hotel' presents you with a wide list of possible venues. The sites listed on page 145 contain thousands of hotels worldwide, in a range of categories. An increasing number of hotels now also offer online reservations.

Booking a flight online

The Internet shopping revolution now means that you can research and book all kinds of travel – including air travel – online.

HERE WE'LL FIND out how to book a ticket from Liverpool to Amsterdam with the budget airline easyJet. The procedure shown is broadly similar to booking a ticket on other airlines that offer online booking. These other companies include British Airways, Buzz (a subsidiary of KLM), Ryanair and British Midland.

1 Type easyJet's address (www.easyjet.co.uk) into your Web browser's Address box and press [Enter]. This takes you to the English part of the easyJet.com site.
When the home page has loaded, click on the important notes link to read an explanation about how easyJet's booking system works and their terms and conditions. When you're ready, return to the home page.

2 Scroll down and use the online sales area to specify what you're after. Simply fill in the spaces with the relevant information, either by typing or by selecting from the pull-down menus. When you've completed all areas of the screen, click on the 'show prices' button (see inset).

3 Now you're shown the flight information for your chosen location, possibly ranging over a number of days both before and after the dates you requested. To proceed you must click on the radio button next to the flights you want to book (ie outbound and return), then click the proceed button at the bottom of the screen.

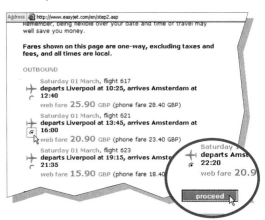

4 The next screen displays the flight you have selected and the price of the ticket. Check your selection very carefully as the next step is to give your personal details.

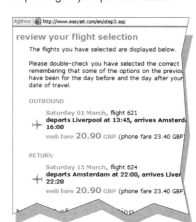

5 If you are happy with the information shown, click on the 'book now with security' button at the bottom of the screen.

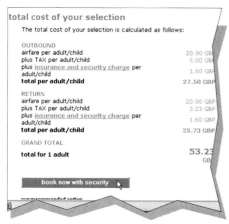

6 On the next screen, all you have to do is fill in the details of the passenger, including your name and address, so that a seat in the correct name can be booked. Scroll down the page to fill in all the details. Next you will need to fill in your credit or debit card information.

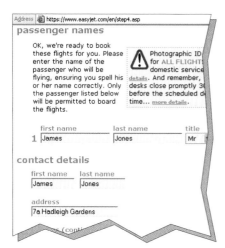

7 Tick the box to show that you have agreed to easyJet's conditions. When you click the 'buy now' button, your card details will be processed and your booking confirmed. You'll receive an email confirmation and a booking reference. Keep these safe – you will not be issued your boarding card at the airport without them.

Finding out about... Amsterdam

The Internet provides easy access to lots of information about any travel destination. So now you've booked the tickets, here's how you can discover where to go and what to do while you're in Amsterdam.

1 A good place to start is a search engine that categorizes content, such as Yahoo!. Go to www.yahoo.co.uk, and start by clicking on the Countries link in the Regional section. Click the Netherlands link when you see a list of countries of the world. Click Travel when the list of sub-categories appears.

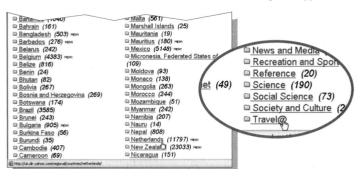

2 Finding a place to stay is a priority, so click on the Accommodation link and then the Hotels link. This page leads to a substantial list of hotels and other places to stay. Read the brief descriptions to see if they're your kind of place. The Hotel Barbacan seems interesting and has a Web site, so click on the link. It offers plenty of information, so you could come back and book, once you've checked out other places on the list.

3 To get a few ideas on what to do while you're in Amsterdam, search Yahoo! for 'Amsterdam', then click on the Local Guides link. TimeOut Amsterdam offers a guide to what's on and where to go. Use your browser's Bookmark or Favorites command and it will remember the page; you can return later to plan your trip by selecting this Bookmark or Favorites again.

4 One of the reasons we're visiting is to see the museums dedicated to Holland's great artists, Rembrandt and Van Gogh. To find out about these, go back to Yahoo! where there are links to sites such as The Rembrandt House Museum (below) and the restored Van Gogh Museum. Both sites give a good view of the respective artists and their work, information on where the museums are and opening times.

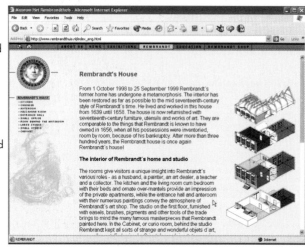

5 It might be fun to do a little shopping – particularly for antiques. Yahoo! has lots of sites under their Business and Shopping link. The Antiques and Collectibles category contains a link to the Aronson Gallery, which gives us a good idea of what's on sale.

6 Finally, to check current weather conditions before you go, click the Weather link on the Yahoo! home page, then choose Europe and then type in Amsterdam. You will get a two-to-four-days' forecast – giving you a good idea of what to pack in your suitcase.

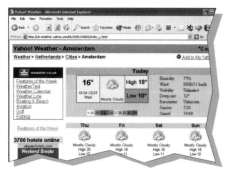

Top travel sites

There are plenty of travel-related sites on the Internet, but a few stand out from the crowd for the breadth and depth of what they offer.

Wish You Were Here

www.wishyouwerehere.com

This is the Web site of the popular TV travel show *Wish You Were Here*. Not only are there reviews on all the current locations but an excellent, alphabetical archive lets you roam around the world from Acapulco to Zanzibar. Every destination has a thorough review and an invaluable fact file, providing flying times, prices and health advice as well as information on best buys and places to visit. Useful links take you to sites covering issues such as travelling with children, senior citizens and those with special needs.

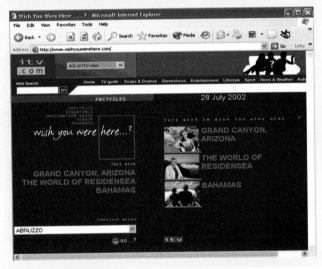

Expedia UK

www.expedia.co.uk

This is the UK version of Microsoft's gigantic Expedia travel site. It's huge, so its tentacles reach just about everywhere that a travel site could think to go; the chances are that you can find information here that might only otherwise be found on half a dozen individual sites. Late bookings, flights, maps, car rental, hotel directories, health advice or insurance – you name it, Expedia's got it. And it's all very clearly presented.

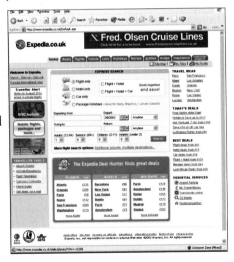

Lastminute.com

www.lastminute.com

If you like to do things on the spur of the moment, this could be the site for you. Lastminute.com supplies last-minute bargains, principally in the shape of package holidays and flights, but also more upmarket city breaks (often in posh hotels at competitive prices). The offers are very tempting and you can subscribe to a free email newsletter to keep you up to date with what's happening.

Lonely Planet

www.lonelyplanet.com

Lonely Planet is the big daddy of printed guides for the 'independent traveller'. The Web site offers plenty of useful information but what makes it vital to anyone thinking of an exotic trip is the Upgrades section, where you find the very latest information on border crossings, visas, and safety, that didn't make it into the printed version.

Internet fan clubs

Whether you're a fan of Doctor Who or Doctor Finlay, you're sure to find a Web site to suit your interests. We take a look at Internet fan clubs, from the hugely popular to the downright obscure.

One thing that the Internet is justly famous for is providing a forum for fans of just about anything. Whether you spend your spare time mulling over the various theories on the TV series *The Prisoner*, or the exact wording of the *Monty Python* parrot sketch, the Internet can guide you in the direction of like-minded people. For no matter how alone you might feel in your own particular interest, you can guarantee that there will be someone else on the Web who feels the same way. To attract these lost souls, many fans create Web sites for their chosen subject and often start up fan clubs around them.

● Official and unofficial clubs

The term 'fan club' can describe anything from a small group of enthusiasts who keep in contact via email, to an extensive organization (either official or unofficial) with its own magazines (print or email-based) and annual conventions.

Many unofficial fan clubs are free to join, but some charge a nominal fee. Most, though, are non-profit making. However, the same cannot be said of the various official fan clubs you might find. Although they usually have the more extravagant Web sites, the amount of information and content actually available on official sites can sometimes be less than that offered by more obsessive fans. Of course, this all varies according to the subject of the club and the company behind it.

Over the next few pages we look at some of the more reputable official clubs and the more enthusiastic fan sites. As ever, be careful about handing over your hard-earned cash when joining any club. A brief chat with an existing member should soon fill you in on what's what...and, of course, this is incredibly easy thanks to the exhaustive email links that many sites contain.

UNOFFICIAL SITES

You might be wondering how it is that unofficial sites get away with using copyrighted words and pictures. The fact is that often they don't. While copyright holders may be happy to ignore infringements and reap the free publicity, their lawyers sometimes like to flex their muscles and try, usually successfully, to ban various sites.

This happens most frequently with valuable brand names, such as *Star Trek* and *The X Files*, and usually results in torrents of abuse from fans, and possibly a retraction from the copyright holder.

A selection of official and unofficial sites

As you can imagine, there is an almost infinite number of fan sites for just about everything you could possibly think of. Many don't actually advertise themselves as fan clubs, but are still just as effective at bringing mutual admirers together.

The Prisoner Appreciation Society: Six of One

www.theprisonerappreciationsociety.com

The Prisoner is the grandfather of all cult TV shows. The programme, starring the British actor Patrick McGoohan, was unique when it came out in 1967 and is still regarded by many as unsurpassed in terms of ambition and execution.

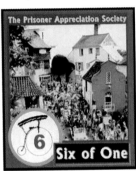

The series told the story of Number Six (played by McGoohan), a top British secret agent who resigns from his job, but is kidnapped and sent to The Village – a surreal town that serves as a prison, and from which he is determined to escape.

This Web site is the focal point for fans around the world to talk about the show and discuss exactly what they think was going on in it.

The surreal nature of most of the episodes has created enough controversy to keep the series alive over the years. Although surfing around the Web site is free, The Prisoner Appreciation Society does encourage you to join the Six of One club. For a fee of £18 you receive a quarterly newsletter and the chance to join the annual anniversary of the show, which usually takes place in the Welsh village of Portmeirion – where the series was filmed.

The ElvisNet

http://members.aol.com/elvisnet/

On the Internet, the King is certainly not dead – with one or two of the sites even claiming to have been created by the man himself. This is one of the more sane sites, which tries to concentrate on the facts of his life and music.

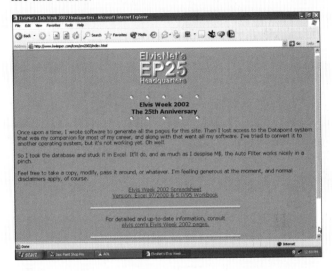

Harry Potter Fan Site!

www.geocities.com/thepottersite

The creators of this site, devoted to J. K. Rowling's bestselling children's books, have done Harry proud, with a fan site that overflows with content – even if it's not the smartest-looking. There are summaries of each of the books and rumours about future titles, as well as behind-the-scenes photos from the first Harry Potter film. There's a biography of the author and a games section, and fans are encouraged to contribute their very own drawings, which could be displayed on the site.

FRIENDS

www2.warnerbros.com/friendstv/

This is the official site for the hugely popular TV series featuring the young, beautiful but not always very happy (or smart) New Yorkers. It's very well presented and has just about anything a fan could want, including cast biographies, story updates and peeks behind the scenes. There are also well-presented and heavily used message boards and chat areas.

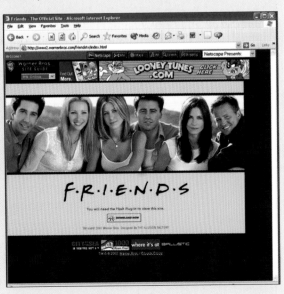

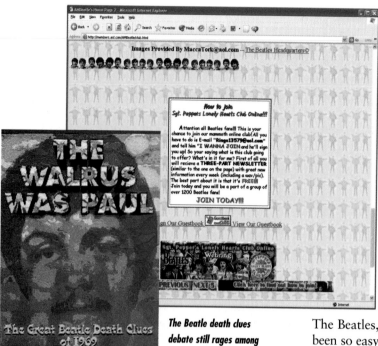

The Beatle death clues debate still rages among fans on the Internet.

Sgt. Pepper's Lonely Hearts Club Online

members.aol.com/AMBeatle/club.html

When you are dealing with a worldwide phenomenon such as The Beatles, it's often difficult to know where to start in terms of finding online resources and fans. Sgt. Pepper's Lonely Hearts Club Online, or SPLHCO, as it is also known, professes to be the world's largest online Beatles fan club.

On first visiting this site, this fact isn't particularly believable as the main page is rather amateurish and very slow to download. However, if you dig just below the surface, you'll find a wealth of interesting content. For starters, the club boasts free membership, via email, and more than 1,200 worldwide members. On the site itself you can find interviews, news, memorabilia, pages created by other fans, the music itself in various file formats, and much, much more besides.

Finding out about the 60s legend that was The Beatles, and making new friends in the process, has never been so easy, especially as the fan club organizes regular conventions all around the world.

The BarryNet

www.barrynet.com

Whatever your musical tastes, you'll find them catered for somewhere. The devotion of Barry Manilow's fans is legendary and they can boast a Web site that is far more professional and attractive than most of its peers. You get a comprehensive biography and discography, complete with pictures and sound clips. There's a lot of emphasis on making pen (or email) pals, as well as taking part in the traditional conventions and, of course, concerts.

This site has information on Barry Manilow's current tours and projects, as well as photos and reviews of past concerts and shows. If you're one of his fans, you need never feel alone; after all, this site has had in excess of 3,000,000 visitors.

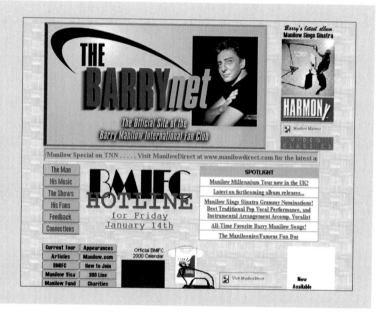

CarryOnLine

www.carryonline.com

This site is a true labour of love that brings together the many fans of the long-running and saucy *Carry On* films. Here you'll find masses of information on the films and their stars. There are extremely good biographies of all the regular performers, interviews with them from a variety of sources and periods, and detailed pieces on posters, books, videos and all the other spin-off products. In addition, there is a substantial gallery of photographs.

One of the major attractions is a collection of sound clips featuring favourite moments from the films. This site also has its own online shop, where you can buy memorabilia.

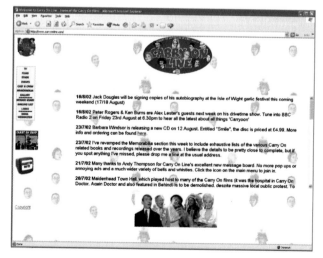

Time Warp – The Official UK Rocky Horror Fan Club

www.timewarp.org.uk

The Rocky Horror Show is a film and stage show that has thousands of Web sites devoted to it. This is the official UK fan club site, but there are many others all over the world. Unlike some fan sites, this one actually goes out of its way to

make visitors feel welcome, rather than frightening them away with obscure lingo and references. In fact, if you haven't been to a live show before, there's a page of dos and don'ts that covers everything from the clothes to wear to what you're allowed to throw on stage and when. Remember, the average Rocky Horror fan does not favour anoraks, but fishnet stockings – regardless of gender.

Despite the potential for lewdness, the whole site is very much tongue-in-cheek, so there's little danger of any children being corrupted by Riff-Raff's devilish ways.

Ricky Martin

www.rickymartin.com

Ricky Martin appeared from nowhere in 1999 to become a world megastar, hence this official site dedicated to the crooner of *Livin' La Vida Loca* and other Latin-flavoured tunes. It's a curiously understated

site but there is some solid content, including a decent size biography, a generous stack of Real Audio sound bites from the music and a similar amount of videos.

MAILING LISTS

One of the most refreshing aspects of fan sites is the genuine, heartfelt input from the fans themselves – an input you can have delivered to your own email address, courtesy of a mailing list. Here's how it works. You send an email to the mailing list address asking to subscribe. Any subsequent mail sent to the list – in much the same way as a message is posted on a newsgroup – will also be sent to you. Similarly, any email you send to the list will be sent to all the other subscribers. The amount of traffic varies from list to list, but it's not unusual to find yourself getting dozens of emails per day for each list you've subscribed to. The level of policing varies from strict to very lax, but it is generally commensurate with the subject matter; anyone sending offensive mail can be struck off the list.

Bollywood Babes

www.bollywoodworld.com

Forget Hollywood. The film world's new power centre is none other than Bombay – hence the name Bollywood. Films from the Indian subcontinent are becoming increasingly popular with all types of audiences worldwide. This site, which claims to be 'India's Premier Bollywood Portal' is a content-rich guide to all aspects of Bollywood. As you would expect, much of the site is dedicated to the Bollywood stars. Here you will find pictures of them in an extensive photo gallery, as well as a section of their baby photos! There are profiles of all the stars, as well as personal information such as their addresses and phone numbers – not something you'd find on a Hollywood site. The site also features the latest news from the industry, current releases, a large section on movie soundtracks and all the usual Web site appendages such as chat rooms, games, wallpapers and screensavers.

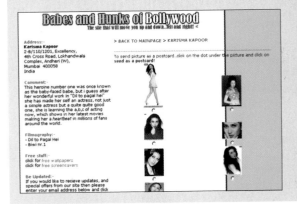

PythOnline

www.pythonline.com

One site that is most definitely not sane – and would be a great disappointment if it were – is this official *Monty Python* page. With input from the stars, this is an impressive site for all fans of the surreal Pythons. There is a reasonably sensible news page – called the Daily Llama – giving details of the former Pythons' books, awards and ongoing projects. Largely though, it's just mad – and anyone who enters the 'chit-chat' room should take note of the warning!

The X Files and the unexplained

From the bizarre to the disturbing, paranormal phenomena are always hard to pin down. But thanks to the global access offered by the Internet, the answers are out there – somewhere.

An American TV show that managed to outdo the turn of the millennium in terms of its influence on the public worldwide couldn't have been doing too badly. For although the arrival of the year 2000 was undoubtedly behind the surge of interest in the paranormal and the spiritual, *The X Files* focused this fascination and made it fashionable in the build-up and after.

For those few who have managed to avoid the show's charms, its premise is quite simple. A hot-shot FBI agent, Fox Mulder, is in charge of the 'X Files' – a series of unsolved cases which appear to have no logical solution, but in some way involve paranormal phenomena.

Although the FBI tolerates Mulder's passion – which is fuelled by his sister's apparent abduction by aliens when he was young – unidentified factions within the US government (and beyond) are less happy. In order to debunk Mulder's findings, agent Dana Scully, who has a scientific background, is assigned as his partner so that she can report on the validity of his work. The pair then proceed

to combat (with varying degrees of success) government conspiracies, UFOs, aliens, ghosts, demons, serial killers and everything in between.

This might not immediately sound like a ticket to mass-market appeal, but a combination of excellent acting, writing, direction and deadpan black humour – plus a couple of attractive stars – resulted not only in impressive viewing figures and a generation of X Philes, but also a fistful of awards.

As the programme ended its phenomenal run – X Philes had nine series to keep them happy – we can look forward to a constant stream of re-runs and no let up of interest in the paranormal.

● Made for the Net

Of course, the combination of TV brand loyalty, bizarre subject matter and good-looking actors is perfect for the wacky world of the Internet. This has led to a veritable invasion of *X Files* Web sites, which only adds to the enormous number of 'ordinary' sites dealing with the unexplained.

Some of the latter have obviously been around longer and might cover an almost infinite range of subjects. However, they usually fall into one of three

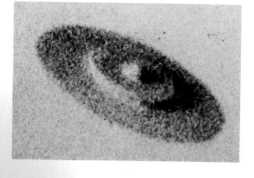

broad groups: the reasonably scientific and organized; the amateurish and illogical – but undoubtedly enthusiastic; and the downright bonkers.

Each category is entertaining in its own way, but you should be careful of the particularly odd sites, as these can be strange to the point of unpleasantness, or even illegality. For that reason, it is always best to keep an eye on children when they look at such sites, and to restrict browsing to some of the more responsible sites.

WHAT IT MEANS

X PHILES

Really obsessive TV and movie fans love to give themselves a name that describes their allegiance, the infamous Trekkers and Whovians being perhaps the most familiar.

Continuing this trend, many pun-loving X Files *fans like to refer to themselves as* X Philes. *So don't be alarmed if you see this term used on any of these Web sites…it's not a spelling error.*

Fox Mulder (far right) investigates the weird and wonderful reports involving anything paranormal, while Dana Scully (near right) applies a more scientific approach, reporting to her bosses on the facts as she sees them.

Exploring the unexplained on the Internet

The truth is out there – and the not-so-true as well.
Visit these sites to make up your own mind.

The Official X Files Web Site

www.thexfiles.com

Supported by the makers of the TV series, the biggest and most impressive section of this site is the guide to each series of the show, split up into all its episodes. Each episode is described in some detail and has an accompanying photo, video clip and credits list. Other sections of the site give biographies of the actors, information on the making of the show and a forum for fans to exchange views.

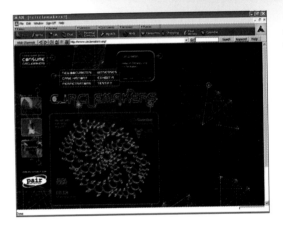

Circlemakers

www.circlemakers.org

This is a curious, not to say weird, site for a variety of different reasons. First of all, it's about the crop circle phenomenon – a relatively new area of weirdness that took off in the last two decades of the 20th century. Second, it appears to be put together by a bunch of people whose aim seems to be to debunk the whole thing – which they do by creating their very own elaborate crop circles. On this extremely stylish and witty site, you can see their and others' handiwork, and, as they put it, 'gain some insight into why this tight band of individuals spend their summers out in the fields of England flattening cereal crops in various intricate patterns'. There's plenty of 'evidence' in the form of photos and real audio files. It's a very odd site, but well worth a look.

GAWS

http://gaws.ao.net

Few fans of *The X-Files*, or X Philes (see opposite), can claim that their enthusiasm for the show is restricted to an academic interest in the subject matter, or an admiration of the cinematography. For although not everyone will agree on whether the two main actors rate as classical beauties, they have both managed to become international sex symbols. There are many sites dedicated to David Duchovny and Gillian Anderson, although not usually to both of them at the same time. GAWS stands for Gillian Anderson Web Site, and is one of the main ports of call for the Scully-obsessed. Here you'll find everything you could wish to know about the red-haired actress.

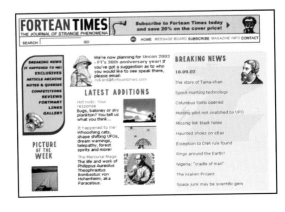

Fortean Times

www.forteantimes.com

Charles Fort was an American-born intellectual who wrote books about science and the unexplained during the 1930s. Fort observed that much research was anything but scientific, noting that inconvenient data was often just suppressed or avoided. He thus became convinced that there was a great deal in the world that could not be explained by traditional science, and he sought to document it in a magazine called *Fortean Times*. This has become widely read and the related Web site features some of its stories and pictures. The site has a good links page and an online form for reporting weird sightings and stories.

Anomalist

www.anomalist.com

The Anomalist is another Web-based version of a printed magazine, which is not dissimilar to *Fortean Times*. The publication certainly shares the same admiration for Charles Fort and his musings, but the Anomalist Web site distinguishes itself from that of *Fortean Times* by having a smaller number of longer articles. These cover topics from UFO sightings to bigfoots. Every story is taken seriously, even though it might be related with a large degree of knowing humour. For the Anomalist site, the truth behind a hoaxed paranormal event is just as interesting as vague facts about a 'real' sighting, since both kinds end up revealing more about human nature than they ever do about how many humps Nessie really has.

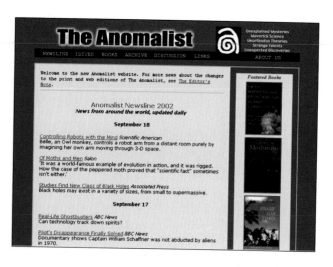

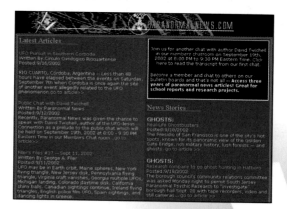

Paranormal News

www.paranormalnews.com

This impressively up-to-date and well-organized site gives you the latest on paranormal activity across the globe. It offers free membership and includes the latest news stories (both recent occurences and sightings, and unsolved mysteries), links to other sites, and a number of other stories and articles. There are plenty of images of aliens, ghosts and gargoyles available, as well as a members' chatroom and a shop selling tarot cards and crop circles board games, amongst other things. The site even enables you to sell your own work on the paranormal – such as a book or article you have written, or CD you have recorded.

CSETI

www.cseti.com

CSETI is short for the Centre for the Study of Extraterrestrial Intelligence, which although it sounds very official and governmental, is actually an organization founded and run by a US medical doctor, Steven Greer, who claims it is 'the only worldwide organization dedicated to establishing peaceful and sustainable relations with extra-terrestrial lifeforms'. There's information on CSETI's projects along with press releases and field reports of 'sightings'.

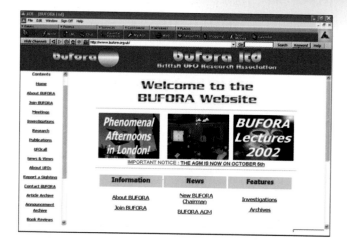

BUFORA On-Line

www.bufora.org.uk

UFO investigation groups are constantly trying to maintain a professional and competent appearance. The British Unidentified Flying Object Research Association (BUFORA) is one such organization and is closely affiliated to similar groups in the USA and around the world. Its Web site is large and well worth a visit. It is split into several areas: a brief history and description of UFOs; News and Views on related topics; a Research section; an Investigations section, where current UFO-seeking is documented; and a section where readers can report their own sightings by downloading and filling in the form supplied.

SITES TO @ VISIT

There is certainly no shortage of unexplained sites on the Web, so here's a selection from the best of the rest:

News of the Weird

www.newsoftheweird.com

Chuck Shepard's News of the Weird is a collection of strange news clippings from around the world. There's no attempt at verification or explanation; you're meant to read and be amused by the stories culled from the small print of every paper under the sun.

Weird Science

www.eskimo.com/~billb/weird.html

Not so much a site in itself as an extensive collection of articles and links to other sites, all of which attempt to put some wonder back into science. There's information on 'scientists' transcended experiences' and well-known but little understood phenomena, such as Tesla coils and ball lightning. Following just a few of the links in the site's long list could shake the convictions of even the most hardened of sceptics.

Weird History 101

http://ferncanyonpress.com/weird/history.shtml

This amusing little site is really a teaser to get you to buy the book of the same name. It offers lots of snippets of wild and wacky facts of history, and a sample from the book recounting some of the more bizarre acts, habits and quotes of American presidents, one of whom (you can find out who in the book) apparently said, 'I have opinions of my own – strong opinions – but I don't always agree with them.'

The Science Behind *The X Files*

http://huah.net/scixf

This is a fascinating site, the author of which has a scientific background. It attempts to cover each episode of the TV programme, commenting on all the scientific and paranormal events featured, complete with possible solutions. What makes this interesting is that each comment is backed up with a hyperlink to a relevant Web site, allowing you to research for yourself.

Conspire.com

www.conspire.com

On the surface, it doesn't really seem that conspiracies – whether committed by big businesses or the government – have much to do with the world of the

unexplained or paranormal. But *The X Files* forged a link, so the paranoid world of conspiracies has become synonymous with that of ghosts, ghouls and aliens.

Conspiracy theories can often be depressing and disagreeable, so it's rather refreshing to come across this site, which takes the whole subject with a pinch of salt. Conspire.com comprises separate sections labelled UFO, JFK, and Rants, which, as well as being informative, together manage to put the fun back into apocalyptic global conspiracies.

Cryptozoology!

www.ncf.carleton.ca/~bz050/HomePage.cryptoz.html

The term 'cryptozoology' was coined in 1959 to describe the search for (and research into) previously unknown animals. To many this might just imply treks in search of the Yeti or Loch Ness Monster, but, in fact, it has a much more mainstream application in identifying new species of insects, birds and mammals.

Of course, many people involved in this sort of research still dream of dissecting Nessie or caging Bigfoot, but no doubt prefer to keep this side of things quiet when talking to more conventional scientists.

This site is therefore a mixture of descriptions and pictures of everything

from a new kind of ape-like animal in Florida, to an interesting picture of one of a new species of large bovines from Vietnam.

Recent sightings of 'large black cats' in remote parts of Britain have excited cryptozoologists and the site has an extensive section on these.

Obiwan's UFO-free Paranormal Page

www.ghosts.org

This site concerns what used to be the major focus of paranormal research: ghosts and the supernatural. The graphics aren't as good as some Web sites, but there is an impressive range of content. Most amusing is the list of haunted hotels, complete with contact details and tourist information.

There's also a large database of supposedly true ghost stories, sent in by visitors to the site. In addition to all this, there's a huge page with links to ghost investigators, case studies and just about anything else that goes bump in the night.

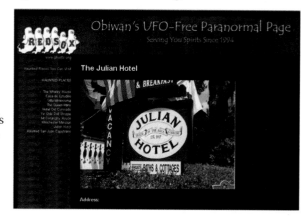

All creatures great and small

If you or anyone in your family has an interest in natural history, the Internet will bring that interest to life, with its rich selection of information about everything in the natural world.

Natural history is a huge topic covering the origins, evolution and ecology of the Earth and the plants and creatures living on it. As such, it cuts across many more specific areas, making it somewhat difficult to find all the information you require in a single book or encyclopedia.

However, the Web offers a vast range of natural history sites, so PC users of all ages can explore their interests in many exciting ways.

● Going batty

For example, if you've just watched a wildlife programme about bats on television and want to know more, you can instantly find information from a 'bats' site on the Internet. School assignments will be enriched by Internet research, with many of the best natural history sites on the Web belonging to great institutions, such as London's Natural History Museum, which prides itself on the educational content and interactivity of its sites.

Quite often there will be a list of FAQs (frequently asked questions) on a given topic and they may well provide just the information you're looking for. You can download text to add quotations to an essay or project, or even save pictures from

a Web site to use in your work. Of course, the interest in natural history sites is not limited purely to those doing schoolwork. The living world fascinates and astonishes all of us, and the Web is the ideal place to follow up even an idle interest in something you've seen on TV or read about in the newspaper.

● Practical pet help

There's a practical value too, at the level of caring for pets and other animals. This is particularly true of

the rarer or more unusual domestic pets. If your taste runs to snakes, for example, you'll find literally dozens of richly informative sites on reptiles, offering expert advice on buying, rearing and breeding these pets.

It's a fascinating world and such a large one that we can only scrape the surface here to point out some of the best sites around. However, you can be sure that whatever your interest, from fish or fowl to beast, you will find not just a couple, but many sites to inform and entertain you.

It's a jungle out there

As the Internet embraces the latest computer technology, the amount of information available about the natural world may prove surprising.

THE SITES we've selected over the next few pages offer an example of the broad range of what can be found on the Web, from the great institutions of the world to small groups of enthusiasts. What they all have in common is that you'll be entertained as well as informed if you visit them.

The major museums featured all have an 'online gallery' of one kind or another – whether it's a guided virtual tour of the permanent collection or a special exhibition on a specific topic. Some of these museum sites also have

excellent interactive and collaborative learning sections, where schools and individuals can contribute to ongoing projects with help from the museum's experts.

We've also looked for sites that will have a special attraction for smaller children – ones that introduce an element of play into learning. Naturally, we've picked out a number of sites that deal with dinosaurs – an enduringly popular subject with both children and adults.

Florida Museum of Natural History

www.flmnh.ufl.edu

This site is notable mainly for its Fossil Horse virtual exhibit, where you can learn about palaeontology and evolution by exploring the fossil record of horses. Clicking on the horse skulls tells you about the creatures, while clicking on the different geological eras explains about the ecology of the period.

This virtual exhibit allows you to uncover the fascinating history of the fossilized horse.

Seaworld/Bush Gardens

www.seaworld.org

This is the site of the aquatic theme parks of the same name, with outposts in Florida, California and Virginia. It's bright, breezy and commercial, but nevertheless contains lots of educational resources. Choose the aquatic safari option and you'll be able to discover a wealth of information about fish. And, by viewing the animal enclosures with the Webcam, you can check out what the animals are up to at that very moment.

At the Seaworld site, you can journey to Florida and visit the wonderful aquarium.

The Giant Squid

bluefin.gsfc.nasa.gov/squid.html

A minority interest, perhaps, but the giant squid is the world's largest invertebrate – and is also very elusive too. This online version of a special exhibition at the American Smithsonian National Museum of Natural History displays the mystery, beauty and complexity of these mysterious creatures.

Discover the mysterious squid – how has such a seemingly fragile creature survived so well?

The Natural History Museum, London

www.nhm.ac.uk

This is a site that does justice to a fine collection. There's a great 3D-surround video tour of the Earth and Life galleries, enabling you to take a 360-degree look at the giant dinosaur skeletons.

There are even virtual reality fossils, such as this trilobite (below), on view. To get the best out of this site, you may need to download plug-ins (see Stage 2, pages 142–143). There's also a Science Casebook section where you can post queries or initiate discussions relating to the areas covered. You might find a discussion of whether dinosaurs really could be recreated from DNA, or even a debate on whether or not the Beast of Bodmin Moor actually exists, or indeed ever did.

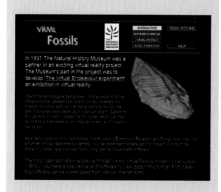

Take a closer look at fossils, such as a trilobite, by downloading data from this Web site and viewing them with virtual reality software.

Chicago is home to one of the finest aquaria. The Shedd Aquarium houses fish, reptiles, birds and mammals.

Shedd Aquarium

www.sheddnet.org

This Chicago aquarium is one of the biggest and best-stocked in the world. The colourful site contains lots of entertaining information about the aquarium itself and is also packed with fascinating information about the creatures of the deep. Fact sheets give you an informative picture of the exhibits and provide you with data – all of which make a visit to this site rewarding.

Smithsonian Institution National Museum of Natural History

www.mnh.si.edu

The leading natural history institution in the USA has an excellent presence on the Web. You can find out all you need to know about the museum and examine a number of well-presented and informative online exhibits. The virtual tour of the museum is interesting and you won't find it hard to get to the dinosaurs. It's a terrific resource for anyone that needs to know about the beasts that once roamed the earth.

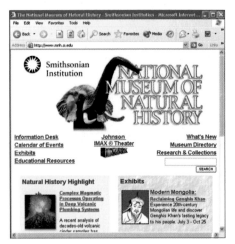

The Fossil Lab at the Smithsonian (left) will have you engrossed in what scientists can find from the rocks of millions of years ago.

The Web site for the Smithsonian Institution's National Museum of Natural History (right) will keep you up-to-date on events, and give you a look at current exhibits – handy if you can't make it over to the US.

Sites for children

Children are well served on the Internet too. Whether it's for homework or just for fun, there's plenty to discover.

Bats4Kids

members.aol.com/bats4kids

This site aims to take the terror out of bats. Designed for children, Bats4kids presents masses of true and fascinating facts about these nocturnal creatures. For example: Where do bats live? Why aren't they birds? What are the myths about bats? All the answers are given in this colourful and entertaining site. You can play a game of bat concentration (a simple memory game), enter the bat quiz, or even visit a bat cave. Children will love this site, but adults may also find much of interest.

Bats may be frightening for some children, but this site quickly explodes the myths, revealing much about these fascinating creatures.

The bat cave provides a bat puzzle, bat crossword and a bat word search game to test young visitors on how much they can remember.

Walking with Dinosaurs

www.bbc.co.uk/dinosaurs

The TV series that outdid *Jurassic Park* in its recreation of dinosaurs has a lavish site, rich in resources. Here you'll find information on the creatures and their habitats.

St. Louis Science Center

www.slsc.org

This interesting site is a rich source of information on ecology and environments of the past, with an online gallery that is sub-divided into several sections, including a geological timeline and plenty of information on fossils. The section Geological Timeline is of most interest, giving a guided tour of living beings since the dawn of time.

Dinosaurs obviously feature, with colourful dioramas, but so do plenty of other creatures, down to the tiny shrew of 200 million years ago. As well as the natural-history content, the site contains a rich vein of other interesting scientific material.

At the St. Louis Science Center site there are 300 pages of photographs, video footage, drawings and informative text – and that's just in the Ecology and Environment Past section.

When dinosaurs ruled the earth

Dinosaurs provide endless fascination for both young and old alike, so step back in time by several million years and search for them on the Web.

The Field Museum of Natural History

www.fmnh.org

This site serves to tell you all you need to know about The Field Museum in Chicago and its marvellous exhibitions. It's packed with educational material too. Most importantly though, the Web site is worth visiting to find more out about Sue – the largest, most complete and best-preserved *Tyrannosaurus Rex* in the world. There is a whole section devoted to finding more out about her past.

UCMP Web

www.ucmp.berkeley.edu

A geological time machine is the highlight of this site from the University of California at Berkeley. It takes you through millions of years of history, discussing the ecology and the creatures that lived in various eras – including the dinosaurs. The site is rich in links to related information and is well illustrated.

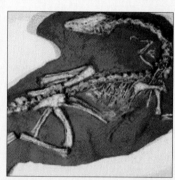

The University of California's Museum of Palentology Website is a vast source of knowledge on fossils and ancient creatures.

National Geographic

www.nationalgeographic.com/dinoeggs

This 'online egg hunt' is developed from a National Geographic-sponsored expedition and the subsequent magazine article. Researchers 'hatch' fossilized dinosaur embryos and you can then follow their progress. Although this is not an extensive or in-depth site on dinosaurs, it's a good source as far as it goes, and there are plenty of links to other dinosaur sites. And, of course, anyone keen on natural history is likely to be interested in much of the content of National Geographic.

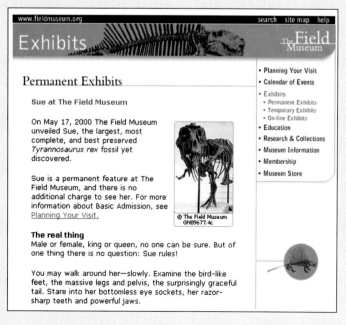

The National Geographic site is of the same high quality as the respected magazine. Discover the dinosaur egg hunt (right) that originally featured in a 1996 issue of the magazine and get a behind-the-scenes view, unique to the Internet user.

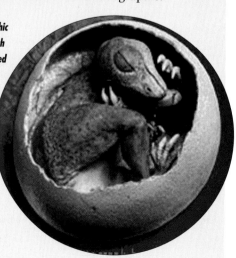

● **Acknowledgments**
Abbreviations: t = top; b = bottom;
r = right; l = left; c = centre;
bkg = background. All cartoons
are by Chris Bramley

8	Lyndon Parker/De Agostini
9tl	Lyndon Parker/De Agostini
12	Lyndon Parker/De Agostini
14	Stockmarket
15t	De Agostini
17tl	Stockmarket
18	Craft Plus Publishing Ltd
22all	Steve Bartholomew/De Agostini
23tr	Steve Bartholomew/De Agostini
26	Steve Bartholomew/De Agostini
28	Jennie Child/De Agostini
30	Lyndon Parker/De Agostini
34	Lyndon Parker/De Agostini
38	Lyndon Parker/De Agostini
40	Lyndon Parker/De Agostini
42tall	Lyndon Parker/De Agostini
45tr	Lyndon Parker/De Agostini
46	Lyndon Parker/De Agostini
50t	Lyndon Parker/De Agostini
50b	De Agostini
53t	De Agostini

54	De Agostini
56	Lyndon Parker/De Agostini
58	Getty One Stone
60	De Agostini
62	De Agostini
64	De Agostini
66	Performing Arts Library
68	De Agostini
70	De Agostini
73	De Agostini
78	De Agostini
80	De Agostini
82	De Agostini
83all	De Agostini
85	De Agostini
86	De Agostini
87all	De Agostini
88all	De Agostini
89all	De Agostini
90	De Agostini
94	Getty One Stone
95	tl NEC PR; tr Sony CNCE
102t	Lyndon Parker/De Agostini
102b	Ray Dunthorn/De Agostini
104t	(family) Imagebank
104t	(computer) Lyndon Parker/De Agostini
104c,b	Warrender Grant/De Agostini

105tl	Hewlett Parkard (courtesy)
108b	Lyndon Parker/De Agostini
109t	Roland UK Ltd
110	Lyndon Parker/De Agostini
111all	Lyndon Parker/De Agostini
115	tr Wincor Nixdorf; bl IBM
116t	(picture) Bridgeman Art Library
116t	(computer) L Parker/De Agostini
116bl,br	De Agostini
117all	De Agostini
120	D Jordan/De Agostini
121	tc D Jordan/De Agostini; cl Paramount pictures; bl Pathe; cr New Line Cinema; br Columbia Pictures
128	Lyndon Parker/De Agostini
132	Steve Bartholomew/De Agostini
138	Lyndon Parker/De Agostini
139t	Lyndon Parker/De Agostini
142	Lyndon Parker/De Agostini
146all	De Agostini
150tr,cr	Fortean Picture Library
150br	The Kobal Collection
152br	Fortean Picture Library
154	(tiger) Getty One Stone
154	(boy) Lyndon Parker/De Agostini
155t	(tiger) Getty One Stone
155t	(boy) Lyndon Parker/De Agostini